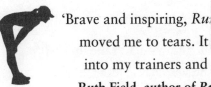

'Brave and inspiring, *Ru...* moved me to tears. It ... into my trainers and out for a run!'
Ruth Field, author of *Run Fat B!tch Run*

'A searingly honest account of Rachel's amazing journey from sedentary teenager, lacking in confidence and self-esteem, through to accomplished and inspirational member of the running community. She kept me engaged from start to finish, with plenty of laughs along the way, and I'd thoroughly recommend this book to runners everywhere.'
Tom Williams, Global COO of parkrun and co-host of the Marathon Talk podcast

'It's so inspirational to read how Rachel's discovery of a passion for running helped her to overcome her mental health struggles. For Rachel, running became so much more than purely keeping fit. It became something which enabled her to fully conquer the battles of severe anxiety and self-doubt. It's heartwarming to learn how Rachel has been able to prove to herself that she really can achieve things that she would have never believed were possible.'
Jo Pavey, medal-winning long-distance runner

'I love this book for showing how with sheer determination and dogged tenacity you can overcome great difficulties, and that sport, from whatever point or age that you start, can change your life. She might even persuade me that one day I too could love running.'

Essex County Council

3013021566100 9

'Written wittily, honestly and with a "take no crap" attitude, I could feel the warmth of [Rachel] as a person in her writing. Anyone who is hungry for change, looking for "the light" or even running their first marathon and needing a little insight; this book is FOR YOU! I loved every chapter of this book.'

Lipstick & Trainers **blog**

'What a heartfelt, moving, honest journey of self-discovery… this is a book you have to pick up in 2018. Rachel is a natural writer… I was laughing out loud at times, feeling sad at others, but most of all I was rooting for her the whole way through.'

Sissi Reads **blog**

'A rich, colourful and brutally honest account of one woman's fight to beat her mental health demons. Written with candid details and dark humour this book is a journey about a quest to live life in the happiest and healthiest way possible – chronicling all the ups and downs, the good, the bad and the downright ugly along the way!'

The Very Pink Notebook **blog**

'Full of heart and beautifully told… inspirational, melancholy and often very funny, it's kind of a road map of the inner soul – I loved it.'

Liz Loves Books **blog**

RUNNING FOR MY LIFE

How I built a better me
one step at a time

RACHEL ANN CULLEN

BLINK
bringing you closer

Published by Blink Publishing
3.08, The Plaza,
535 Kings Road,
Chelsea Harbour,
London, SW10 0SZ

www.blinkpublishing.co.uk

facebook.com/blinkpublishing
twitter.com/blinkpublishing

Trade Paperback – 978-1-911-274-84-1
Ebook – 978-1-911-274-85-8

A CIP catalogue of this book is available from the British Library.

Typeset by seagulls.net
Printed and bound by Clays Ltd, St. Ives Plc

1 3 5 7 9 10 8 6 4 2

Blink Publishing is an imprint of the Bonnier Publishing Group
www.bonnierpublishing.co.uk

To my beautiful Tilly.
Thank you for being my reason why.

CONTENTS

FOREWORD

This story is like many untold stories of superwomen and supermen, who have yet to find and unfurl their capes. It just takes that first step into the unknown and, for so many, that unknown is running.

For Rachel, running allows her to explore openly and rawly her personal and physical struggles. She shares with the reader the pressures of societal expectations and relationships; the puzzle of life that can take so many years and so many tries to get right. The hardships of our world are right here for us to relate to, giggle at and be heartbroken by.

We have all been on some sort of journey like Rachel and, because of her words, we can see that we are not alone. Her openness to share her story has created a pathway for us all to follow, to unfurl our own capes.

We can become aware that, even under all our negatives, we too are actually super.

Anna Frost, 2018
Trail and ultra runner

PROLOGUE

I'm on the train down to London. I'm listening to other runners on the train talking about the marathon, which is taking place in a couple of days' time. Some women in front of us are mid-chatter: '... Yeah, I hear Paula Radcliffe is running with us regular runners this time. We may see her!' Gav and I quietly chuckle to ourselves at the conversation: she's hardly likely to be overtaken by Barbara in a tutu or Ronnie the Running Rhino.

I'm standing up next to a guy who's waiting for the loo – it's his first marathon. Small talk reveals we've both been fixated on the weather report for the last week. 'It's supposed to be a monsoon for us on Sunday, isn't it?' I figure a brief weather synopsis is always a good way to break the ice, shortly followed by the obvious: 'Have you run the London Marathon before, then?'

'Nope – it's my first time,' he replies, resembling a rabbit in headlights. 'I ran my first 23-miler last week which seemed to go OK.'

I daren't mention the word 'taper'. For the uninitiated, this is the theory that you should reduce the amount of training you do just before a race to get your body to peak condition. For a marathon, it's generally thought to be a pretty good idea.

Fortunately, the loo becomes free.

The first destination for most of us once we reach London is the Expo, the big pre-marathon exhibition for runners held at the ExCel conference centre in the east of the city. As the train pulls in to King's Cross, we've already got our Oyster cards in hand, ready for the next leg of the journey.

The Underground is swarming with people, many clearly in town for Sunday's race. Some – unsurprisingly – look like experienced, fully fledged marathon runners. There is a cool stereotype: well-worn trainers and the running equivalent of 'shabby chic': '*What? These old things? Nah, I've just thrown them on!*'

Those kitted out head to toe in fully branded, last year's Virgin London Marathon (VLM) merchandise with all but '*HEY, LOOK AT ME! I'M RUNNING THE MARATHON, DON'T YOU KNOW!*' tattooed across their foreheads are trying too hard. They somehow can't quite carry it off. It's the others who fascinate me: what's their story? Have they been running all their lives? Has running saved them, too? How confident are they, and are they likely to run past me on Sunday? I've learned from experience that you never can tell.

I see a man and his partner getting onto our Tube. He's clearly running – he has the requisite well-worn trainers. She isn't – she's wearing a flowery dress and sandals. Ridiculously presumptuous, I know. She could be planning on smashing the course record in her age category for all I know.

It's standing room only on the Tube. I lean over and make my offer of polite conversation to Shabby Chic man. 'Are you all set for Sunday, then?' I'm genuinely interested in how he's feeling.

'Oh yeah – yep. Sure am,' he replies, seeming surprised that I've spoken, and even more surprised that I somehow 'telepathically' know he's running the marathon. It really doesn't take a genius.

We quickly establish that neither of us are novices, and bond over our shared love of marathon running.

'Yeah, I've done it a couple of times before,' I tell him, when prompted. He has no idea of my fifteen-year journey to carve myself into any semblance of a runner. Why would he? I'm interested in his story: does running help him to tame the mad, Bastard Chimps cavorting around in his mind? Did he once have a long-term relationship with Prozac too, or is running less of a therapy for him than it is for me? Did running become his drug of choice, and, if so, when did he realise he was hooked? I probe a little further.

'Are you going for a time, then?' I ask, unable to help myself.

'Yeah, kind of. I'm hoping for around 3:25. I've been trying to get sub-3:30 for a couple of years now. This is my third attempt. I got 3:32 here last year. Close, but no cigar,' he says quietly, with a slight whiff of understated arrogance about him. His wife stands alongside in her flowery dress. She looks every bit the silent running widow.

'Great! Well I may see you somewhere on the course, in that case,' I retort, smiling. He looks surprised, and I try not to take offence. He asks the same question of me, and my ego thinks it's appropriate to join in the party.

'Well, I'm hoping for around the same kind of time I ran at the Yorkshire Marathon back in October, 3:16.' I hear the words 'THREE' and 'SIXTEEN' coming out of my mouth and still wonder if it was actually me who ran a marathon in that time, or if I dreamt it. 'Or something similar to my time last year here at London, 3:22. Either of those would be absolutely fine by me!' I say, trying my best to sound relaxed, and not like an egotistical wanker.

'Oh really? Woah, you ARE a speedy one!' he says, unable to conceal the look of slight disappointment in his face, like I've just pissed on his bonfire. I suddenly check myself and wonder if I sound like a complete cock. I try to bring myself firmly back to reality before my ego goes on a rampage, and I dare to believe that I may be capable of such times again.

'Yeah, but I'm not sure if I'm in the same form for this one. Anything can happen on the day, can't it?'

My fragile ego is back in its box.

The VLM Expo straddles the line between inspiration, possibility and excitement on the one hand, and propaganda, hype and commercialism on the other. You take from it what you will, but it's easy to become sucked in. Money is burned like litmus paper. *'Try our new beetroot bar – it delivers nitrates to parts that other root vegetables can't reach'* … *'Our high-carb energy bar has THREE different types of carbohydrates, whereas most energy bars only have two …'* Does the third type of carbohydrate *really* make all the difference? I wonder.

I'm as susceptible to the hype, the promises, and the possibility of anything that could conceivably make me run that millisecond faster, as all the other wannabe Paula Radcliffes and Mo Farahs meandering around the pop-up stalls. Coconut water; fancy strips of support tape to make pretty patterns down either thigh; springier trainers with more bounce for your buck; a hi-tech watch that can tell your heart rate, run cadence, and when you need the toilet – a mile underwater. I tell myself I don't need one: I'm not even fond of baths.

The running attire is endless. Alongside the watch, I spot some new 'performance-enhancing' socks and a state-of-the-art vest made from the latest breathable mesh material, which is miraculously capable of regulating your core temperature and was tested by NASA in a lunar module. The socks look very much like regular socks, the vest looks scarily like a normal vest, and the watch looks smart, but I'd run into a lamp post messing about with its many gadgets whilst on the move.

Finally, having succumbed to my own limited toleration of the one-stop-marathon-shop, I pick up my annual London Marathon souvenir teddy for Tilly, apologise profusely to the man at the checkout for contributing to the madness, and head for the nearest glimpse of fresh air.

I wonder how I got here. *How on earth was it possible for me to do this – to be a part of this?* At times, it overwhelms me to look back at my journey to arrive at this place.

And breathe …

INTRODUCTION

I've often thought that my life is like a book filled with many – too many – contrasting chapters, or a play whose creator couldn't quite decide on the lead role, and so threw in a number of options, just in case. I've played a different character in each one: no two parts have been the same. Who knows how many more there will be.

I've lived and breathed each one.

I know how it feels to be unfit – to feel trapped in a not-fit-for-purpose, defunct body which doesn't work or look like it 'should'.

I know how it feels to be ashamed of my size and shape, even – and especially – in the 'prime' of my youth; to be unable to jog on a treadmill for ten minutes without feeling like my lungs would burst or my legs collapse beneath me.

I know how it feels to be called FAT – for peers and partners to mock and make comments about my appearance ('Honey Monster' was one such stinging jibe), and to wish the ground would silently open up and swallow me whole.

I know how it feels to be desperate for approval – at any price; to be in a cruel, bullying relationship where an already fragile sense of self-worth was further trampled on and eroded, and yet to still feel as though I should be grateful enough to settle for even that.

I know how it feels to want to shrink – to simply be smaller, neater … to be invisible.

I know how hard it feels to begin to run, and to push through the mental and physical blocks that scream, '*You can't do this – you're making a complete fool of yourself!*'

I know how it feels to repeatedly come second-to-last in cross-country races at school, and to be jeered at for my efforts, as pathetic as they may have been.

I know how it feels to hate putting those damn trainers on – especially in the early days when even the steadiest jog was so ridiculously hard and monotonous that I loathed every single, miserable step.

In fact, I know how it feels to pray every single night to be someone else – anyone else – other than my own pitiful self.

BUT

I also know how it feels to have run well over fifty half marathons, eight full marathons and around 500 races across all distances and terrains. I have an ever-expanding personal archive of amazing running adventures. They are some of the happiest, most incredible experiences and memories of my life.

I know how it feels to have taken my running fitness to a level that I never believed was possible for me – to have run marathons in times ranging from well over four hours down to three hours and sixteen minutes; half marathons from over two hours right down to just ninety minutes.

I know how it feels to have won countless prizes in my age category; to have my name and mug shot in the local paper for my own mini-victory, small-fry race results.

I even know what it feels like to win a race, having only last year experienced being the first lady to cross the finishing line. *Me! First female finisher in a race!* At thirty-seven years old. If I were telling my teenage self that this would occur in her future, she would quite understandably laugh me out of town (as opposed to run me out of town: she couldn't have done that).

I know how it feels to have a body my misshapen seventeen-year-old self used to pray for (let's keep it real; she would have been easily pleased), and to look better in jeans now than I did as a teenager – jeans without an elasticated waist.

I know how it feels to be so proud of my achievements that I can look my daughter in the eye and know that she sees a mum who has some degree of self-worth.

My hope is that she sees what I never did: what is possible, instead of what is pitiful.

START

PART 1

THE BEGINNING

AGED 4

I'm standing in the driveway. Mum and Dad are packing up Dad's small Transit van ready for the house move.

I look up and flinch as next door's demented Alsatian hurls itself repeatedly against the enormous, towering fence – our one and only line of defence between us and it; the fence that guards us from the rabid mutt's salivary jaws and its demonic bid to eat us all alive. I hear its frustrated, maddening barks and the repeated *THUDS* as it slams its body into the wooden panel fencing for the fiftieth time. I look up and see its drooling chops hanging loosely over the barrier. It's getting closer, I can feel it. Surely it will break through the barrier and eat us all like Birds Eye potato waffles before we have a chance to pile into Dad's Transit van and make a quick escape. I squeeze hard onto the Fairy Liquid sponge mum got free with a recent promotional pack (she's a clean freak). I wish they'd hurry up packing the van.

I am four years old.

The house we're moving to stinks of wee. The carpets are varying shades of turd brown, albeit they have 'modern' circling, swirly patterns akin to 1970s bus seats. When we arrive, Jane and I run around in circles – chasing each other through the kitchen, into the lounge, round to the dining room, and back into the kitchen again. 'Don't take your shoes off. Or touch anything,' Mum barks through from the lounge. I see why: our shoes stick to the peeling kitchen lino floor. The cacky brown carpet patterns clash between rooms, and the stench of wee eventually overwhelms us so that we have to go outside.

The garden is vast, wild and unkempt. I wade through the grass that comes right up to my ears and itches my arms and legs. Dad scoops me up, and I get a clearer view. There are apple trees down in a small orchard, and a little rockery which looks like it'll make amazing stepping stones across to Dad's new homespun barbeque. I can see fields all around.

This is their dream. We've escaped from the incarcerated Demonic Dog, and we've moved to 'The Country' (well, it's actually less than a mile away from our old house, but it *feels* like we're now living in an episode of *Countryfile*). Once the turd-coloured carpets have been binned, and the garden is hacked back to resemble a lawn, then we will spend our days skipping through the fields. We will pick apples from our orchard, and gooseberries from the bushes that stretch the entire width of the bungalow. I can see the cows chewing grass in the field from my bedroom window. One of them is scratching its chin gormlessly on our garden wall. This is like heaven – or at least it will be, eventually. My mum won't be sad here. And we'll be safe, away from the frothy-mouthed Alsatian. Maybe that's why we've moved? Maybe *that* was what was making her feel sad.

I have a painfully well-intentioned, manic-depressive mother and a loveable, largely bewildered, hard-working father. They are as mismatched as steak and custard. My older sister, Jane, is seven. She's a ballerina. I am not.

I'm a sensitive child. I see and hear everything. I *feel* everything, too. Nothing goes unnoticed. Mum thinks she can hide her sadness from me, but she can't. It hangs around her like the smell of cat wee does in our new lounge. I wonder if her sadness has moved house with us. Has it come to this new place, or has it been left behind, still living next door to the child-eating, rabid dog?

I try to make her happy. In my intrinsically shy, understated and obedient way, I stick to the rules. I am as far removed from being a 'troublemaker' as it is possible to be. All I want is for my mum to be happy. Genuinely happy – not feigning a smile because I'm contentedly weighing out penny sweets on my Post Office set, but to simply be happy in her own skin; at peace with herself. I know she isn't. I hate that she is sad.

The new house move has coincided with my starting school. We drive down to the tiny village car park in Mum's black Allegro and pull up next to the playground. I know that in the distance, just beyond the Big Slide, is SCHOOL. It will become my school, only I don't want it to. I don't know *why* I don't want it to, but I know it will take me away from my mum, and that's not good.

Panic bubbles up inside me as we sit silently in Mum's shiny black Allegro. I'm apprehensive, waiting for something bad to happen. My seat is getting clammy and the windows begin to steam up.

'Come on, Rach, it's time to go,' she pleads pathetically, as she motions for me to get out of the car. I don't move.

She gets out of the car. I slide across the shiny back seat to the passenger's side. She starts to walk around to my side of our trusty Allegro. In a second, I pounce on the locks. First the driver's side, then mine – best cover all bases. She stands in quizzical bemusement as I leap from door to door, lock to lock. She goes to try another door. I'm on it. The car is now fully steamed up and stinks of my nervous farts. I wipe the window with my sleeve.

My terror feels overwhelming. I see her turn and walk away, towards the school. *Where is she going? What is she doing?* At least it's a temporary reprieve, and I can remain within the safety of our Allegro's steamed-up windows for a little while longer.

A few deafeningly silent moments pass, and I see the two of them approaching. The willowy, fragile figure: that has to be Mum. But who on earth is that Monster with her? A mountain of a woman thunders towards our car. She is thickset with heavy, deliberate strides. Mum can hardly keep up. They finally reach our car and, between the pair of them, I don't stand a chance. I am inevitably dragged out from the safety of my temporary Allegro incubator.

Mum looks on silently as the Monster throws me over her shoulder and makes an about-turn in the direction of the school. I can feel my heart beating so fast, like it could burst out of my body. I kick and squirm, pummel and protest, but to no avail. I look at my mum, and she is crying. She seems helpless and weak.

'I hate you, you stupid fat pig!' I thrash with tiny fists on the Monster's spongy, inflated flanks, as we charge off in the direction of school.

Unfortunately, this is my introduction to Mrs Bottomley, my new headmistress, on my very first day at primary school.

It is also the introduction to my own fragility, and the chronic interdependence between my mum and me. It's when I first become aware of feeling panicked, and also – more worryingly – of absorbing her anxiety too.

AGED 5

My older sister Jane is popular at school. She has lots of friends, and looks good in a ballet leotard. When Nathan Brown teases me, saying I have poo in my sandwiches, I go and tell her. She stands up for me, although I don't want to be a burden. Sometimes she huffs loudly as I go running up to her in the playground when she's with her friends (mostly when I'm by myself, and mostly when I'm upset), as if she's thinking, *'God, what now, Rachel?'* I wish I could be more like her and stand up to Nathan Brown myself. I don't even have poo in my sandwiches.

We go on holiday to Whitby every year with Mum, Dad and Grandma Cullen. Dad lets me buy a small pink cling-on monkey to clip onto my green swimming cozzy. I love it. I wonder why I look so different to Jane in my swimming costume? Mine is green and hers is blue. I know she's older and taller than me, but still my legs look like sausages next to hers, and I don't know why.

The other day at school I fainted and fell back off my chair. My head felt funny, as though I knew something was going to happen but there wasn't time to tell anybody. The adults call them 'petits mals'. When it happens, I'm taken to my grandma's. She's nearly always been baking when I get to her house – usually fruit scones or chocolate buns. She makes me mugs of hot chocolate and lets me plop cubes of *real* Dairy Milk into them (my favourite). The chocolate cubes disappear and sink down into a gooey pool at the bottom. I love licking the spoon after drinking my warm chocolate milk. She doesn't make hot chocolates for Jane, or let her lick the mixing bowl clean of bun mixture. She calls her a 'beautiful ballerina' and says she is 'elegant' and 'graceful'. I wonder why she doesn't say those things about me?

Because of my petits mals, I'm not allowed to go swimming. They think I might have an episode in the water, so they say it's not worth the risk. I'm not bothered – I don't even like swimming. I always get cold and need a wee in the pool anyway. Jane loves swimming. She swims like a dolphin, and has loads of certificates and badges which Mum has sewn onto her blue cozzy. Maybe one day I will get a certificate for swimming a measly length of the pool, but I think it'll be a while until I can dive for a fake brick.

I sometimes feel sorry for Jane. She's good at ballet and swimming, but Mum and Dad seem more concerned with me and my petits mals. I went for another appointment at the hospital last week. A lady rubbed this disgusting jelly stuff all over my head and then fixed wires to it in all different places. Then a machine set off loads of flashing lights, and I had to sit still whilst the machine made a whirring noise. I was worried that the jelly wouldn't come out of my hair and I'd have to go to school like that, so I cried. The lights weren't nice. They were mainly red and green and flashed at me so fast they gave me a bad headache.

Mum seemed tired when we left the hospital. When we got home, she gave me a new board game called 'Guess Who?' for being good at the hospital, and then argued with Dad about the purple tablets I'm taking. I heard them from my bedroom.

'I think we should start to wean her off these tablets, Dennis. I don't care what those bloody doctors say. We should cut it down to half a tablet and see how she goes ...'

'I'm not so sure, Kay. They know more about these things than we do. I'd rather wait for these latest test results to come back. But no doubt you'll go ahead and do whatever the hell you like anyway, regardless of anything I say!'

Dad has been going to church a lot recently. I don't think he knows what to do about my petits mals and the purple tablets.

It was the same as usual last Sunday morning when we were hoiked from bouncing ridiculously high on Mum and Dad's bed once again and carted off to Sunday School. I don't think Mum is overly keen on going to church, but Dad likes some of the old folk there. Mum doesn't really speak to anyone. She likes to head straight off afterwards, whereas Dad lingers in the foyer and chats with kind old folk about 'how lovely the sermon was' and how he 'gains strength' from coming here. They often place a wrinkly old hand on his arm, looking at him with their head tilted to one side, and sad eyes. I'm not sure how it's making him any stronger.

After church, Mr and Mrs Speight came back to ours for a coffee. We were no sooner out of the car than Jane had donned her pink leotard and pointe shoes, and was spinning around doing pirouettes for them in the kitchen. I stood watching her, eating Bourbons.

They had a few cups of tea with some biscuits (all the Bourbons had gone, so there were only Mum's plain digestives left) and Mum spent most of the time pretending to be busy in the kitchen sorting out cups of tea. I don't know what she was doing, but she didn't come and sit down with us.

Just before they left, Jane did one last fancy twirl for them. Mr Speight clapped and said, 'Ah, what a beautiful performance from an equally beautiful ballerina. Bravo!'

They both smiled at each other and nodded. Mr Speight dug into his trouser pocket and pulled out a shiny, gold pound coin which he carefully pressed into the palm of Jane's hand, wrapping her fingers around it tightly for safekeeping. 'This is well deserved by the budding ballerina!' the old man said to her, with a wide smile.

I was still munching on the final few mouthfuls of my last remaining Bourbon, when the old lady eventually turned to me. '... And not to leave you out, young lady,' she said, smiling weakly. 'We've got a little something for you too!'

She sounded kind, yet a little uncomfortable. I smiled and brushed the biscuit crumbs off my dungarees whilst I waited for my shiny pound coin.

And then she handed me a dull, battered old ten-pence piece. It wasn't even shiny.

Maybe someday I'll be good enough to earn a shiny pound coin, like my sister.

My Bourbons were nice, anyway.

So, a 'quiet, sensible girl' I was. I once got my bum smacked for helping another girl roll up a PE mat at school when I was five – I was trying to help – but other than that, my record was clean. Had there been a goose, I wouldn't have volunteered myself to say 'Boo!' to it.

Along with reinforcing what I was purportedly good at, it was also made very clear those areas in which I was not expected to show any natural flair, interest or talent whatsoever. Sport and physical activity was one such area – and so, true to form, I didn't show any interest in it. Also predictably, when I was forced to engage in sport of any description, I was rubbish at it. No one expected anything else.

'Pick me up, Daddy. My legs are tired.' I hadn't walked more than a handful of steps.

'Come here, sweetheart,' he would say, scooping me up and putting me onto his shoulders. I'd look down and smirk at my older sister who would have to trot alongside us. It happened every time. I wasn't made to walk another single step. The mildest hint of tears and my mottled little limbs were spared any further duress, whilst Dad became my very own puppet on a string. This is perhaps my first memory of effective manipulation and exercise-avoidance game play. I became very good at it.

Perhaps for this reason alone, I was also labelled the 'brains of the family', aged five. I'm honestly not sure if this is more of an outrageous (and unwarranted) compliment to me, or an absolute insult to the rest of my family. They were hardly the telly-addict, beer-swilling Wormwoods I would come to read about in my favourite book, *Matilda*.

I always loved reading and writing. I loved words – the rhythm and flow of sentences, and seeing how they could be put together to create a world all of their own. However, that didn't mean I was necessarily interested in academia or bland, one-dimensional educational texts. I just loved stories. Arguably then, a rather sizeable misconception was made about me right there, and from very early on: that I was some kind of sedentary Child Genius. I really wasn't. I could learn quickly – especially where reading and writing stories was involved – but the fact that I would frequently beat my dad in games of Travel Chess and Connect 4 didn't warrant the involvement of Mensa, or a *'quiet word with the teachers'*, to forewarn them of my innate and profound intellect. In fact, they'd have been better off telling Mrs Kirk how I was frequently chased around the playground by the little bastard Nathan Brown, as he hollered 'Ha ha, you've got poo in your sandwiches!' at me for the hundredth time that day. Perhaps they thought I could cleverly negotiate myself to a peace settlement with the little horror. Instead I ran away and hid in the corner of the playground shelter and cried (yes, I was *that* clever).

From being allowed to keep pets – including George the hamster with his *Dynasty*-style four-storey luxury apartment, complete with fitness wheel and penthouse chill-out area – to the latest Amiga 500 computer (it was 1989), I wanted for nothing. And yet a kind of eternal sadness pervaded our house. I felt it all around me. I saw it as clearly as I saw the cows chewing on the grass from my new bedroom window; I smelt it as distinctly as the stench of cat piss had stung my nostrils when we first moved in; and it felt as real as the overgrown lawn that itched my legs after years of horticultural neglect.

I *hated* the fact that my mum was sad. I hated the fact that we were her only joy in life. I didn't want Mum to only *want* to exist because of my sister and I, yet she admitted at times that this was so. Our happiness was paramount. Mum's wasn't even relevant: hers didn't matter, so long as we were bouncing around with glee.

We weren't.

She didn't understand that it wouldn't – and couldn't – ever work that way. Who would want to feel the heaviness of that burden? I often felt it, but as a child I didn't realise or understand what it was. I still remember the weight of that emotional baggage. Feeling frustrated, even resentful, towards her at times, but not knowing why. *How could I possibly be happy knowing that she was sad?*

The sadness was a silence so deafening that I wished I could make it stop. It was so loud, it hurt my ears.

Mum's awkwardness in company was palpable. From legging it out of church the second the last hymn had been warbled by Mrs Hewitt, to making a last-minute dash from her car and grabbing me from the school playground, her active avoidance of social situations became legendary. None of the '*hanging out, chatting with the other school mums*' daily frivolities. Hell, she didn't even have the convenient distraction of an iPhone back then to make her appear to be 'otherwise engaged'. No option to stand looking busy and aloof whilst fully engrossed in *An Important Email from Work*, or *A Vital Text Message Informing of Imminent Global Disaster* (which we all know is in reality a YouTube video of 'Bros: where are they now?' or pricing up the latest Dyson hair dryer on Ebay).

Mum successfully managed to navigate her way out of a whole array of outings, events, parties and even the most mundane social interactions. When family get-togethers had been planned well in advance (Dad's side of the family was ironically very sociable), she would predictably fall foul of a crippling migraine on the day itself. Parties were unheard of; friends didn't just 'call by'. Small talk in the school playground simply caused embarrassment.

Dad had it worst. Before he left to carve out his own self-employed path, he was the manager of a showroom for an international printing engineering company. One year, he was asked by his boss if he and his 'lovely wife and girls' would present the Mayor with a bouquet of flowers at the opening of their new all-singing, all-dancing UK headquarters. Dad was understandably thrilled and flattered at the invitation. Jane and I were bought matching sky-blue *'aren't they just adorable?'* dresses and white patent shoes. They even had kitten heels! Thrilled was not even the word.

Any 'normal' wife would have immediately booked in to have her nails done, along with ten sessions under the grill at the local 1980s tanning salon. She'd have used it as an unbelievably convenient excuse to spend a fortune on the latest garish puff-ball frock, and as a more-than-justifiable reason to revive the slightly sad-looking shaggy perm for the occasion. Not my mum. To be fair to her, she *told* Dad she couldn't go. She *forewarned* him that it was beyond her social anxiety safety zone to be in that place, to be so entirely visible, and – quite literally – on show. And so, poor Dad had to take ... his mother. Yes, our grandma stepped into the breach, God love her. So, rather than his recently permed, tanned and fully manicured glamorous wife, standing next to him on the stage that day stood ... Grandma Cullen: a cross between Mrs Doubtfire and Tootsie.

Christmases were particularly gruelling. It must be the worst possible time of year for a socially anxious, introverted bipolar sufferer. The emotional equivalent of running a couple of marathons back-to-back ... in clogs.

Dad had a friend he played squash with most Friday nights. For a few Christmases – presumably to ease the sense of social isolation for himself at least – he invited his squash pal, Bernard, and his brash, overly confident wife around for Christmas Eve drinks. It was hell for my mum. I could see her clock-watching, counting down the hours, minutes and seconds. Not to Christmas Day! No, not that. To the time when they would leave and she could return to her own insular world. One without the trivialities of small talk or inane chit-chat; where socially acceptable 'norms' didn't need to be adhered to; a world away from the feigned laughter at pissed comedy anecdotes. I would listen from my bedroom as Dad's half-baked belly-laughter broke an otherwise heavy, awkward silence. I'm sure the booze helped to lighten the mood for the others, but Mum stuck to her lemonade.

Way back in the early twentieth century, Carl Jung was the brains behind a theory of psychological types, and he came up with the concept of introversion and extraversion. He theorised that each of us falls into one of these two categories. In basic terms, the introverts amongst us focus on our internal world (i.e. our sorry little selves), whereas extroverts are more drawn to the external world around them (think *X Factor* contestants and Royal Variety performances). As with life, nothing is ever quite so black and white, and Myers and Briggs later developed this theory to reflect the idea that each of us exists somewhere on a sliding scale. I quite like the idea of this. I'm hovering around the middle of the scale somewhere, whilst clinging on at the very introverted edges is most definitely my mum.

Despite seeing myself as floating around in the middle, I am naturally more of an introvert, and happily so. I don't want or need to be surrounded by swathes of people. I choose smaller, quieter groups where I feel more at home. Amid life's busyness, I crave time by myself. However, as with the Myers–Briggs theory, I can dip in and out. I can appear to be nothing short of a social butterfly at times, exchanging pleasantries with the School Mums, or hobnobbing with work affiliates. It's a learned skill – survival, you may say.

At other times, I can be crippled by the thought of even going to Tesco's – dreading bumping into the lady from the gym down the bread aisle and having to act 'normal', whatever that means. I have adapted to both extremes, although I'm well aware of my own shockingly low tolerance for playground small talk. I may dislike it with a passion, but I can exist in that world. My mum just struggled with it all … and it wasn't her fault.

What is important to remember here is that being an introvert does NOT infer any kind of mental health issue. It doesn't walk hand in hand with bipolar disorder (or 'manic depression' as it was known, back in the day). There is nothing *wrong* with being an introvert, wherever that places you on the sliding scale. It's taken me many years to get my head around this as a fact, but yes, folks! It's perfectly fine to enjoy one's own company; to not feel inclined towards rowdy karaoke bars on a Saturday night; and to feel utterly over-whelmed in claustrophobic, godforsaken shopping centres – avoiding them at all costs during the Boxing Day Sale. These idiosyncracies are all part of my personality, and they're all perfectly OK. I'm not flawed by any of them.

Bipolar disorder, and/or 'clinical depression', however, is an entirely different beast. It is as distinct and separate from any 'personality trait' as it is possible to conceive. It is an illness; a thing that envelops and ravishes whatever personality you might have; hijacks it, and assumes its identity (think John Travolta and Nicolas Cage in *Face/Off*). Mark Rice-Oxley expresses it brilliantly in his memoir of depression and recovery, *Underneath the Lemon Tree*: 'The next day is so bleak it surely can't be a Saturday. Thin rain persists, as though someone left it on and went to the pub. I am constantly on the edge of something ... The feeling is that I feel so wretched I think I'm going to ... what? Going to what? There is nowhere to go, nothing to be going to do.'

Perhaps Mum thought that I didn't see her painful desire to be transparent to the world, and to take up as little space as humanly possible. Maybe she convinced herself that I wasn't aware of her silent, daily battle as so beautifully described by Mr Rice-Oxley. But I saw it all. I felt her pain, and it became my pain too. This wasn't about her being 'introverted'. I didn't need her to suddenly take up amateur dramatics, or join the school's PTA committee and transform herself into a proactive supermum, rousing the parental troops to knit animal egg-cosies for sale at the school's Summer Fayre, or sit in a bath of beans for this brand new Comic Relief charity thing. I simply needed for her to be comfortable in her own skin, and stand tall on her own minuscule square footage of the planet.

People talk about 'energies' and 'vibes'. I know they exist. The feelings I had around my mum were of overwhelming discomfort, awkwardness, being ill at ease, and many times a yawning, indecipherable sadness.

Nowadays, we (thankfully) speak openly about myriad mental health issues, and the term 'depression' is bandied about without a second thought (although it can frequently fall foul of being thoroughly misinterpreted and therefore misused as a generic term to cover a multitude of complicated factors). Obvious caveats aside then, at the very least, acknowledgement and support is more readily available now than it ever has been. It's an upward curve – a forward trajectory. I'm not delusional enough to suggest that we live in an entirely non-judgemental, cotton-wool-lined utopia, but at the most basic level, acknowledging such conditions as *actually existing*, and not being some fanciful pseudo illness to mask difficult life events, is a huge advancement on what has gone before.

For my mum, there was no such support on offer. She did what she could at the time. What choice did she have? Who would she have spoken to back in 1982, and what response would she have received? What would the diagnosis have been? Sadness? Madness? Could she have confided in her employer with any confidence that it wouldn't be held against her, or seen as a 'weakness' to exploit within promotional negotiations/bun-fights? She knew the answer back then, as we do now: it simply wasn't an option.

From her, I believe I inherited my deep-routed discomfort of self – the apple not falling far from the tree. Witnessing my mum's struggles only heightened my already pre-programmed, overly acute sense of self. If my own mother couldn't even convince *me* that she felt worthy of taking her square-footage on the planet, then really, what chance did I have? Was I simply demonstrating 'personality traits' as per the Myers–Briggs 'introvert/extravert' scale, or was I absorbing and then projecting my mum's mental health illness as it washed over me daily, each time dousing me with an increased predisposition to suffer from its cruel and maddening effects?

Whether accredited to nature or nurture, or a concoction of both, I was exhibiting the exact same traits. My thoughts at a very young age were often consumed with 'self'. Afraid of how I may appear to others, of looking foolish, of somehow being judged as falling short in one way or another, of simply not being 'good enough', whatever that meant, whatever it looked like; feeling afraid and anxious, and about what? Well, nothing really, other than just being me.

I wanted for nothing. And yet it was the icing without the cake. My cake wasn't baked, or even in the oven. Despite the best of intentions (I was surrounded by those) and the most amazing outward-facing opportunities, it is still possible for a child's essence – its innermost needs – to somehow fall between the cracks. An unbaked cake simply cannot be iced. There is no blame or admonishment attached: it is just a fact.

Growing up in the only world I knew – alongside my troubled mum – was damaging me. Thoughts of fear, inadequacy, heaviness, and a sense of peering in on other people living this thing called 'life' became my normality.

That's what depression does. Believe me: I know.

SHAPES

My sister is a ballerina. She is built like a runner bean. She is long and straight; bendy and stretchy. I often stand watching in amazement as she demonstrates her latest ballet skills in the kitchen. Mum's scrubbed the lino floor, and it stinks of bleach instead of wee now. Plus, it isn't sticky any more. Jane flings her leg onto the (bleached) work surface, then gracefully scoops down to the floor. I stand pot-bellied in amazement and watch. My fingers are still sticky from scraping cream off a butterfly bun when no one was looking. My body is not balletic. I am 'well built', 'healthy', and every other offensively polite euphemism for FAT. I can get away with it at six and, admittedly, I do like my food.

Mum has identified some early warning signs that my activities of choice appear to be coat-tail-clinging and spoon-licking. I don't think there's anything wrong with either of these as hobbies (I do also like to dress my miserable ginger cat up in Strawberry Shortcake hats) but Mum seems hellbent on carving out a hobby for me.

'How about coming along to Miss Clegg's and trying out one of her ballet classes, like your sister?' she suggests. I already know I don't want to go. I won't be able to wear my blue and brown corduroy dungarees for starters. Jane was designed to be a ballerina: I was not. I know this for a fact, at

six years old. *Why doesn't she?* However, in terms of gladiatorial 'battle of the wills' showdowns, on this occasion, age
matters. I lose, by virtue of my being six.

I have to borrow one of my sister's pink leotards. 'Ahhh. It
looks lovely on you, Rach! You look beautiful!' Mum cajoles.

We park up outside the ballet studio, and trudge inside.
Usually, I feel OK, but this time I'm not in my normal role as
silent observer. This time, I am *being* observed. And it feels
dreadful. We walk into the studio, and it's teeming with little
pink waify girls and heavily made-up mums. I feel ridiculous
in my costume. I want to sit on the sidelines and watch, like
normal. I love watching. The teacher comes over and tries to
take my hand to make me join in. I begin to cry.

I feel different. I know a bit about shapes, what with
being six years old and all. The other girls are straight shapes
– up and down. I am round. It makes my pink leotard look
different. Mine is stretched and taut around my tummy:
theirs isn't under such apparent distress. *Why am I not the
same shape as them?* I wonder. *Why isn't my round shape
the best one?* The long, thin, up-and-down shape is WAY
more popular. Perhaps there is something wrong with my
shape? Either way, I don't like it. I want to be the popular
shape: long and thin.

'I want to go home, Mummy,' I plead, in between hyperventilated sobs.

'But you haven't even given it a go, Rach. Why don't you
just go and join in with the others and see how you feel then?'

'But I look fat in this, Mummy. I don't want to ever come
back here. Please don't make me come back. It's stupid and
I HATE IT. PLEASE [sob] CAN I [sob] GO [sob] HOME?'

My very apparent distress is more than my mum can bear. I can see that her heart is breaking. She doesn't want me to be sad, like her.

'OK, Rach. Let's go home. Of course you don't have to come back, sweetheart. There are plenty of other things you can do.'

And so, after watching my sister pirouette and arabesque along with the Pretty Pink Girls, we thankfully head home.

'Right. Who's up for fish, chips and bits?' Mum says, looking at me with a wry smile. I smile back at her, wiping the snot from my face with my sister's ballet cardigan. The morning has ended infinitely better than it began.

You never know, we might be back in time to watch Big Daddy wrestling on the TV.

AGED 7

I am at one of my best friend's birthday parties. It's a strange kind of venue for a kid's party. It's big, dark and dingy with a long bar and fridges full of glass bottles. There are bottles everywhere – fancy ones hanging upside down; smaller ones stacked neatly behind glass doors; and loads of empty ones thrown into big crates at the side of the bar. It looks like a scary street on a dark night, only indoors. Over the door it says 'Maine Street' in bright, swirly letters. I think it's where adults come to hang out at the weekend – like my dad when he goes for a beer with his squash pal, Bernard. I hope it's more fun than this when he comes down here.

There are a few small, round tables scattered about, but they have been pushed aside to make way for Charlotte's pink bouncy castle. It looks stupid in the middle of this enormous, dark, stinky room.

There's no one here but the group of us, and a couple of bored-looking adults wandering about collecting glasses and making endless *chinking* noises behind the bar.

I know I'm tall for my age. Adults always say I'm 'well built', and I'm much bigger than most of the other girls in my class at school. Charlotte and her two sisters are tiny and blonde. People call them 'cute' and 'adorable'.

I've just come off the big pink bouncy castle and I'm standing next to one of the lonely round tables. I'm tucking into a hot dog from the big silver plate. The bouncing was fun, and it's made me hungry.

I'm listening to some of the mums gossiping in a little huddle. I like listening to adults' conversations. I play a game in my head trying to guess what they're talking about as quickly as I can. I'm very good at it – maybe from lots of practice sitting slumped behind our frosted-glass lounge door, hearing Mum and Dad talking/arguing/just being silent and stomping around.

I've tuned in to my friend's mother's chatter. She is laughing and guffawing along with another pink-lipsticked mum.

'Ha ha, yeah, did you see?' She cackles like a witch as she flicks her shoulder-length perm away from her face, and takes another drag of her cigarette. The packet says they are called Silk Cut.

'My little Alexandra went flying! She's only a tiny dot. Always has been,' the other mum replies.

I suddenly feel uncomfortable and anxious, but I don't know why. As I tune further into their adult chatter, my heart thumps loudly in my chest as I realise they are laughing ... at me. I put my hot dog down. I'm not hungry any more.

They think that I knocked the other, smaller girls out of the way when I jumped onto the bouncy castle. The Dainty Blondes were sent flying off and propelled across the dark, stinky room. *That didn't happen, did it? I didn't knock anyone over, did I?*

I feel confused, because I like Charlotte's mum. She wouldn't intentionally be mean or hurtful towards me. I'm sure they have no idea that I've tuned into their adult conversation, and that my hearing is so good. I stand as still as a statue. There is still some hot dog in my mouth, but I've stopped chewing it. All I can feel is my heart beating fast, and my cheeks are burning.

I don't want another cheap hot dog, or to bounce on the stupid pink castle any more. I suddenly hate the dark, dingy room and the dirty stench of Silk Cut fags.

I want to go home – away from the cackling witches and the Dainty Blondes.

At least I'm not laughed at there.

I'd crashed and burned at ballet; starting school had been the childhood equivalent of being made to walk the plank; I'd even taken offence at Brownies, wondering why the hell anyone would wear those God-awful cacky brown dresses, sit around discussing 'badges' and (literally) jump over a pretend toadstool in the middle of a church hall. None of it, *ABSO-LUTELY NONE OF IT* made any sense to me. When my unquestionable disdain at such orchestrated activities became apparent, I was typically given a consolatory ice cream, and watched the telly instead. I was far happier tottering around in my favourite blue and brown corduroy dungarees anyway – the ones that Mum had to routinely shoehorn me out of. At least my round shape felt happier in those.

I also became increasingly aware of my sister's sensitivities around our respective labels. I was 'the well-built, clever one', whilst she was '*ever* so good in pointe shoes, but no academic'. Maybe she didn't want to be a Prima Ballerina just as I was no Child Genius. Yes, there was some element of truth in our apparent strengths. BUT (and it's a big but) it shouldn't have meant that either: I grew up believing myself to be physically capable of little more than watching Nigel Mansell racing in the Grand Prix on TV, or that my sister considered herself to be lacking in intelligence and believed that she wouldn't amount to much, outside of the tippy-toe spins she'd recently mastered on her trusty pointe shoes.

Neither could have been further from the truth.

My parents had no reason to even consider that sports could be a way for me to discover who I really was, and more importantly, who I could be. It just wasn't my 'thing' and equally, it wasn't theirs either. I guess the truth of the matter is that a child is influenced far more from what he or she absorbs whilst growing up, day in, day out, than by being steered in any particular direction. Lifestyle osmosis perhaps …

To be fair to my mum, she tried hard with the 'lifestyle osmosis' approach. There was surely more chance of discovering my hidden talent through the timeless Mozart I heard Mum play so effortlessly (and endlessly) on the piano as a child. But after only just mastering 'Chopsticks' and grappling with 'Walking in the Air' after countless lessons, this was looking increasingly unlikely. I even cried going to my piano lessons – the clues were there. I must have been the one pupil my elderly piano teacher dreaded walking through the door.

Every week, I would be plucked from my Tuesday tea-time Happy Place – in front of the TV watching *Danger Mouse* whilst heartily tucking into my carb-loaded tea – and cajoled into Mum's Rover 200 (we'd moved on from the traumatic Allegro). There, I would sit in resentful silence as she attempted to make small talk around the nothingness of the day. I was missing *Chuckle Vision* for this.

'You *know* I hate going to Mr Steiner's house, Mum. His front room stinks of old people and wet dogs. I haven't practised my scales, and I can't even remember what I was supposed to do from last week. I'll go, but only if I can have some sweets afterwards. What treats have you got?'

'Oh, Rachel. It doesn't matter about the scales – and anyway, we've got a Sara Lee double-chocolate fudge cake in the fridge. You can have some of that once we're back home,' she promised weakly, inevitably falling for the con.

This was the beginning of my reward/bribery relationship with sweet, sugary, calorie-laden treats. I was on a steep learning curve regarding the power of such tactics with my mother, who was conversely unaware of the future damage of such effortless negotiations. The deal was this: I sucked up her laborious attempts at hobby-finding in exchange for an unlimited supply of chocolate-flavoured, sugary comfort. She fell for it.

Nowadays we have countless kids' incentives, out-of-school clubs and novel ideas to assist with this very scenario: *what latent (or non-existent) talent do I encourage my child to pursue?* In fact, the opposite problem now exists: which class or activity do I *not* take my Little Johnny to? From Baby Ballet to gymnastics, Tae Kwon Do to Sea Scouts, all have their merits. Back in the day, though, the 'pick a club, any club' dilemma faced by today's parents simply didn't exist.

To be honest, I'm not a fan of the overly contrived nature of such an approach. Maybe some kids don't want to belong to a 'club', wear a branded uniform, have orchestrated, structured fun and play 'follow-the-leader'. I know I didn't – hence the ballet ending before it had even begun.

Progress has been made on this score: the phenomenon of Parkrun has come along to offer a genuine solution to the modern-day likes of my parents. Having taken the nation by storm with the adults' weekly timed five-kilometre running events, it has now been extended to offer a Junior Parkrun two-kilometre model. It offers dungaree-wearing snot-bags just like I was a regular platform from which they can become familiar with putting on a pair of trainers, and with discovering their own fitness.

The kids may have a manic-depressive for a mother, or Seb Coe lurking somewhere in the family gene pool. Parents don't need to be super-fit or shining examples of a modern-day Adonis: they simply need to be bothered enough to take their offspring along to a local park. Competitive dads can run alongside hollering at their talented and gifted doppelgangers, whilst Starbucks mums can stand on the sidelines with a full-fat latte if that's their bag: it matters not. What does matter is that kids can turn up, and just run.

As in life, the best ideas are simple: simple and brilliant. For that, thank you, Parkrun. I just wish you'd been around in the eighties.

THE FOIL
BLANKET

AGED 9

Amanda Walker has brought in her mum's silver foil blanket from the London Marathon to show our class. *Wow! Her mum has run the London Marathon!* I have no idea what that is, or what it means, but I'm impressed and intrigued nonetheless.

Mrs Kirk unfolds the crumpled foil blanket, and holds it up by the blackboard at the front of the class. It's huge, crinkly and shiny – like something an astronaut would wrap himself up in after a bath.

The class is invited to ask Amanda a few questions about her mum's marathon. I've got loads of questions I'd like to ask, but I'm too scared to put up my hand. Jack Patterson is the first with his query. 'Is London a long way away?' he quizzes, more interested in the glamorous-sounding location than the event itself.

'Yes, Jack. London is England's capital city. It's where the Queen lives,' Mrs Kirk replies kindly. She steps in for Amanda, who looks confused and lost behind her owlish specs. The class give a collective '*Oooooohh*' at the mention of the Queen, but soon settle down again. Craig Crossley is the next to put up his hand.

'Did she run further than the school gates to the car park?' he chirps.

'Yeah I think so,' Amanda replies, looking over at Mrs Kirk who gives her a reassuring nod.

I visualise the route from the school gates to Mum's Rover. *Crikey. That is a long way.* I go home, and tell my mum.

'Amanda brought her mum's big silver running blanket in to school today, Mum,' I say to her. She seems preoccupied, with half her body out of sight and hidden in the deep chest freezer. She's rustling around trying to locate the frozen chips.

'Really? And how did she get that?' she eventually responds, sounding out of breath, like she's had a fight with the bag of chips.

'She ran the London Marathon. I think it's quite a long way. And she ran past the Queen's palace, too!' I reply enthusiastically.

'Wow! That sounds amazing, sweetheart. And I bet it is a long way – I couldn't walk that far!' she half laughs.

I've never seen my mum in a pair of trainers. *Does she even have any?* I bet she couldn't run from the school gates to the car park. Mind you, I bet a packet of cheese and onion Space Raiders that I couldn't either.

'You do want chips with your pizza, don't you, Rach?' she asks, as though justifying her efforts rummaging through the various Cornetto boxes and eventually locating the crinkle cuts.

'Yes please, Mum,' I reassure her.

My attention is suddenly diverted from thoughts of running past the palace and waving at the Queen to the plate full of bubbling cheesy loveliness I will shortly be tucking into. I *love* pizza and chips.

In my youthful, ignorant bliss, I couldn't possibly have known that what Amanda's mum had achieved was a pretty big deal. Women had had a tough time taking part in running the marathon distance. It had been concluded – *by the far more knowledgeable sex* – that 200 metres was the maximum distance that women should be permitted to race, as anything beyond this was considered to be 'too strenuous'. It was all for our own good, of course.

Kathrine Switzer was the first high-profile female runner to seriously challenge the concept that women were 'too delicate' for marathon running. She ran the Boston Marathon – illegally – in 1967 whilst listed as entrant '*K Switzer*', and presumed male. In the unbelievable sepia television footage from the event, we see the race director going onto the course and attempting to physically remove her from the race.

Over the subsequent two decades, women continued to push on the door of the elusive marathon distance. It was only in 1984 that the women's marathon was made an official Olympic sport, after decades of persistent refusal to allow the event to take place.

Amanda's mum was a pioneer. This was only a few years after that momentous breakthrough in women's distance running: she was one of a small number of ordinary, everyday superwomen taking on the marathon distance and going into battle with it, just because she believed that she could. Although significant progress had been made since the days when women were manhandled and physically ejected from marathon races, we were still a hell of a long way off any kind of '*This Girl Can*' encouraging – and inclusive – female mantra.

To put this into some perspective, fewer than 5 per cent of the first London Marathon finishers in 1981 were female – and I'm sure the numbers weren't much higher just a few years later when Amanda's mum took part. Contrast this with 2014 when – although it was still predominantly male – 37 per cent of finishers were female (of which I was one).

I've often wondered how many marathons Amanda's mum ran, and why she did. I wonder what kind of times she got, and what it was like being one of only a small handful of pioneering females brave enough to take part in the race back then. I wonder if Amanda was encouraged to run the marathon herself in her later years, like her mum. Did running become a lifeline for her, too?

And I wonder if either Amanda or her mum ever realised what an achievement it was back then – to tackle the naysayers, and be one of the very first unassuming and quietly defiant women who actually *did* say, 'You know what, This Girl Can!'

Hats off to Amanda's mum for being on the start line that year, and for letting Amanda bring in her crumpled-up spaceman's foil blanket in to show our class.

Maybe – *just maybe* – this planted the very first seedling in my mind that one day, perhaps I could take on the London Marathon and run past the Queen's palace: maybe one day, I would have my very own spaceman's foil blanket.

For that, thank you, Amanda's mum.

May 2015

I only went and bloody cried after Tills ran Parkrun this morning. Me? A melodramatic mother? A sentimental fool? Yep, indeed – guilty as charged. But I couldn't help it. I saw an almost exact replica of myself from over three decades ago.

She's just like me. She's exactly like I was. She worries about not being 'good enough' or 'fast enough', or even just 'enough'. She's only five years old, for God's sake, but she feels the same anxiety and fear of somehow falling short that gripped me and wouldn't let me go.

I can tell she's apprehensive about the run first thing in the morning, when she says to me with a genuine look of concern on her face, 'But what if I can't run two laps today, Mummy?'

I think back to my own, insecure childhood self, and I remember how I felt. I say to her, 'Don't worry about that, Tills. All that you ever need to do is to try. Just being brave enough to try is more than good enough.'

Her slightly furrowed brow relaxes a little, but I can tell that she isn't fully convinced.

She stands on the start line holding my hand, surrounded by a liquorice assortment of kids, Lycra Mums and Competitive Dads. She goes quiet.

Then we're off.

We're still holding hands and she runs. Her little pink trainers launch her forwards, and her face looks focused on the task in hand: two laps of the park – 2km in total. We approach the first hill, and I can hear her breathing heavily.

'I'm thirsty, Mummy. My throat is dry,' she gasps. I glance down to her – I'm trying to read the signs: she looks like she might cry. I pull out a water bottle from my overly stuffed rucksack, and she stops for a second to take a sip.

'It's OK, Tills. Just go again in your own time, and slow it down a bit if you need to,' I say to her, wondering what she'll do next.

She starts running again, her legs like mini pistons firing their way around the park. She's concentrating hard. She settles down and finds her five-year-old rhythm again. And then she says, partly to me but mostly to herself, 'I can do this, Mummy. I can do this!' And I can actually feel my heart soar with pride.

'Yes, Tills. You can do this, sweetheart, you really can do this!'

I'm still holding her hand. Her legs are still powering forwards; her face is still focused, and her heavy breathing tells me she is working as hard as her little body will let her.

'Nearly there, Tills! It's the last corner now

– last time seeing High-Five Man. Keep going, you're almost there!'

She gives High-Five Man the last generous slap on his palm, and then she lets go of my hand. Both her arms are pumping now as she reaches the finish line.

We cross the line, and I'm overcome with an entire chemistry set of emotions. She doesn't understand what she's just demonstrated about herself and her own little character. I know only too well. She's just proven to herself that she CAN tackle her fears: she really CAN do two laps; she really IS brave enough to stand on the start line; she really IS fast enough, and she really IS ... enough. She doesn't know why I'm so emotional.

'Stop crying, Mum!' she says, like an embarrassed teenager.

'I'm sorry, Tills. I can't help it! I'm just so proud of you today.'

We get back to the car, and I feel mildly pathetic for my heightened emotional state.

'So, did you enjoy Parkrun today then, Tills? You did ACE!' I say to her, trying to stop myself from sounding overly fawning.

'Yeah. I loved it!' she says, pushing windswept hair out of her eyes, with her pink cheeks still glowing from the effort. 'And I got a PB too!'

I remember when I was her age, and how my own self-absorbed anxiety felt.

I thank God she's already learning how to tackle it.

PART 2

PART 2

ANXIETY

AGED 13

May 1991

Oh God, why is Mum so unhappy? It's as if she's sick
of life altogether. I really don't want to fall out
with her. I love her so much, but it's just hard to
know what to do for the best.

She told me today that she's cutting down
her working hours by two afternoons a week.
I'm glad. I think maybe we should just leave her
to sort herself out, but then she always makes
such a bloody mess of it! Tonight, she has looked
so pathetic and depressed. It makes me feel
unbelievably sad to see her like that, but what
can I do?

I wish her and Dad would get back together
— for her sake more than ours. I know she can
be hard work, and I do feel sorry for Dad. Like
him, I don't know how to help her, although I'd
do anything.

Mum took me out to Brighouse earlier today
— we needed some more hamster bedding for
George. When we got back home, she let me order
a takeout pizza and I watched TV — on my

own like normal — whilst I heard Jane and her boyfriend of the Month getting off with each other in her bedroom.

Why don't lads ever go for a good personality over prima ballerinas? I'm <u>way</u> funnier than Jane, but she looks better in jeans than I do, and hers don't have an elasticated waist. Anyway, I'm sick with jealousy, and so I have just eaten one large bag of fudge, one piece of caramel shortbread (homemade) and a (big) bar of Lindt chocolate. I'll have doubled like bacteria in the morning.

I've also cried listening to my Lionel Ritchie album (again) whilst cutting bits out of a magazine to stick on the front of my new diary. It's all very sad when a thirteen-year-old girl has nothing better to do to occupy her mind.

Newsflash: Mum's just actually come into my bedroom and said, 'Oh, Rach. I feel like a right fat pig.' Ha! What the hell does that make me then?! She's the skinniest bloody pig I've ever seen!

Maybe it was a REALLY big scone she had... last week.

Dad saw Mum as being highly intelligent, rather detached from the regular humdrum of life, and more than slightly aloof. He loved the fact that she was different to anybody he'd ever met. She was admirably stubborn and tenacious, ensuring that any arguments with Dad were over before they'd even begun: she would have even the most illogical wrangle wrapped up before Dad realised what was going on, his head still spinning around in bemusement.

What he didn't know, and what he couldn't see (neither of them did) was that she was ill. Mentally, she was unbalanced. The admirable stubborn quality would often turn into self-loathing masochism; the illogical decisions and subsequent, impulsive, knee-jerk reactions just didn't stack up. Even as a child I knew that. As a teen, it only got worse. I listened to them argue whilst I sat on the swirly patterned hallway floor, slumped down with my back against the lounge door.

'There's never any bloody reasoning with you, Kay, is there? Only ever black and white. It's YOUR way or NO way!' he would throw at her. And he was right.

Arguably too, there was far more black than there was white: the loneliness she felt and her disconnectedness to the world was a far deeper wound than it should have been. I felt it. The heavy black cloud that hovered over her had far outstayed its welcome. I wished it would leave us all in peace and never come back.

Mum was – and still is – beautiful. Her features were dainty and pretty in a natural, understated way. She was always slim in photos from my very early childhood, but there were precious few photographs of her before this time as she'd destroyed them, hating how she looked.

At some point – or more likely over a gradual descent – she changed from being slim and healthy to just being thin … then skinny … and then painfully so. Looking back, it was a potent combination of her mental illness, an intense dislike of herself, and her desire to be invisible. The result was disordered eating. I call it this as opposed to an 'eating disorder' because she didn't have a specific type of eating disorder with a convenient label, such as anorexia or bulimia: she simply ate in a manner that was so restricted and minimal it enabled her to exist and function, but only just.

Most weekends, Dad would take us all out for a mooch around to some random place, and – as a default – out for a meal. Mum always *appeared* to join in and eat normally, like we did, but in reality, she didn't. I knew she didn't. She would order something small like a scone, and spend ages prodding and poking at it, the rest of us having demolished three entire courses by the time she'd finished messing about trying to skewer minuscule crumbs up with her fork. I would watch her in frustration, sometimes having to stop myself from blurting out, 'For God's sake, Mum, just eat it! It really can't be all that difficult!'

Then, she wouldn't eat again for ages, like a bear holding out for the arrival of spring to break the winter hibernation. It seemed like entire days could go by and she'd exist on only a couple of biscuits, washed down by endless cups of tea.

I believe it was a subconscious effort to literally take up as little space on the planet as she conceivably could.

It worked.

Around the age of thirteen, our family spontaneously combusted, courtesy of Mum's mental health problems alongside Dad's inability to work miracles. Jane had escaped by virtue of her 'coming of age' around the worst of it all. So, most of the time it was just the two of us – me and my troubled mum. And despite her own minimalist eating, she was a feeder – at least where I was concerned.

Mum worked all manner of unsocial hours, but she always made sure I was well fed. She would prepare meals from scratch and keep them foil-wrapped for my return from school. The portions were huge. If I'd been working fourteen-hour shifts down the mines, I'd still have struggled to clear my plate. And yet she somehow existed on a diet of digestives and cups of tea, often using 'busyness' as a well-worn excuse to mask her disorder.

Digestives were such a staple part of Mum's diet that one winter, we did a pre-Christmas big shop at a discount wholesalers. Obviously, Jane and I could throw any amount of sugar-laden crap into the trolley: it was Christmas, after all!

'Can we have some of these chocolate profiteroles, Mum? And what about a cheesecake? We could freeze it?' I half asked, knowing I was pushing on an already open door.

'Yes, of course, love. Just put them in the trolley,' she replied, without question.

Mum's treat to herself was a catering-size box filled with forty-eight large red packets of McVitie's plain digestives. *Who needs meals anyway?* Like a squirrel with his nuts, she'd be good right through until spring with such a stash.

Mine would be a long and painful journey with food. Over the subsequent years, it would be my best friend, my comforter and my haven ... but also my prisoner, my tormentor and my nemesis. Once I figured out that food was only *pretending* to be my friend, I stopped hanging out with it. But my understanding of the relationship I had with food (and drink) was not a constant, upward curve: it fluctuated.

In later years, I became so entirely consumed with my own lostness that I could not eat properly. At times, I became my mum. Like her, I learned to restrict my eating to the point where I could exist, but only just. And yet I still felt full.

Perhaps that was the case with my mum: maybe there was literally no room left for food.

Dad must surely have seen Mum's decline, as her mental health gradually deteriorated, and the grip that she'd once had over her bastard inner demons – however feeble it was – became ever weaker. But it's quite possible that he didn't see it at all. A combination of his not wanting to accept the fact that his wife – the woman he loved – was broken, whilst at the same time unwittingly succumbing to the fact that she was the master of deceit. Mum hid her sadness and her disordered eating from him as best she could. I saw it all. I observed; I watched. I studied her, like a keen student observing the trickery of an expert magician, and I learned the secrets. *Keep busy. Always busy. Cater for the others. Focus on them. Are they otherwise occupied with their plates piled high? Deflect attention; distract. Look busy; always busy.* And then, eventually, when the pressure was too much to bear, there was no option but to push him away. He didn't see it happening right in front of his eyes. Her smoke and mirrors had worked – he had no idea of the depth or extent of her misery. But I did.

Was it simply denial?

Dad was as oblivious to my continuing daily internal battles as he was to my mum's decline. Was it simply too painful for him to accept? Did their separation during my early teenage years and the fact that he was kept at a safe distance, away from the worst of it all, account for his lack of insight into what was happening? I have to assume so.

As a result, he doesn't understand my running: he never has. I've had to learn to accept it. Arguably, I don't particularly understand his fixation with tinkering around on old motor-bike engines, or watching very fast cars zoom around a track seventy-eight times on a Sunday afternoon. But I would surmise that he doesn't partake in these things as a way of managing a tribe of uninvited Bastard Chimps as they threaten to stomp all over his otherwise well-maintained garden of sanity, and leave it like a squalid, muddy pit: dark and dank, and entirely devoid of pretty flowers. Therein lies the difference.

He is a loving dad, albeit a fearful, fretful one, and my passion for running frightens him. Whether it stems from my early years of coat-tail-clinging and 'petit mal' seizures, or whether he somehow associates my running with risk-taking, and purported self-induced masochism, I'm not quite sure. Maybe he was *actually listening* during the 1970s/early 80s when it was deemed that running further than the kitchen sink was simply 'too dangerous' for our weaker, female species. I sincerely hope that isn't the case.

Having enjoyed playing rugby as a young man, he rarely spoke about those days, and instead seemed to have resigned himself to some tired old rhetoric that he was now in a 'different phase of life'. Having a dysfunctional family to support and being driven in his own entrepreneurial way to create financial success were justifiable reasons to leave his sporting interests behind him. He appeared to be of the view that sport would be equally irrelevant to us.

Prior to the marriage break-up, he would disappear most Friday evenings to play squash with one of his pals. The main up-side to this was the Mars bar he'd bring back for us to share afterwards (he was a Yorkshireman, after all), or the Bird's Nest Chinese takeout bag of sweet-and-sour pork balls which would ignite my nostrils with excitement the second he walked through the door, together with the biggest grease-sodden bag of deep-fried, piping hot crunchy chips. He may have earned them thrashing around on the squash court for an hour and a half, but I hadn't: I'd spent my evening eating Cornettos whilst pondering over the recommended retail price of a caravan on *The Price Is Right*. He seemed oblivious to the fact, and so I devoured them nonetheless.

He was also a keen, semi-serious walker. A group of them tackled some pretty heavy-duty European climbing holidays, but it wasn't something I was encouraged to take any interest in. Why? I have no answer. Perhaps my incessant moaning and bleating as a lazy, manipulative toddler to be carried *absolutely everywhere* had worn him down. Instead, I observed his activity from the very distant sidelines. Perhaps as I hit the horror of puberty, he assumed I had better things to do.

I didn't.

How did he not see me steadily balloon in front of his eyes? How could he not sense the boredom, or see the sadness hanging around me like a second skin? Why didn't he know that the purported 'clever girl' label he'd given to me felt like the heaviest of jail sentences?

I didn't want to be clever: I wanted to be happy, and free.

I've got to presume that at times, when my dad looks at me, he sees an exact replica of my mum and her ever-present Black Mist. Undeniably, my mum and I have travelled along some of the same paths in life, and shared some of the same struggles. It must have filled him with fear and sadness. But he was always able to escape. He could drive away and be spared the tortuous depths of both mine and my mum's despair. There was some small comfort for him in the distance. Ignorant bliss, I believe they call it.

All I know is that devouring endless bags of greasy sweet-and-sour pork balls would never hold the answer.

June 2015

It was Thursday night Club run tonight.
We turned off the road and began to climb,
zig-zagging our way up through some woodland.
I got my head down and settled in for the grind.
My tortoise-paced granny climbing gear was
proving to be steady but effective.

As I inched slowly past a guy who I didn't
know by name, he said in a voice loud enough
for the entire group to hear, 'It's all right for you
running up this hill: you don't weigh anything!'
He sounded genuinely put out that I'd been
able to nudge myself forwards and up the steep
woodland track in a way that he couldn't. I
responded with a mild, fake laugh and what felt
like appropriate – if also fake – banter.

'You cheeky bastard,' I thought to myself. 'If
only you knew,' as the memory of my melting
Mars bars against the radiator in my bedroom
flashed through my mind.

MY BFF: FOOD

AGED 14

June 1992

My friggin' chair only went and broke in maths today. I couldn't believe it! And what's worse is the whole class was silent when it happened. I was just so embarrassed I could have died. I thought that everyone was laughing at me, and I'm pretty sure I went bright red, because my cheeks were on fire. I felt like such a fat, heavy cow.

Mum and Dad took me out to Harry Ramsden's for fish and chips for tea, but the queue was too long, so we ended up going to a burger restaurant close by instead. I ordered a cheeseburger and milkshake. The burger was drenched in relish — it was so gross. I figured I may as well have a decent dessert, so I ordered a Knickerbocker Glory. When that arrived, it was loads of slimy melon balls swimming about in melted ice-cream. Rubbish! Meanwhile, Mum pushed a few anorexic-looking chips around on her plate. All in all, what a crap meal! I can't fasten my jeans now, I feel uncomfortable and bloated, and it wasn't even worth it!

I've felt unhappy within myself for most of

> today. I've got to be more confident answering
> questions in class, but I feel so self-conscious,
> worrying that people are laughing at me. I
> know they probably aren't (except when my
> bloody chair breaks!) and I know that I've got to
> somehow stop this ridiculous way of thinking.
>   I just hope tomorrow is much better — and
> I hope I can sleep now after that enormous,
> disgusting meal! Euugh!

I wrote diaries throughout these angst-ridden, formative years. Predictably toe-curling, melodramatic and full of largely teenage nothingness; yet they show a girl who felt trapped in a body, a mind and a world where she didn't know how or who to be. Always seeking the approval of others, looking for validation – to be 'liked' by one of the popular girls; to be spoken to by the cool gang and invited to the party; to have one of the boys acknowledge my mere existence. All of it based on seeking; yearning; searching. *For what? For whom? What was the prize?*

My world began to shrink as I regressed and withdrew further into myself, in line with my ever-decreasing confidence. Feeling constrained within the virtual 'clever girl' box in which I'd been pigeonholed, I would watch endless drivel on TV, and spend empty hours comfort-eating in hidden solitude. It felt like a part of me was missing, but I had no idea what.

The juxtaposition between knowing my end destination, courtesy of a one-way ticket to university via grammar school, and yet knowing so little about myself caused me some degree of inner turmoil. *Who am I? Who could I be? Who do I even WANT to be?* I didn't have any answers. Instead I was going to be defined by pieces of paper. Little slips of paper known as 'qualifications' would tell people all they needed to know about me. I would collect them, and they would represent me. Where there was once a person now stands a collection of letters. No further work needed on scratching any deeper into discovering who Rachel is: the pieces of paper would be enough.

It wasn't enough for me: it would never be enough.

To add insult to injury, my absolutely shrinking world of Not Very Much induced me to seek refuge and comfort from somewhere. And quite understandably, food was the easiest, most convenient place to find that belly-filling reassurance. Things that tasted nice made me feel nice. Usually they were sweet, chocolaty, fudgy, gooey things. I don't ever recall experiencing a rush after eating an apple, or battling my cravings for a few seedless grapes.

It very quickly spiralled out of control and (excuse the clumsy pun) my mum's love for me only fed the problem. Even at the time it felt as though she was actively trying to compensate for something she knew I was lacking.

She wouldn't dream of discouraging me from devouring some sugary indulgence, or cutting my portions down to even a reasonable adult size; she wouldn't dare question where all the cookies had gone which I'd baked only an hour since. She wouldn't even ask why I felt the need to demolish an entire half of a Sara Lee chocolate fudge gateau in one sitting, followed by two iced buns. *Half a cake!* I mean, really. I look

back in horror at those times and I thank God that somehow
– eventually – I got a hold of it and I made it stop.

I even had a ritual for eating Mars bars. Whilst seated in front of the small television set in my bedroom, I would carefully gnaw the chocolate off the sides, exposing the nougat bottom and gooey caramel top. I delicately devoured the top caramel layer, and then set about processing the nougat. It felt a bit like play dough as I rolled it into small balls between my sticky fingers. I'd slowly work my way through the newly formed nougat balls whilst mindlessly gaping at whatever inane drivel happened to be on the box at the time (it could have been *Watching Paint Dry: Live!* – I wouldn't have cared).

One particularly experimental day (maybe when *Paint Dry: Live!* was actually on), I peeled off the wrapper as usual, and felt the heat being pumped out from the enormous radiator next to me. I wondered what it would be like to have my Mars bar *melted*, and before pausing to consider how random/odd/entirely grotesque it was, I pushed the entire bar against the scorching white radiator. I held it there for some seconds before scraping the warm, sticky, melted fudgy modge off with my fingers. As comical in hindsight as it is disgusting, it was indicative of both sheer boredom and desperation in equal measure.

I could recount endless similar tales. Food satisfied me. It gave me some pseudo sense of comfort, focus and, sadly, even purpose. However, in reality, all it did was to accentuate my lostness and feed my increasing isolation.

Those mid-to-late teenage years for me were crippling. The more I sought refuge and solace from my sadness in empty calories, the heavier I became, and the worse I felt. The worse

I felt, the greater my reliance on dietary comfort, and the more insular my already solitary existence became. And so my world shrank as I grew. This was the cycle, and so it continued.

Now, after fifteen years of learning, my mind and my body have grown to look to running for sanctuary. It gives me a focus; a place I can go to which is all mine – some quiet place where my over-thinking mind can rest and process the madness. Back then, that place was with my best friend – food. Although time and time again it let me down, I always gave it another chance.

The solace I thought I'd found wasn't that at all: it was a prison in which I was trapped.

November 2015
Inter-financial Services Cross Country Race,
London

We came down to the Big City – as we did last year – for the off-road, short, sharp shock: a bugger of a race. It's the annual cross-country running competition of the banking sector, with all the major financial institutions represented – including Lloyds Bank [Gav's work], whose glamorous pea-green vests we raced in today.

There are two races: the ladies' race – a one-lap 3.5-mile route around the capital's Richmond Park, and the men's two-lap 5.8 miler. The distances look like a breeze, but they're not. The course is surprisingly tough. There are some shocking little climbs, and the distance forces an uncomfortably fast pace, particularly for the ladies' shorter race. There is no time to build speed gradually, or settle into a rhythm. It's hard work with fast climbing right from the off. I always know when I've done this kind of race because I get the same burning, sickly feeling rising in my chest towards the finish. I could run many times that distance a minute-per-mile slower: that bit faster just hurts.

Unbelievably, the three of us Lloyds ladies won second place overall in the ladies team prize, and first in the vets ladies team prize ('vets' prizes are awarded to those over the age of thirty-five at the time of racing. We're considered to be the 'oldies'!). The medals weren't quite as shiny and spectacular this time around as last year's booty (we won then, too) but they were equally hard-earned.

Although thoroughly knackered and hungry, a few of us posed for team photos before we headed off. The others were already planning beers and a curry, but Gav and I were contemplating nothing more than curling up in front of Masterchef with room service and a beer. Maybe we're getting old!

I can't help but wrestle with my own grip on reality, when my modern-day experience of cross-country races is so unrecognisably different to that of my teenage years: when the words 'WINNER' and 'RACHEL' were, at that time, mutually exclusive.

AGED 15

July 1993

Had an OK day at school today, I suppose. Half-decent morning. Lunch was good — I helped out in the tuck shop, so bagged myself a free Choc-Dip and bag of Frazzles.

Completely crap afternoon, though. It was TRIPLE games, and I was in deep shit right from the start. I didn't have half my kit with me, and Miss Hunter accused me of being 'a lazy piece'. She told Jo that she should 'tell me where to get off'. Is she even allowed to say that to my best friend?! Silly cow. Anyway, I ended up in a small group along with the other non-sporty girls who also can't play hockey, so we had a bit of a laugh 'coz we're all as bad as each other. Miss Hunter ignored us anyway (once she'd stopped telling Jo how useless I was, that is).

I'm still upset though. Why does Jane get picked for the hockey teams, and I don't?! I get so jealous of her. I know I shouldn't, but I can't help it. She doesn't realise how lucky she is. I'm like a lumbering oaf next to her. No wonder they call me 'Honey Monster'. That's exactly what I feel like!

I'm just thinking — I wonder who will read this in years to come — a boyfriend or husband maybe? (Yeah, right!) I may let Mum read it when I'm grown up. Hopefully I won't look the same on the outside, but I'm quietly confident that at least my personality is OK. I'll probably look at this diary and piss myself laughing at the L-O-S-E-R sitting here now.

Oh well, I think I'll make some chocolate cornflake buns, eat them, and do some more of my project work. It's got to be better than sitting here staring at my spots and feeling sorry for myself.

PE was a necessary evil to the extent that it was a (tiny) part of the school timetable. Even then, it was pathetically easy to avoid. Not being particularly talented at team sports – or in the least bit interested, actually – I would dread the moment when netball or hockey teams were picked, and positions screeched and contested.

The loudest, most popular girl always seemed to be given the position of Centre at netball. It may just have been coincidence, but from personal experience they tended to also be small, cute and blonde with a distinct ability to deliver a glass-shattering screech. Meanwhile, the quieter, more useless drabs (such as myself) would sweep up the leftover positions such as Goal Defence. I don't wish to appear disrespectful; I am quite sure that the position of Goal Defence – when played properly – requires a myriad of skills and abilities, which I would neither be aware of, nor possess. Anyway, I was *never* Centre. Not ever.

My rare selection for Goal Defence required me to jump high repeatedly on the spot, with my arms flailing around in my opponent's line of vision. Simply being tall, of sturdy build, with an ability to jump (albeit for very short periods of time) would apparently suffice. The girly screeching and persistent hollering drove me insane, although I did try my best to continue boinging, Zebedee-like, for fear of 'letting my team down'.

And then there was getting changed in the school changing room: another opportunity for me to have to acknowledge my self-loathing. Especially so since I was bursting at the seams, largely as a result of my Sara Lee chocolate gateau/iced finger comfort-eating. Already tall for my age, I was now just big – far bigger than my netball-playing peers. I felt cumbersome, awkward and heavy, and I looked significantly older than my young years.

As well as feeling physically heavy, I also carried the burden of my inner hatred. If only I was smaller, shorter, petite, thinner, lighter, prettier, happier.

If only I wasn't me.

If this was sport, fitness, exercise, then you could keep it.

I *hated* my body. Being – as I perceived – a different size and shape to my peers meant that I was extremely self-conscious, and would do anything to escape the dreaded inter-house cross-country spectacle. I regularly came second to last in the annual public humiliation in ugly, unforgiving grey gym knickers. Knickers that were so hideous and vulgar that they must have only narrowly avoided being labelled pornographic and banned, as endless psychological abuse claims must have posed a real and imminent threat to the national education system.

My 'house' was called Waterhouse. We waited inside the canteen until it was our turn, my corned-beef goose-bumped thighs already bulging irrepressibly out of my unnecessarily rigid gym knickers. *Shit. It's us – we're on.*

The rest of the school stood alongside the elevated grass banking, ready to spectate as each house would take it in turns to drag their sorry grey backsides around the cruelly visible course. It couldn't have been more than a mile long – two at the most. Endless, meandering laps of the varying levels of playing field that were almost all within full view.

I can still feel the burning humiliation of wearing the aforementioned vacuum-packed gym knickers; the horror of having the rest of the school witness my arse and muffin-top battling their way out of the grey, unforgiving pornographic attire.

My internal mantra went something like this: *'Oh shit – here we go … I'm not even one lap in and I'm already knackered. I'll have to stop running. We've only gone 600 metres, and I'm the slowest person here other than Nadiya (and she's virtually walked around the course in silent protest from the second the gun went off). I bloody hate this! How can this be any good for me at all?'*

I was utterly convinced that the rest of the school – the spectators – were ALL focusing entirely on me, waiting for the pitiful comedy spectacular to commence, willing the suffering of another in the name of 'sport' or (worse) 'entertainment'. *Is this how it felt during the gladiatorial games of Emperor Nero?* As we all know, kids can be cruel. They sniff out weakness, exploit it and become a silent victor over the weaker specimen. Or in my case, maybe the majority of them couldn't really care less. The gladiatorial games were perhaps only taking place inside my head. Either way, it felt cruel and it felt painful: emotionally as much as physically.

If there were some way – *any feasible way* – of escaping the imminent torture, I would have jumped at the chance. *Burrow my way with bare hands through the playing fields to the burning centre of the earth?* No problem – I can do that. *Stand on one leg facing the corner of a room with an orange in my mouth for a week?* Yep, I'd seriously consider that too. Nothing of the like presented itself, and so – quite paradoxically – there was nowhere to run and – equally traumatising – nowhere to hide.

It was all reinforcement of my million-and-one reasons to hate exercise. I didn't associate it with feeling strong, empowered, or filled with kick-ass *'This Girl Can'* motivational mantra. I felt demeaned, humiliated, useless, and a whole host of other negative associations.

At best, it validated my role as a studious, geeky girl who was thoroughly crap at sports. Activity wasn't for me – I wasn't 'built' that way. At worst, it filled my mind with a whole host of negative associations about sport, fitness, exercise and running – and about my own ability to take part in any of the above.

It made me fearful of even trying.

My take on it now is this: had I been familiarised with running; had my body grown up having adapted to such basic feats as being able to run steadily and confidently for just one or two miles, then yes – put me in front of the gladiatorial crowd. Challenge my apprehension and encourage me to take on those inner fears and tackle them head-on. However, don't put me into the arena unarmed, without any weapon.

Don't expect me to find anything positive from such an experience when you haven't even taught me to see running as anything but The Enemy.

July 2015

I've just come off the treadmill at the gym. Bloody hell, it was a tough session. Speed work is hard at the best of times, but it's a necessary evil: in order to run faster, you have to … run faster!

I wore my headphones today. I like to sink into my own thoughts and not be distracted by the sound of my feet hammering the treadmill, as the belt whizzes around so fast that my legs can barely keep up. I sometimes wonder what people in the gym think when they see me kicking my own backside so hard, at a speed that to some may appear to be insanely fast. It FEELS insanely fast.

My music also helped to drown out the dulcet tones of the two young girls who were walking with minimal effort on the treadmills next to me: both gripping tightly to the front handrails, whilst chattering on about last night's Eastenders.

I somehow can't reconcile it with my memory of my very first time on a treadmill ...

HELLO HOOCH!

As we got older, more freedom ensued, and we were allowed to venture further afield to seek out a wider range of fitness activities. My trusty sidekick Jo and I caught the bus into town, and headed to the main leisure centre where we could choose to either take part in nineties step classes, or to roam free around the metallic gym without daylight. Jo and I chose the gym: I'd cleverly figured out that it was easier to become invisible in there.

Donning my oversized T-shirt and non-Lycra leggings, I reluctantly stepped onto the treadmill alongside my best friend. I looked at us both in the spitefully placed full-length mirror straight in front of us: Jo was far more compact than me, although she was such a lovely, sensitive friend that she never made me feel like the lumbering oaf I saw staring back at me. She increased the speed on her treadmill to a (very) steady jog. I reluctantly followed suit.

'Blooming heck, Jo – this is hard!' I felt shocked at the difficulty – and we were only a couple of minutes in. *Crikey – can I last the ten minutes we've set ourselves?* I could feel my already shallow, laboured breaths struggling to take in enough air.

'Jo—' I wheezed, in between hyperventilated breaths, 'I'm going to [gasp] have to [gasp] walk.' It was becoming clear that this was a bridge too far for my struggling sixteen-year-old body to handle. I hopped off the barely moving treadmill, panting profusely after just six minutes.

'God, that was awful, Jo. I don't think running is for me.'

She didn't disagree.

We left the gym and headed for the vending machine where I found some comfort in a 30p Summer Vegetable/Salty Chalk Cup-a-Soup.

I was sixteen years old. I weighed the best part of 12 stones (76kg/170lb).

According to the NHS BMI online calculator, this put me in the ninety-second percentile of girls in my age group, which means I was OVERWEIGHT: not 'big-boned', 'sturdy', 'a growing girl', 'bubbly', or any other polite euphemism. I was simply that: OVERWEIGHT. If I scroll down the page a little, there is some advice on 'Healthy eating for teens'. *What about how to avoid comfort-eating for teens? Self-esteem for teens? Perhaps either of these options would have been more useful.*

Equally concerning – if not more so – was the fact that I couldn't run at a very moderate pace for just ten minutes on a treadmill. This was my level of fitness, in the prime of my youth. It would be the benchmark that became etched in my memory bank for years to come. I would always be able to say that when I was sixteen years old, I couldn't run at a steady pace for ten minutes – *TEN MINUTES* – on a treadmill. It surely couldn't get any worse than that.

And so, I opted out of this painful, pitiful debacle and created my very own personal fitness regime. It was somewhat

off the curriculum, and very much based on my active avoidance of anything vaguely exercise-related, which I'd learned
to so detest.

From the bus stop in town, I called at a bakery close to the
bus station, where I'd pick up a couple of cheap bread rolls.
Jo and I then took a gentle stroll over to the leisure centre,
where she did at least partake in some semblance of genuine
physical activity, whilst I vanished. I sloped off to the recently
discovered vending machine, found a darkened corner to sit
in, and dunked my cheap white bread into the horrible, yet
comforting, salty soup. There, I waited for the time when I
could escape and get the bus home.

I had succeeded in becoming invisible. No one knew, or at
least no one was bothered even if they did.

I look back at photos from those years with sadness at
the squandering of my youth. The more invisible I wished
I could be, the larger I became. I would stand next to my
school friends in photographs in a semi-squat position, as
if trying to shrink to fit the minuscule version of myself I
wished I could be.

Even in later life when I *had* proven to myself time and
time again that I could challenge such crippling beliefs
about myself, these were demons I would never rid myself
of completely. I remember thinking at the start of one of my
London Marathon races, '*What right have you got to be here,
Rachel? To even think you can do this? Remember where
you've come from, Rach: remember who you are.*'

April 2015

It's now Thursday – four days post London Marathon 2015. I set off running from dropping Tills off at school – I was yet again the only mum in the playground wearing ridiculously short shorts and particularly bright knee-length socks!

My plan was to take it very steady, my legs still wobbly and grumbling at the mere mention of trainers. The route I had in my head was around eight miles. The first half was (thankfully) mainly meandering downhill, which would then flatten out to meet the canal, where I would wind my way back along the wretchedly familiar marathon training route. I felt entirely thankful to be free and able to run on my own terms, and not stuck in some life-sapping commuter traffic jam, or slowly letting my soul crumble at a sterile office desk somewhere.

Whilst trotting along the canal towpath I happened to spot my old geography teacher, Mr Gladwell, coming the other way. He was heavily into his sports, often doubling up as PE teacher, and he seemed only concerned with those who showed particular talent in the sporting arena. He had no time to waste on those like myself, who had been written off and thrown onto the sporting scrapheap.

'Hi, Mr Gladwell!' I ventured, having gambled on him still recognising me after all these years.

'Hello there! I remember that face. How are you?' I was right. He looked slightly taken aback at my greeting him, and we stopped for a brief chat.

'I'm good, thanks. Just out stretching my legs. I ran the London Marathon on Sunday, so I'm still suffering from that!'

'Oh – oh right. Good grief. How did you get on?' he asked, looking genuinely shocked. I knew that times were everything to the likes of Mr Gladwell. I told him my time.

'3:17! Oh, that is good!' he said, with an understated yet undisguisable look of amazement on his now older, lined face. 'Did I see you in the Evening Courier the other week too, in the race reports?'

'Erm, yeah, quite possibly,' I offered, suddenly conscious of sounding narcissistic. 'I've no idea what race it would have been, but I've had a few mentions recently.' He would no doubt have caught sight of a small-fry post-race report sent in by the running club.

We exchanged some banter around races, pacing and times, speeds, distances and goals. I clearly now understood the 'Runner's Lingo'. He couldn't help looking taken aback.

'You've lost some weight too – trimmed down quite a bit, haven't you?' he said, stating the bleeding obvious.

'Yes, I guess so. It's been a few years since those good old school days though, hasn't it?' I replied, my head swimming with memories, and flashbacks of cringe-worthy PE lessons.

We exchanged a few more pleasantries, and then I ran (or more like hobbled) on my way.

Why didn't I know back then, when I was in my pitiful teens, how much joy, happiness, and confidence it was possible for me to gain by simply pushing through my own self-imposed boundaries, and discovering running? I would have done something about it far sooner, had I known.

For me, his acknowledgement of my running achievements today was testament to my journey since those days, when – to the likes of Mr Gladwell – I was invisible.

I'm not invisible any more.

AGED 17

It was an inevitable path. We were teenage girls, for goodness sake, and our unequivocal naivety and quest for validation was palpable. We were seventeen, and all the Cool Girls had started going out into town on a weekend. It was the dawning of a new era, and the opening of floodgates that wouldn't shut again for well over a decade. This was our chance to get a life, and to find someone who would want to be with us – even if we could barely tolerate our sad little selves.

Mission: Get a Life was about to commence. Just like an inseparable motorbike/sidecar combo, my faithful companion Jo and I were going to hit the Cat's Bar nightclub in Halifax. It would be our first experience of 'clubbing', and all the endless possibilities that entailed: freedom, excitement, finding love (this was particularly high on our agenda), and putting our deposit down on securing 'a Life'.

It would make all the previous, desolate years of stifling boredom and loneliness worth the wait. That was all in the past now: no more watching *Every Second Counts* on a Friday evening whilst silently devouring a semi-frozen cheesecake; no more nothingness to report back to the Cool Girls on a Monday morning when faced with the *'Did you go out at the weekend?'* popularity auction. I couldn't wait to volunteer my pre-scripted, over-rehearsed response, *'YES! Yes, actually, we did. And it was ACE. Unbelievable. Totally amazing – the best night ever. Yeah. You?'*

I was already at a huge advantage to my peers. I say a huge advantage – excuse the pun – because quite literally, at seventeen years old, I looked like a naive 35-year-old with bad dress sense. With my weight and body shape being as they were, I could easily pass for a grown-up. *No ID problems for me!* The other girls would have to prepare their emergency 'what ifs' and fallback plans on the (high) chance that they weren't allowed in to the pubs and clubs. Not me. *Ha ha, there IS a God!* I knew there would be payback for them being small, cute and blonde, and some benefit to me being big, bouncy and bland. *This is it, Rach. This is your time to shine!*

With that small comfort, Jo and I commenced our preparations for the Big Night Out. Jo opened up the Clothes Conversation.

'So, what are you wearing tonight then, Rach?'

'Oh, erm – I've no idea, really,' I mumbled, as my mind began racing through a damage-limitation exercise. What *could* I wear to disguise the fact that a) I was fat, and b) even more crucially, the fact that I was me? 'I was thinking of those ribbed cream leggings. What about you?'

'Denim shorts over my black tights, I think,' Jo replied, innocently. *Shit. I knew she'd say that.* She was going for the 'small and cute, in tiny cut-off denim shorts' look. *Bloody typical. Great – thanks Jo!* That'll just be me having to find something more flattering with soft, flowing lines and elasticated contours then. I guess 'sexy' is off the radar and propelled into some other galaxy far, far away from me.

Armed with my 'more is more' approach to clothing – I was heavily into the camouflage scene – we trotted off into town, and headed for the Brass Cat. I never fully got the feline theme running through some of the nightlife hotspots in Halifax at the time, but they did tend to stink of cat piss, so perhaps that was the link.

The Brass Cat was heaving and we could barely see the bar, let alone reach it.

'You'll have to get served, Rach – I've got no chance!' She was right. She looked fifteen.

'OK, well don't go anywhere, 'coz I haven't got my glasses on and I can see fuck all. Is there anyone in here we know?'

She scanned the bar. I felt utterly overwhelmed with busyness and bodies. Chatter to my left, raucous laughter to my right. I didn't know where to look or what to do as mild panic arose inside me. It was made infinitely worse because, quite literally, I couldn't see very much at all. On the off-chance that I could somehow align myself with the distant-galaxy 'sexy' look, I'd opted to leave my Coke-bottle-bottom specs at home. This meant that I could see just about in front of my face, but no further. People had no faces; chatter had no origin. I was completely and utterly dependent on my trusty lifeline Jo to be my eyes, as I was her ID.

'Yeah, I think there are a few people I recognise over there,' she eventually volunteered. 'Let's get our drinks and head over.' And so, armed with our bottles of paint-stripper Hooch, we did. After schmoozing with God-knows-whom about God-knows-what, we took our leave from the Brass Cat in order to reach our final destination: the Cat's Bar. *Yes! We're in!* Jo gleamed with delight at the fact that her tiny cut-off denim shorts had made their way past the bouncers. I wasn't overly fussed: I knew I looked like her mum.

We were now shuffling up and down next to other sweaty non-faces on the cattle-market dance floor. 'Shit, it's hot in here, Jo,' I hollered to my sidekick, who was all of six inches from my face. She looked at me quizzically, whilst hopping about in time to the music. *'I SAID IT'S TOO HOT IN HERE!'*

My turtleneck felt like it was strangling me. The sweat and heat made me feel sick. I kept dancing. *Maybe this is just how it is*, I mused to myself … *this is 'clubbing', after all.*

After much deliberation, my outfit of choice was as follows:

A pair of thick, ribbed, elasticated leggings. These were s*eriously* structured – think a very early version of Spanx. The heavy panelling around my tummy would hold secure a multitude of Sara Lee-induced sins. I hated the fact that I even had to *think* about disguising various parts of my body. Jo didn't have the same issue – and anyway, there was no room for control panels in her River Island denim hot-pants. It was a consideration she didn't have to entertain. As much as I hated that being a truth, I was eternally grateful for my control panels.

A cacky brown turtleneck 'body'. This was during an unfortunate phase in fashion when a whole manner of women's garments used to fasten with press-studs underneath the crotch. 'Bodies' were – I would hazard a guess – designed by men, as going to the toilet became a military operation (especially if said 'body' happened to be sitting underneath stiff, control-panelled ribbed leggings). That said, they served a purpose: the harsh, structured nature of the beast made me feel secure. I was fastened in – ready for take-off. No spongy flesh could spill, pour or dribble out of anywhere. The feeling I had was akin to a modern-day body-wrap at a luxury spa: the tightness pressing against otherwise loose flesh, making it feel more solid and compact than the reality. Jo, meanwhile, poured her tiny self effortlessly into a crop top. For a millisecond, I hated her.

A heavy, ribbed, chunky-knit jumper. This was (predictably) oversized, and shapeless. One of the classic 'getting it wrong' delusions of figure-enhancing tips I'd fallen foul of went as follows: *Hide it! Hide it! Throw something big and baggy over it! They'll never know!* (And by the way, the 'it' I refer to was me: it was my body.)

Finally, to complete the ensemble, an *oversize black leather jacket* slung over the top (it was real leather and stank of cows). I actually have no explanation for this one. Simply that I was far too Captain Sensible to go out without a coat, and it was yet another place to hide. So I kept it on.

And to top it all off, my dancing shoes were a pair of well-worn black Doc Martens.

I couldn't help but notice that all the other girls were in pretty, short skirts partnered with crop tops and no coats on: I could have survived a night in sub-zeros in my 'clubbing' gear. I would have given anything to be free of such worries as *How to Hold (Whatever) in Place* and *Top Ten Ways to Disguise 'X'*. I dreamt of putting on a pair of hot-pants, but I knew that wasn't a part of my reality. The thought that sport, fitness, and managing my abusive relationship with food may hold the magic answer didn't even dawn on me. I was too satiated with my own sorrows to actually think of this as a possible solution, or any solution at all.

'God I'm starving, Jo,' I said, suddenly feeling entirely consumed with drunken hunger as we staggered in through Mum's front door. It was just after 2 a.m.

'Yeah, me too,' she replied, unconvincingly.

'Ahhhhhh, can you smell that? Mum's made a fresh loaf. Do you want some crusty bread and a bowl of cornflakes?'

'I'll be OK with just the bread, ta.' Jo was already half asleep and had her 'sensible' head on.

Mum's bread maker had been busy in action whilst we'd been slopping our way around the Cat's Bar dance floor. It smelt like heaven. Freshly baked bread complete with post-binge drinking munchies in the early hours of the morning: it was a combination I would become accustomed to.

I hacked two enormous doorstop wedges off the crispy, tanned loaf. No messing about with dainty slices. It was almost a panic to ingest the food quickly enough. There was no time to waste, just get it eaten. I reached for a bowl. *What's the biggest one I can find?* Perfect. It held at least four of the 30g 'suggested serving size' portions as detailed on the packet. *Are those portions for toddlers?* I wondered. I filled my bowl full of cornflakes, drowned them in milk, and inhaled them like my life depended on it. I couldn't wash it all down fast enough. Once the bulk of the flakes were crunched and only soggy remnants floated in the bowl, I picked it up and poured the final quarter pint of milk plus the sodden cornflake crumbs down my throat. Phew! My tummy felt full again.

Oh. Oh no. Wait. 'Jo. Jo, wake up. I don't feel too good,' I squeaked so as not to alarm my exhausted mum upstairs.

Jo had fallen asleep at the kitchen table, her head nestled on her neatly folded arms. The bread was just enough to send her into a carb-induced coma. I shot across to the kitchen sink, where the acidic Hooch/milk combo had spontaneously combusted in my gut. Soggy cornflakes shot out of my nose and mouth as I heaved and spewed up the contents of my night out.

Exhausted, I sloped off to bed, safe in the knowledge that at least I had something to tell the Cool Girls at school on Monday.

Same again next week?

August 2015

Whilst doing my usual reluctant pre-Parkrun warm-up trot around the park this morning, I glanced up to my left, and I saw them: two of the Cool Girls from school. I haven't seen them in twenty years. They clocked me, too.

'Hi!' I chirped automatically, wanting to appear friendly.

'Oh, hi!' they replied in sync, more of a stunned response than a considered one. They both looked older and rounder.

I immediately felt seventeen again. My heart pumped with adrenalin. I remembered those days, and my yearning for their approval; wanting to be invited to the party. I had to put it to the back of my mind, as the race was due to start.

3,2,1, GO! We were off. My focus was on my race, and nothing else. It felt hard today. I pushed myself around the first two of the three hilly laps. On the third lap, my throat burned as I motored up the hill for the last time.

As I approached the top, I noticed that the Cool Girls had pulled over for a rest, under the common guise of fiddling with their trainers. I lapped them as they huffed and puffed and caught their breath whilst (ahem) 'tying shoelaces'. I knew they saw me go flying past.

All of a sudden, I felt like I was in my very own Cool Gang, at my very own party. I didn't want – or need – to be invited to theirs any more.

PART 3

FLAWED

Following our first outing to the Cat's Bar, and after learning from my initial mistakes of over-layering and consequent heat exhaustion, Jo and I had at least commenced with our plan to Get a Life. It consisted of going out into town, drinking copious amounts of wretched teeth-rotting Hooch, whilst on an endless search for Mr Right somewhere on the revolving dance floor. This was followed by an equally depressing trudge home once it became clear that Mr Right was – yet again – not out in Halifax town centre on that particular night. It was only made slightly more palatable by our routine stop-off for some greasy fried chicken and oil-laden fries on the way home.

And so, it continued.

Now, the obvious points to note here are these:

Firstly, our *getting a life* consisted only of activities that would perpetuate the existing problems with my weight, body image, fitness levels and self-loathing. Guess what? Following the introduction of vat-loads of sugary Hooch, and the equally gut-busting greasy chicken takeouts, my weight steadily ballooned. It was inevitable.

Secondly, it was all based on searching – yearning – for something outside of ourselves. Validation from some unknown, external source that we were OK and that we passed the test. For me, my sole focus was on getting a boyfriend. I needed to prove to myself that I was worthy of someone else's attention, and their love. It didn't even dawn on me that this would be an entirely futile exercise in the tragic absence of any kind of self-acceptance. I simply didn't know any better.

So, my empty quest for validation commenced at full throttle. It would be the start of a very long, painful and lonely road.

What strikes me now is, firstly, how absolutely desperate I appeared to be, and secondly, the indiscriminately chosen, random and often completely unsuitable guys who would find themselves on my radar. In a nutshell, the main requirement for said boyfriend material was for them to a) be male, and b) have a pulse. That was pretty much it, really. So, with those boxes ticked, they could confidently assume a position on my Hit List. *Low standards, you say?* And there's me thinking I was picky.

Well, be careful what you wish for, because just around the time of my A-level exams, all my wishes came true. I met my first serious boyfriend, Josh, and things went pretty much from zero to pseudo middle-aged relationship bliss in the blink of an eye.

The world stopped. *Friends?* Who needs those! *Exams?* A bloody inconvenience. This was the break I'd been waiting for – the dawning of a new life: a new me.

I threw myself wholeheartedly into my new role, and I took great care to demonstrate that I could cater for his every whim. If I could hold on to my boyfriend, then the world – my world anyway – would be a happier place. No sooner had we met – predictably on a pissed night out in the Brass Cat – than he was staying over at my mum's house regularly; very regularly in fact. The traditionalists amongst you may ask, 'What about doing simple things like going to the cinema or meeting up for a romantic walk in the countryside?' Nope – none of that. No popping out for a coffee, although to be fair this was before Starbucks took over the world. Even a dodgy ice-skating date never happened. Hell, I'd barely spoken to a boy throughout the entirety of my sixth-form years. Talk about going from the frying pan into the fire. I bunny-hopped both and jumped directly from a flickering tea-light into a blazing inferno.

I was also slap-bang in the middle of my A-level exams. This was it, my future: the culmination of Phase One of my Lifetime of Education. I'd been working up to this point for almost all my life. *What else had all this been for?* All those years of endless study: surely I couldn't be sidetracked by the first willing taker for the 'Rachel's Boyfriend' vacancy?

I was also still virtually a child. I still needed parenting, and I still needed protecting. I simply wasn't able to put those boundaries in place for myself, even if I had argued the toss in my best Kevin and Perry teenage melodramatic strop.

My mum, in her bipolar head-fog, thought she was doing the right thing by giving me freedom and allowing me to do exactly what I wanted, pretty much without exception (remember the trolley scenario at the discount wholesalers? This was like that, but on a whole new level). She had also eroded the ability of my dad to step into the breach. He didn't know how to go about even trying to influence what was going on in the broken family home he was no longer a part of.

AGED 17

November 1995

How many times can I cope with him being so bloody cruel? I was so looking forward to seeing Josh last night, but he was such a bastard ... again. I'm beginning to think he hates me. I hate myself. I feel terribly lonely and I'm still so confused and upset that I've been treated like this. What have I done wrong?

Jane rang earlier and I couldn't stop crying. I don't think she likes Josh any more — I wish I didn't, but I do. I couldn't bring myself to tell her what happened when he came over last night.

We were cuddled up on my bed watching The Lion King. A couple of the girls from school were heading out into town, but I wasn't fussed about going to dingy old Maine Street anyway — I'd rather be with Josh. I was lying on my side, as he lay behind me with his arm draped over onto my chest: think 'spoons'. I felt happy enough, watching the film. It was the part where cruel Uncle Scar lines up the buffalo stampede to do away with Simba's dad, Mufasa. It gets me every time.

Anyway, Josh was groping around my chest area when quite out of the blue he piped up, 'Oh my God! Your boobs are different sizes! One's bigger than the other!

> I froze — utterly stunned. I felt my body stiffen up. My eyes widened and I couldn't speak. I broke down and cried. I cried because I knew he was right, and I cried because I hate my body enough, but most of all I cried because he said it in such a cruel, thoughtless and insensitive way. How could he do that to me?
>
> I cried until I thought I couldn't cry any more. I had no words. I couldn't explain to him how much he'd just hurt me; how my heart was in a million pieces and strewn all over the floor. I didn't even know where to begin.
>
> After a while — once I'd cried my bodyweight in tears — he said sorry and told me that he loved me. I forgave him — he didn't mean to be so cruel.

So, this boyfriend then. He began staying over under my mum's roof. In *my* bedroom, during *my* A-level exams. And it gets worse. He:

- Called me names
- Made fun of my weight and my 'wonky boobs'
- Belittled me in front of his friends (and mine)
- Kicked me out of *my own bed* the night before one of my most important A-level exams – including a three-hour Economics paper. I had to sleep on the floor, if I slept at all
- Seemingly made it his mission to completely erode any hint of self-confidence I may have once had – and that wasn't very much at all

On the night of the wonky boobs revelation, I felt like I'd been hauled into an arena and publicly humiliated. *Look at her! Next best thing to the Bearded Woman, we bring forth … the girl with the odd-shaped breasts!* One of nature's freaks, I'd just inadvertently hopped on board the travelling circus. Or I was put there by Josh. Had he delivered the news of my physical misgivings to me in a more sensitive, caring way, then my tears may not have stung quite so badly. As it was, my already pitiful levels of self-esteem were eroded even further.

Just a few weeks later, I reluctantly agreed to go on a Girls' Night Out – a most irregular occurrence. I'd forgiven Josh for his recent insensitivities (that was just a blip, of course), and had long since stopped bothering with sticky revolving dance floors ever since bagging myself my beautiful, caring Josh.

I didn't really want to go out. I felt fat and frumpy; I *was* fat and frumpy. The Pot Noodle and Walker's crisps diet I'd been on with Josh had equally done my weight no favours. It was easier to stay in with him and tuck into a Sweet 'n' Sour Pot Noodle than it was to face dressing my odd, undesirable body shape, or trying to contort myself into the persona of a carefree young girl on a 'fun' night out. It was never that simple.

I must have felt brave on this particular night, because I reached inside my wardrobe and took out a skirt. It wasn't short by any 'young girl about town' standard, but it was for me: it was above the knee. I put the barely worn skirt on over my thick black tights, and together with loosely fastened baggy shirt draped over my hold-everything-in 'body' I was ready for off.

'Do I look OK in this?' I ventured nervously to Josh, looking for a kind, reassuring response.

'Yeah, I guess so ...'

Phew! I almost heaved a sigh of relief, before he inter-jected, 'But your legs look fat in that skirt.'

My heart fell out and onto the floor. I didn't want to go out any more. What little confidence I *had* mustered was now in the dustbin along with my apparently unflattering, frumpy skirt. *Hang on a minute, maybe he's doing me a favour ... Maybe he's being kind, and telling me I look fat so I don't make a fool of myself.*

Perhaps he isn't so bad after all ...

And I thought all of this was OK. Of course, it seriously wasn't. It was the makings of a controlling, emotionally damaging relationship, which was based on eroding my sense of self-worth in order for him to feel better about his own. Where was my pride? My dignity? Where was the filter? What about a selection process whereby I would *CHOOSE* a suitable mate, someone with whom I had something – even just one little thing – in common; someone who I genuinely wanted to spend my time with? Josh should have been sent packing at the very first round of auditions. The truth is, I didn't think myself worthy of that choice. I made do with what I could get, and I convinced myself that I was lucky to even have that.

I have cried many times at the memory of thinking like this. I would weep if my daughter ever had such maligned, warped beliefs about herself, and what she deserved. I would want her to be asked out by a thousand potential suitors, and to turn down the whole job lot of them if she didn't believe any were right for her – for any reason, be that having an irritating laugh, or simply for being a wanker.

I would implore her to hold out for the one person who is worthy of her affection. Or at the very least select a small number to go through to the Judges' Houses stage, where I can turn all Sharon Osbourne ('*We're eliminating Number 4, Tills. He's got a monobrow.*').

All of it was wrong, and it shouldn't have been allowed to happen. Not at that time. Not at any time.

AGED 18

June 1996

Surprisingly, Josh and I are still together. He had all last week off work and stayed over every night except Christmas evening. He is my life now, and to be truthful, I'd be lost without him, and unbearably lonely. But I'm pretty sure he's going to dump me. Mainly because:

I'm too insecure and possessive;

He's cold and unaffectionate;

I'm worried;

He isn't.

I also realised today that I have a real problem accepting myself for who I am. I know that I have some good points, and I know that some people find me attractive (I'm no supermodel, but Jesus — I'm not exactly Quasimodo either) but sometimes I have such a low opinion of myself that I can't even think of ANY of the good things about me.

It's got so bad that I can't even convince myself that Josh could love me. What does he see in me? We could be so happy together if only I'd let go of this self-conscious paranoia. I know it's my fault, not his.

Josh was in the paper on Monday, and he looked quite gorgeous, unsurprisingly. Mum wouldn't shut up about it today, saying, 'His eyes are so beautiful, aren't they, Rach?' and 'Isn't his hair lovely?' I KNOW HOW FIT HE IS MUM — I DON'T NEED REMINDING, THANKS!

I wish I was HALF as good looking as he is, but I think he loves me — even with my wonky boobs and fat legs. I'm lucky to have him — I know that.

He's cooking me a meal on Saturday night, anyway. Saying that, it'll probably be a Pot Noodle. Good job I like them.

I was the tender age of eighteen. Having already experienced an unhealthy relationship courtesy of a boyfriend who had revelled in reinforcing my painfully low levels of self-worth, something inside me changed: I had to change.

The very same wanker who'd kicked me out of my own bed the night before a three-hour Economics A-level exam unceremoniously dumped me. Even worse is the fact that I was beside myself with feelings of loss and abandonment after he discharged me of my girlfriend duties and condemned me to the dreaded Reject Bin – the place I feared the most. I realise now, of course, that his behaviour towards me was only reflective of my own levels of self-worth at that time. If only I'd known …

Two of my best friends took me to Blackpool to divert me from my warped sense of loss. Prior to this, I'd concentrated mainly on driving up to his mum's pub to beg and plead with him to give me one more chance to redeem myself, and prove that I was still worthy of his affection. The main problem being that I didn't even believe it myself, and so, understandably, my pleadings fell on deaf ears. He could do better, and so he set me free.

My head felt fuzzy and strange. I was there with my best friends in Blackpool, but at the same time, I was utterly absent. I played crazy golf. I fake-laughed for the photos: *look how much fun I'm having!* CLICK! But inside, I felt dead, having only valued myself by virtue of the desperate relationship I'd been in – and I wasn't even worthy of that any more. *What do I do now?* I didn't have a Plan B. In photos, I look to have given up. Standing on a crazy golf course wearing a horrible, baggy old grey jumper, sad sloppy jeans, with tired, jaded eyes. I was a pitiful sight to behold. Living but not feeling alive. Is there an emptier feeling in the world?

I had only just turned eighteen, and I felt utterly hopeless; hopeless and lost. I could cry now for those wasted years. If only running had found me sooner, I could have grown some confidence, happened across so many amazing adventures and experiences, and discovered my own joy – and my own worth.

As it was, I'd have a bit of a wait before I received any such epiphany, but it was on its way …

July 1996

Qualities I believe I lack:
1. Patience
2. Tidiness
3. Thinking of consequences
4. Rationality
5. Physical self-acceptance
6. Physical endurance

Things I can't do now but would like to learn how:
1. Swim front crawl
2. Write a book (and have the patience to finish it)
3. Ride a horse confidently
4. Learn to sew and make a (basic) item of clothing
5. Flower arranging (actually, scrub that one)
6. Cake decorating (and have the patience to learn in the first place without just eating the pre-decorated cake)
7. Run, even just a little bit

Fantasy wants (no matter how ridiculous):
1. Become naturally blonde
2. To be able to see further than the end of my hand (generally, to have good eyesight and not have to squint for the rest of eternity)
3. To have matching, non-wonky boobs

> 4. A flat tummy (yeah, right!)
> 5. A walk-in wardrobe
> 6. To like myself, even just a little bit

My experience of that God-awful relationship, together with the unceremonious dumping by my ex-boyfriend, was the catalyst I needed to take some long-overdue action, and reclaim my life.

I found an article whilst flicking through one of Mum's recently discarded lifestyle magazines. It was titled 'Mind Power' and it quizzed me about my current hopes and aspirations. *Where am I now?* it asked. *Where do I want to be?* I didn't know. I answered the questions anyway, and a couple of things became pretty clear.

Firstly, many of the things I *wanted* to learn to do required the very thing I lacked the most: patience. So, of my list of seven things – one of which had been eliminated immediately upon writing – six of them were non-starters. I was not prepared to be taught how to ride a horse by a snotty, naturally blonde slender fifteen-year-old in jodhpurs, nor was I about to join a group of OAPs on a cake-decorating course advertised at the local library (this was *way* before *GBBO*. There was nothing sexy about bread-making back then, and Paul Hollywood was still in short trousers). I still hated swimming with a passion, and it had only made it onto my list because I thought I should want to learn how to front crawl. Actually, I couldn't give a shit.

It appeared as though the ONE THING on my list that would actually be possible for me to try immediately was … going for a run.

Question one: *Do I have a pair of trainers?*

Answer: *Yes.*

Question two: *Do I know where they are?*

Answer: *No, but I'll find them.*

Question three: *Is there ANYTHING stopping me from putting them on (once found), and going for a run/jog/walk/ just getting out of the front door? Anything at all?*

Answer: *No. No – there isn't.*

Question four: *So, there is simply NO GOOD REASON for NOT going?*

Answer: *Shit. No. There really isn't.*

I continued to ponder the article, and read about a lady called Veronica who, once she'd realised the power of her mind, was able to change her mood. She was instructed to use affirmations from the moment she woke up, even if depression was lurking. She would tell herself, *'This is going to be a wonderful day!'* and every time she had a negative or depressing thought, she was told to create an alternative 'better' one. *Brilliant!* I thought it sounded like the easiest and most magical of magic spells. *Is that seriously all it will take?*

I wondered if I could make it work for me and my trainers. I dug them out from under the dusty old sledge in the cellar, and said out loud, *'Today, I am going to go for a wonderful run!'* Like Dorothy looking down and expecting to see a pair of glistening ruby slippers, I stared at my trainers. The sledge had been sitting on the front of them for well over six months, and so they looked more like Ronald McDonald's clown shoes, only smellier.

Regardless of the reason, and the negative, masochistic motivations still looming in the background, I decided I would go out for that run. Make no mistake here: there was no intention of ever enjoying this, nor expecting to. It was a necessary evil, and nothing more.

I glanced over at the magazine article again, and wondered why the Magic Spell had worked for Veronica, and not for me. Either way, I *STILL* didn't have any good excuse to *not* go for a run.

And so – reluctantly – I did.

DIGGING OUT THE TRAINERS

It was hard going. I set off from my mum's house and I saw the road ahead of me all bendy like a cheap, warped tablespoon handle that's come off worse in a battle with some overly frozen Ben & Jerry's. *Mmmmm. Ben & Jerry's.* The pathetic rises in the tarmac threatened to defeat me long before my trainers even got close: the fear of the 'hills' was enough. And so, I walked. Just until the bendy, warped-spoon road flattened out enough for me to believe I could face it.

I was eighteen years old, and I was as unfit and miserable as I'd ever wish to be.

Jog/walking along the road, I suddenly felt foolish and paranoid. *Are people laughing at me?* I panicked. *Will I see anyone I know? God almighty, I hope not.* This – the main (and worst) – part of the route wasn't along a busy road, thankfully. And then I reminded myself of the reason why I was doing this in the first place: *You HAVE to do this, Rach. You can't be that person any more. You NEED to do this to change.* So, I kept on putting one foot in front of the other.

I trudged up the endless, gradual incline of Albert Prom, and berated myself for being unable to cope with the half-mile ski-slope I saw ahead of me. That's what it felt like – running up a ski-slope. But I couldn't run up it. *I'll NEVER be able to run up it! When will this get any easier?* My mind had to resign itself to the fact that it might not. Not ever. That was the harsh reality.

I stopped for a breather at the end of Albert Prom, near the spooky old people's flats or sheltered housing, which was ironically situated next to the graveyard. I pulled over panting and wheezing, grateful at least for the most torturous part of my ordeal to be over.

Supporting my aching body against a conveniently placed wall, I met the pitying stares of fascinated onlookers. Dog walkers risked collision with lampposts due to their barely disguised fascination – at least, that's what it felt like to me. *'Oh, fuck off,'* I telepathically transmitted to them, along with a fake, tired smile.

Eventually, I set off again.

I prayed for a stream of endless traffic on the main road just before the park. *Is it safe to cross? I hope not.* I mastered the fake hand-on-hip stance indicating mild frustration at being somehow held back from continuing 'effortlessly' on my way by inconsiderate drivers going about their business. *Shit. It's clear to cross. I'll have to start running again. Oh, hang on – there's a learner driver approaching a quarter of a mile away. Best wait until he's gone …*

Safely in the park I happened across other runners. Some were ambling around, chatting idly to each other, barely breaking a sweat. *They're chatting! Do they have no respect?* They made it look so easy. *How do they make it look so easy?* Nothing about it was easy.

And then – finally – came the downhill bit. *Thank God!* At last, a brief reprieve from the lung-busting humiliation of the previous two miles (at most). This was the part I grew mildly fond of (love is far too strong a word), when just for a short while I could *pretend* to be a runner. I could seemingly float down the side of Manor Heath Park and make it look as though it wasn't actually killing me; I could begin to vaguely comprehend what that feeling of 'wind through my hair' felt like, and perhaps then, the very first seedlings of feeling freedom through running were sown. *But why can't it all be downhill?* That part seemed *so* unfair.

Once back on the flat, I had a half-mile plod back to my mum's. Each time, seeing her driveway come into view felt like the first glimpse of the finishing line of the London Marathon. It was the visual cue for my mind to tell my body in no uncertain terms that it was done in, and couldn't possibly take another step. And the truth of the matter is that every single time I walked back in through her front door I *felt* like I'd run my own personal marathon. I'd beaten the demons in my head that told me I shouldn't even bother trying.

'Did you enjoy it, love?' Mum called down from the upstairs bathroom, as the sharp aroma of bleach crept down the stairs and told of a motherly cleaning frenzy.

'No. It was bloody awful,' I shouted back up to her.

Why lie?

I wasn't motivated to change by any deep-rooted desire to 'find myself' or excited by the prospect of kicking ass with my newfound freedom and '*This Girl Can*' positive self-talk, but – disappointingly – by sincerely and wholeheartedly believing that I wasn't good enough; not fit for purpose. The desire to change was a kind of self-punishment, you may say – and a need to be something other than what I was.

I'd been rejected. Cast aside on to the dunce pile, and – despite the fact that in retrospect I can see my ex was an absolute arsehole – at the time I believed it was my fault because I'd let myself go. I was fat. Ugly and fat. *No wonder he'd dumped me! I'd have dumped me too!* This is a horrible truth to admit, because even then I took the blame. Not only for my relationship, but also for it ending. I didn't celebrate it and feel free; I turned on myself and stepped up the self-loathing instead.

Fortunately, my fragile self left for university, where I was (predictably) focused on beginning a new chapter, meeting new friends and making my acquaintance with 30p pints – along with the rude awakening of a law degree.

On returning home that summer, I picked up from where I'd left off a few months earlier, and found myself on a mission to transform. My burning desire for metamorphosis had begun and, over the course of the summer months, I was utterly committed to my goal. The bubbly, beer-drinking, 'curvy' law student would be gone; to be replaced by a sleeker, slender, fitter, new and improved version. Everything around me was changing, but most of all, me.

My one and only running route was from my mum's front door. It was no more than three miles in distance, and I couldn't run all of it by any stretch of the imagination. I struggled with even small inclines (I had the audacity to call them 'hills' at the time) and felt beaten by every single bump on the road.

However, it became my own personal commitment to run/walk this same route every single day. It was an obsession, my own verbal contract with myself, and I stuck to it without fail. It would only be on the very rare occasion – in exceptional circumstances – when either illness or force majeure (forgive the legal reference) would prevent me from adhering to my side of the contractual obligation. In hindsight, maybe I was taking this law degree thing a bit too seriously ...

Familiarity grew with putting on a pair of trainers, leaving the house, and run/walking the same old route; and each time on returning home thirty-five minutes later being utterly thankful for the miserable experience to end. None of it was comfortable; none of it 'flowed'; I didn't feel a rush of endorphins – I'm not sure I believed they even existed. It was only through sheer bloody-mindedness that I kept repeating the whole sorry saga.

Summer is a challenging time to begin running outdoors. For the self-conscious – or self-obsessed – it's the dreaded season of vests and shorts. *What?! There's no WAY I'm going to run through my own neighbourhood in a strappy vest. You've got to be kidding!* So, hot summer days were by far the worst. To circumvent this mental stumbling block, I would deliberately over-layer. Baggy tops and jackets accompanied me at all times.

Even when the sun was cracking the flags outside, I still wore my safety-net running jacket. One day, I foolishly left it at home, and for the whole of the three-mile loop I was entirely consumed with paranoia. *I'll take my jacket along with me next time, and tie it around my waist,* I planned, so as to avoid a repetition of the unnecessary mental turmoil. And that I did, but it kept slipping down and spinning around, making my T-shirt act like a corkscrew as it was pulled in the direction of my rotating midriff-disguising cagoule. The jacket arms flailed around in the wind, rhythmically cracking me on the thighs, making me look like an irritated Mr Tickle.

But I was slowly beginning to grow in confidence. I began to feel proud of myself for putting my trainers on every day: it would have been *so* much easier not to. As relieved as I was to crawl back through my mum's front door after my torturous daily outing, I also tingled with fresh air and a feeling of aliveness. *Yes – I felt alive.* From slumber, solitude and inactivity, my body had been jump-started into life. And I felt *so* much better for it. Was it the cumulative build-up of endorphins, or the steady, incremental steps in my gaining confidence, like a toddler building its first Duplo brick wall? Was it the fresh air and the mystical therapy it delivers in combatting an otherwise stale, sedentary lull? Did the feelings of mini-progression drive me on, as every day an increase of even just 1 per cent in my fitness made the following day's outing marginally more palatable? Or was it because this was something I was never 'cut out' to do, and yet, here I was, with my plan, my route, and my commitment, and I was sticking to it despite my Bastard Inner Chimps telling me it was entirely foolish and futile? In truth, it was all of the above.

I didn't have the confidence to vary the route, and it wasn't an option to lengthen it – *I can't even run THIS one yet!* I didn't believe I had the fitness or ability to run for any longer, or go any further.

However, just like Eric when he turns into Bananaman, a miraculous transformation was starting to occur. My weight was dropping off, and I was morphing into someone who was no longer invisible.

And people were noticing the changes …

AGED 18½

May 1997

I saw some of the lads from school out tonight, on Maine Street. One of them came over to talk to me. 'Wow, Rach! Look at you! You look amazing!' he said, his eyes sparkling at me.

I'd never seen him that close up, or even look at me before. 'Oh (ahem), thanks. Yeah, I've been trying my hand at some running lately, so I guess a bit of weight has dropped off,' I replied sheepishly, followed by an unnecessarily nervous laugh.

'I didn't think you had any weight to lose, did you? But whatever — you look great!'

I appreciated his kind comments, but really — what other reason could there have been for my invisibility for the past five years? Surely it's not just down to a few blonde highlights?

'So, erm, will you be coming out on Sunday? A few of us are meeting up in here and heading out clubbing afterwards,' he continued, whilst nervously peeling the label from his bottle of Bud.

I didn't know what to say or do. And then I panicked. What if I go back to my sad old self? What if I can't keep up this façade? I'm still the same old ME. Does it make me a fraud, now? Am I pretending to be something I'm not?

It's funny how people talk to you when you look a certain way, and treat you differently.

Anyway, best not get into a head-mess about that now. At least he spoke to me, and it was kind of him to comment on my apparent transformation. I must be worthy of a conversation now!

A BLESSING, OR A CURSE?

I thought I'd found a Magic Spell: like the one Veronica had discovered that could make her feel happy 'even if depression was lurking'. The only difference was that mine required a pair of trainers.

The excess baggage I'd been carrying around with me throughout my teenage years was falling off – and fast. My body shape was changing so rapidly, I could barely keep up with the momentum. My legs – remember how gorgeous Josh had told me they looked 'fat' in my knee-length skirt only a year or so earlier? They now felt lean and firm. In fact, over the summer, they'd come into their own, and I'd made friends with them to the extent that they were now allowed to see daylight. I became brave enough to wear shorts: *short* shorts, at that. *YAY, LEGS! GOOD JOB!*

My bum now had some evidence of muscle developing, and veered me away from the flat-arse-that-looks-like-it's-melting-and-pouring-down-my-legs look. Again, a mini-victory!

One weekend my trusty friend Jo and I went to visit a pal at university in Manchester. We went shopping, and I honed in on some jazzy-looking skin-tight red trousers in Warehouse. I bravely went to try them on. 'Bloody hell, Rach! You're a size eight!' my Manchester friend hollered at me in the changing room. 'They look ACE!'

I couldn't believe it was me. My legs looked like drain-pipes in the full-length mirror; I could fasten the size eights with ease; I didn't feel like an alien who had landed and walked into a high-street store, only to realise they don't sell clothes for foreign bodies. The sales assistant looked at me and smiled. *Did she know that this had NEVER happened to me before? Could she tell that I'd only recently got my new body?* It was *that* I was trying out – not her fancy clothes.

My stomach – well, reminding myself that having a flat one had made an appearance on my list of 'fantasy wants', together with a *'yeah, right'* written next to it some years earlier, then this was a little harder to achieve. But at the very least, we were heading in the right direction. I would still *never* wear a bikini in public, or even utter the words 'crop top' out loud. Neither of these would ever be a part of my reality, but I was certainly happier with the progress I was making.

And then there were the boobs. The famous circus-freak wonky boobs. What happened to them?

Well, they didn't behave quite so well.

AGED 19

September 1991
God, that was awful. I've just been to the gym at uni. I did my usual twenty minutes' steady plod on the treadmill, but I couldn't help thinking that the other girls were laughing at me. I felt like some kind of paranoid schizophrenic!

I had my regular baggy T-shirt on to try and disguise my body, but I felt humiliation with every pounding step on the treadmill — plus the fucking full-length mirror right in front of me didn't exactly help! I know my shoulders were hunched over as I tried in vain to hide myself away from view (which is difficult under those bloody fluorescent lights).

They were doing that snide girly giggling at someone else's expense thing, and I couldn't help but convince myself that they knew — that they could see my flaw. I felt so utterly consumed with paranoia, and embarrassment — I just wanted to crawl away and hide.

I know I've lost weight, but I'm unhappier now than I was before! I just want to feel normal, in a normal body. Why is that apparently so hard for me?

The other girls in our house have just gone up to the Union for a drink, but I've stayed put. It was the same yesterday. I couldn't face going out. I feel so distant from them — it's like I'm living with complete strangers.

And I've been doing my own head in staring endlessly in the mirror again. The longer I fixate on myself, the more I can find to hate about the person looking back at me. I sort of don't know what to do about feeling this way. I know something's seriously wrong, but what can I do about it? I'm sick of crying — I'm actually bored

> *of it. I can't talk to any of the girls here. How*
> *would they understand any of this?*
> *I'm going to have to book in to see the doctor*
> *because I can't carry on like this.*

With some effort to eat healthier, and by virtue of my religious three-mile daily run/walking routine, I was morphing into a different person. But with the emergence of a new slimline, 'more attractive', seemingly more confident Rachel, came the realisation that all was not as it seemed.

The weight loss had revealed that my wonky asymmetrical breasts were more ill-proportioned than I'd realised: even though my wanker ex-boyfriend had done me the favour of pointing out my physical defect a few years earlier, my old flab had disguised the extent of the misalignment. Of all the ironic and cruel twists of fate. All I'd wanted was to like myself, and accept my body. Now, having put in so much hard work into losing weight, it had betrayed me. My recently deflated breasts had lost their shape, were saggy and a not-insignificant two cup sizes different. I was heartbroken.

I ran on the treadmill at the university gym and watched obsessively in the full-length mirror as I saw – and felt – one breast bouncing around, whilst the other didn't move. I can laugh about it now, although at the time, any such comedy value escaped me entirely. I was riddled with anxiety and utterly self-absorbed as I struggled mentally to accept myself as I now was. *It was easier being fat!* At least I could mask the reality then, and I wasn't obsessively monitoring the eyes of other girls, who could surely see my deformity.

Living in a student house full of girls – pretty, confident, fun, carefree girls – was tantamount to torture. I was ostracised, but I'd done it to myself. My deep unhappiness and depression pushed me further and further away from any kind of friendships. I told no one about my problems. I just vanished – my soul disappeared. The laughter stopped. The other girls must have wondered what the hell had happened. *Why is Rachel acting so weird? Why is she so thin? Why doesn't she come out any more?* They just saw a shell of a person: a very unhappy, troubled soul who was difficult to be around, because she couldn't even bear to be around herself.

Feeling like I was trapped in my own body with nowhere to go, I confided in my mum. *How can I tell my poor mum that I now feel disfigured, abnormal, deformed, ugly, betrayed and completely lost in my own self-absorbed world?* I risked breaking her already fragile heart, but I was out of options.

This wasn't about me aspiring to have the 'perfect body'. I was simply aspiring to feel normal; to be able to wear normal clothes, and not have to pad one side of a bra, or feel like I had the breasts of a ninety-year-old woman. I should have been carefree, confident and full of laughter; going topless on the beach, and experimenting with non-wanker boyfriends. Instead, I was crippled with self-loathing and hatred of a body that didn't serve me.

I became introverted, depressed and obsessed with controlling my weight. It felt like the only thing I could control at the time.

And so, I became a recluse.

Thank God Mum acted quickly. We swiftly made arrangements to see a surgeon in Leeds. My options were to have one breast implant to balance out the size difference, or to have both breasts uplifted and reduced. So, beach balls or bee-stings. *Which would I choose?*

I'd hated having big boobs, and the mere thought of attracting attention to myself with false, pumped-up balloon boobs horrified me. I still wanted to hide: I just wanted to feel *normal* and hide. So, I opted for a double breast reduction. I was told that it was quite a big operation. This was an all-singing, all-dancing re-augmentation of my boobs as I knew them. They would be virtually taken off and rebuilt from scratch, but it's what I needed to have any chance of feeling normal, and not like a one-woman freak show.

Dad cried the night before my surgery, pleading with me not to go through with it. 'You're beautiful just as you are, Rachel,' he wept. 'You don't need to do this.'

But I *did* need to do it, and I trusted in my gut instinct. It was the best chance I had of ever feeling normal, and I refused to write myself off from that possibility. I was young enough to heal well, and to get over the physical and mental trauma. I knew there would be scars – and significant ones at that – but at least I could be confident in my clothes, and somewhere in my future, I could even visualise wearing regular bras. I was prepared to deal with all of it if I could realise my dream of wearing a fitted T-shirt in peace.

What excited me even more was the prospect of running with small, pert, symmetrical boobs bouncing in unison with the same amount of (minimal) 'swing'. Maybe then I'd be able to run on a treadmill without mental anguish.

It sounded ideal to me.

SURGERY

AGED 19½

December 1997

Thank God that's over. It all went well, and I'm strapped up like a mummy with bandages all around my chest area, plus a (very) tight sports bra to hold everything in place. It's actually quite comfy and, although it's a right pain because I can't get my new breasticles wet for a couple of weeks or so (until they change the dressings and take the stitches out), everything feels so much better already.

I feel like I have a body which is at least in proportion now, and I can try to move on from that horrible place. Who knows — I might even start enjoying my life a little bit!

I never thought I'd hear myself saying this, but I can't WAIT to start running again. I can't wait to see how my body feels now that I don't have to wear two sports bras (with one side padded) and stare obsessively in the mirror at the gym. What will that feel like? Will I run better? Faster? With a new sense of freedom? Will I feel lighter?

It seems ages since I've put my trainers on. I bet my usual route seems tough when I do *eventually get back out there. Ah well, it's been worth it. I'm excited to find out!*

I'm back at work in Yates's tonight, so it will be good to have some kind of normality resumed ... Plus, I've tried on a T-shirt — a fitted one — not my usual wretched XXL number (which is already in the bin) and I can't believe the difference! I think it'll take some getting used to, but I can stand tall for once, and I don't feel like I need to stoop to try and hide myself away, or balance out my lop-sided cup sizes. It's a revelation!

I'm really excited about going out again, too. I can go shopping and try on some tighter, skimpier tops (well, the right size, at least — it's all relative isn't it); I may go completely crazy and try on a colour other than BLACK!

God, these past six months have been awful. It's such a relief to FINALLY see a glimmer of light at the end of the very dark tunnel.

Following the surgery, I was elated. I was strapped up in a well-scaffolded sports bra for weeks with the dressings held firmly in place. Other than the obvious care and immediate aftermath, it was as if nothing had happened: I only told my best friend Jo what I'd been through, and she was her usual quietly supportive, endlessly considerate self. All 5' 4" of her did what she could to protect my newly sculpted boobs from sharp elbows and clumsy, drunken punters at crowded bars. As tiny as she was, she was both my radar and my bodyguard all rolled into one very compact package. I could press 'play' once more, having had my life on pause whilst I rectified my disobedient body. I'd shown it who was boss, and perhaps now I could live in harmony with a body I could grow to accept, and a future I could begin to visualise positively at last.

Initially, the combined feelings of freedom, relief and normality were euphoric. The surgery was a gamble that had paid off. Or was it a gamble at all? I'd suggest not. It wasn't my peeling back the ring-pull on some dangerous and alarming quest for bodily perfection, or the slow leveraging open of the floodgates of desire for further nips and tucks as seen in the glossy cosmetic surgery brochures. People have asked me in the many years since, 'Did you not consider speaking to your doctor about possibly getting help accepting yourself as you were rather than resorting to surgery?' and my resounding answer is, 'NO! I felt like a freak, and I didn't *want* to accept myself as I was!' I wanted to be normal, and feel like I had the body of (almost) every other nineteen-year-old girl, not resign myself to having tits like my grandma when I was barely out of my formative years.

That said, I understand the argument. As women, we are encouraged to 'love' and 'accept' ourselves as we are – lumps, bumps, curves, lines, crows' feet, sags, bags, flaws, and all. *Amen to that!* We should *all* be kinder to ourselves, and accept that some days – most days in fact – we need the L'Oréal Paris Touche Magique to conceal the Bags for Life permanently residing under our peepholes. It doesn't mean that we should necessarily have *surgery* to remove said bags, just as wearing a bit of lip-liner doesn't nudge us ever closer to the filler-induced 'trout pout'.

In my mind, the difference in my choosing the surgery option over a less extreme alternative is this: it was my aspiration for normality, as opposed to any aspiration for perfection. The two are markedly opposed, and I simply wasn't on a quest for perfection. I chose to have thick red tramline scars for the next ten years over wonky, deflated boobs, for God's sake! That's some compromise on perfection, and quite a price to pay for feeling 'normal' – but it was worth every penny.

I wasn't out of the woods yet by any means, and my quest for self-acceptance remained something Frodo Baggins would have been challenged to undertake, but my search for normality had resulted in the opportunity for me to experience fully clothed non-freakishness for what felt like the first time. It was a start, at least.

I'd found the confidence to start working in Yates's Wine Bar in Halifax town centre a few evenings a week with a group of old school friends during the never-ending summer break. I say friends, but they had no idea at all what I'd been through over the previous six months. They didn't know about my meltdown at university, or the hours of mirror-gazing in my solitary, soulless room. They had no idea about the bandages underneath my Yates's denim work shirt; or the painful red tramlines that would often make me wince at the sudden effort of pulling pints without due care. How would they? I'd hidden it from them all.

They just saw a different Rachel emerging, with 'fetching' blonde highlights and a less heavy fringe. I'd almost succeeded at venturing into their carefree world, at last.

Well, almost …

RUNNING AWAY
... FROM MYSELF

January 1998

Yayyy! I've been back out running today for the first time since the major boob-refurb. God, it was such a relief!

It felt strange; strange but good. My mummified chest was held together so tightly by my ever-present sports bra that even a nuclear blast wouldn't make those babies shift. Seriously, I couldn't believe the lack of movement. I'm not sure what I was expecting, but the absence of my usual 'double-bra/mono-bounce' scenario was hard to get my head around. I felt SO much lighter, though. My body is healing unbelievably well, and I feel like I've finally been freed from some heavy, invisible chains that were holding me prisoner.

My running route is just as I remembered, only my body felt lighter, and my mind less burdened. I noticed a few things that surprised me: my arms could swing freely as I ran today, whereas they used to be held in a semi-fixed position trying to camouflage my chest: I hadn't even realised I was running semi-paralysed before — maybe that's why my arms and shoulders ached after only one frickin' mile!

And for once, I didn't have to keep looking down at my chest to monitor myself on the freakish scale. I could look around me, and I saw things I hadn't noticed before — beautiful things — because I was looking up instead of down.

Saying all of that, a complete miracle hasn't occurred, unfortunately. I still wrestled with myself whilst I was out pounding the pavements today. It was STILL bloody hard work; I was STILL breathing out of my backside, and I STILL hate that nasty little hill just as I approach the woods near Mum's. I seem to have to walk every single time I get to the bastard thing — will it never get any easier?!

Also bizarre is the fact that I've genuinely missed running. I came back through Mum's front door today and felt strangely happier. That always seems to happen — it remains a complete mystery: how can something so utterly painful make me feel so much better?

I know I've been increasingly worried about putting weight back on since I've not been able to run whilst recovering from the op — and I've been cutting down on my eating to try and mitigate the calorific damage, but I have genuinely missed running all the same. Who'd have thought!

My running resumed pretty quickly after the surgery, and the very first indications were good. I'd discovered a newfound freedom whereby I could hop onto the treadmill without mental torment and trot along with minimal, synchronised bounce.

But it didn't last long.

Running to me had sadly become nothing more than the magic weight-loss tool I was obliged to integrate into my daily life in order to never again go back to how I used to be. It was forced; laboured; still hard to step out of the door most days, and it was my own contractual obligation – the price I had to pay for the *'Wow, you look great!' 'Crikey, you've lost some weight!' 'Good grief, you look amazing!'* comments I was rapidly becoming familiar with.

And running was becoming addictive – only for all the wrong reasons. If I missed a run, I was one step back down the ladder to the sad, lonely, invisible old Rach. I'd seen the other side, and it was the fear of regression that kept me hooked on my self-induced running regime. I had no grand aspirations of progressing with it. If I could get away with the minimal effort required to remain at a safe distance from my old self, then I was happy with that. My journals hold no mention of the mental adjustment I may have needed to enable me to keep pace with my rapidly decreasing jeans size, or the alien comments from newfound admirers. *JUST KEEP RUNNING, RACH. KEEP ON RUNNING AWAY FROM YOURSELF. THAT IS WHAT RUNNING IS TO YOU. THAT IS ALL IT IS, AND PROBABLY ALL IT EVER WILL BE.*

What about my mind? What did *that* need to keep me sane throughout all of this madness? What about those fleeting moments that I'd only just discovered since my recent physical liberation – the ones where I could look up and witness the magical cloud formations, or marvel fleetingly at the view ahead and feel the wind in my face? They simply vanished, having been usurped by some invisible, insane pressure to run away from myself. Any epiphany that may have been hovering just around the corner to release the joys, freedom and magic of running was entirely kiboshed by an endlessly heavy, crippling pressure to transform my outer shell at the expense of my inner peace.

So, I continued with this burdensome, uninspiring running plan: one with no end date, and at the same time with no real purpose, other than to keep me from becoming my sad old self.

AGED 20

> May 1998
> Where have I gone? Why do I feel so sad? I've been through all of this, and I still feel dead inside. I can't understand what's gone wrong. Wasn't the dawning of a 'new and improved Rach' supposed to make things easier, to make me happier? It doesn't seem to have worked out that way. I'm even more confused now, wondering who I am — who I'm supposed to be. How do I act? What do I say? I don't know where to go from here.
>
> I run, but I don't know why any more. Is it only so I can fit into my skinny jeans? Is that all?! I hate that it's turned into this for me.

I went on a night out in town with Jo at the weekend. I know I've just had some more blonde highlights flashed through my hair, but people who haven't spoken to me throughout the entirety of my school years began to strike up random conversations. I stood there and felt my Inner Geek protesting: 'Hang on a minute — I was still ME last year, and the year before that. I was funny then — remember? I may have been quiet, with a heavy fringe and thick glasses, watching you "cool guys" from the sidelines, but I still wanted to be invited to the party and to be asked out on a date. Where were you then? Why was my conversation not worthy of your attention then?'

Now that I look a certain way, in a certain size clothes, with a certain colour hair, I appear to be validated — stamp of approval received. But it all feels so hollow and false. I don't want those empty conversations. It makes me sad to think that I was right to want to run away from myself in the first place — like I was never good enough as I was. And it's nothing to do with the boobs. It's the shrinking, blonde imposter I'm faced with in the mirror every morning. I want to like her — I really do.

The metamorphosis I'd gone through over such a relatively short time had taken its toll. From the angst of my mid-teenage years, I'd battled with ugly, overweight invisibility: I'd become comfortable with not being seen. I'd lived in the background, settling for unsupportive boyfriends, accepting that as my lot.

And I was kind of comfortable with all of that. I knew how that felt, and I'd learned how to act. Over the years, I'd figured out how to compensate for my shortcomings with the other things I had in my armoury (being 'clever' was a good one; 'funny' another). I'd grown into my role. It may have been a small audience, but over time, they responded well. If truth be told, I was settled – if not perhaps even happier – knowing myself in this way. And I actually quite liked those aspects of myself. I made people laugh, over even the most desolate teenage years.

What did mess with my head was when the show changed. *Enter stage left the new, improved, radically transformed … Rachel!* I naively thought it would be so much easier being a neater, 'prettier' (subjective) package. I'd surely have an outpouring of social ease and confidence: I'd laugh in all the right places and throw my head back as I guffawed at the in-jokes, my blonde hair swinging effortlessly around my shoulders.

It never happened.

Instead, I felt like an alien who'd been trapped in head-lights on the M62, made massively visible by the direct glare of luminosity. *'Whoa, whoa, WHOA! Let me stop you there. This is NOT what I signed up for. I just wanted to feel normal – to be accepted. It should be easier than this. It has to be!'* My Inner Geek didn't waver. It hadn't been consulted as part of the transformational process, and so simply refused to play along with the new, improved outer version of myself. In fact, it was worse than that. It actively tried to sabotage my efforts, and even grieved a little for the old me.

Whereas I used to be funny (the subjectivity theme continues ...), my Inner Geek wasn't laughing any more. Instead, I was preoccupied with my newly assumed role. I had to adapt to conversations I hadn't needed to before, and see things in a way that my old Coke-bottle-bottom specs found unfamiliar. People spoke to me now, when they hadn't bothered to before, in a way that was different to before. It all seemed so confusing, and so false. I didn't know what to think, or what the truth was any more.

And then my Inner Geek asked *why*. It probed a little further. Based on the fact that all this was happening now, my logical reasoning confirmed that there *had* in fact been something inherently wrong with the old me! *I was right all along! I WAS flawed. Defunct. Not fit for purpose.* This realisation hit me hard, because it appeared to validate all the previous years of self-loathing, and my being undeserving of visibility.

But I couldn't accept it. My Inner Geek wouldn't let me. It knew the real me, and it loved the real me. This new, polished, blonde imposter was no replacement for the old Rachel, who my Inner Geek had loved and found funny *regardless* of the fringe, the glasses, the weight, the hair colour, and the wonky boobs. It tried to reconcile the two, and together we muddled through. But my physical metamorphosis simply wasn't the Golden Ticket to inner peace and personal freedom I'd been fooled into thinking I'd bought.

And then I began to ponder, '*Well, if the reaction to me losing a bit of weight is so dramatically different, then clearly I need to lose MORE weight. I need to be thinner ... I need to be blonder ...*' The messages I'd received as a little girl at my friend's birthday party with the pink bouncy castle were right all along!

Inside, my Inner Geek wept, as it couldn't understand where the real me had gone. Being consumed with self – again. Only this time, in chasing an ever-elusive, unobtainable goal, it had left my soul dead: cold and dead.

I was now well on board the body dysmorphia and depression bus: I didn't know when, or where, I would eventually get off.

September 1998

I dragged myself to the university campus gym today to execute my usual daily dreadmill calorie-burning obligation. I'm feeling tired, sluggish and hungry, but I also feel ridiculously guilty when I eat.

I trudged up to the counter and showed my membership card to the guy on the desk, barely looking him in the eye. 'Gym, please,' I said, feeling tired before I'd even got in there. He looked at me, glanced down to the photo on my Union card, and then back up to my face for a double-take.

'Crikey. What's happened to you?' he said. He didn't mean to be hurtful, and I'm not even sure he realised that the words had slipped out of his mouth. I knew exactly what he meant: my Union card photo shows a bright-eyed, healthy, vibrant young woman, whereas the person standing before him was a twenty-year-old scrawny, hollow, distant shadow of a girl barely resembling the photo ID. His words hit me like a train — but I know he was right.

What has happened to me? Why am I so broken? Where have I gone?

Then I came back home again to hide.

THE BLONDE IMPOSTER

As I struggled to align the new version of myself alongside my stunned yet faithful Inner Geek, I simply didn't know how to be, or who I was any more. Trying to get back to the pretence of some normality during my third year at university whilst living in a house full of girls who I wasn't close to only heightened my sense of not-belonging. Perhaps I'd been too embarrassed to confide in them about my body image issues; perhaps I'd judged them, and assumed that they wouldn't understand. Either way, I chose to push them all away.

My running was now an energy-depleting, laboured chore with the sole purpose of burning calories in a wilful attempt to shrink: I was turning into my mum! I'd reduced my food intake to such a degree that I was only just able to exist. I measured out measly portions; I missed meals; I went teetotal (alcohol contains bagloads of calories, don't you know?) and I turned into a version of my mother I had never in my wildest imagination thought possible: minimal energy intake + maximum energy output = shrinking and once again invisible Rach. The irony was so ridiculous that I didn't even see it until years later when I realised – I'd come full circle.

I hid myself away in my cramped, lonely bedroom. I simply lost the will to go out. It became harder to summon up the courage to even go to the corner shop. I stared endlessly in the mirror, as if trying to see the real me through all of the confusion. *Maybe if I stare long and hard enough, I'll see glimpses of the real Rach, and it will prove to me that she's still in there, somewhere.*

I was now suffering from severe depression, and increasingly concerning levels of body dysmorphia. I had absolutely no idea at the time that such a condition even existed. However, in retrospect, I exhibited all the classic traits of somebody crippled by the disorder. The Body Dysmorphic Disorder Foundation website describes a sufferer being someone who has a 'disabling preoccupation with perceived defects or flaws in appearance' which makes them 'excessively self-conscious, causing devastating distress and interfering with the ability to function normally, particularly socially'. Yep. That was me.

Within the confines of my (very) small bedroom, staring endlessly into the mirror, all I could see were flaws. I'd almost go out of my way to find blemishes that would then justify my obsession. Perhaps if I took my eyes off the mirror even fleetingly, I'd miss a trick and I would be ambushed by ugliness. I couldn't take the risk, and so I remained vigilant. Just in case.

I didn't want to see anybody at all, and the worst relationship in the world I had at that time was the one with myself. It was a particularly bleak period of inner turmoil.

Everything about me must have screamed that I was someone on the edge, only just managing to cope.

My quest for normality ran in parallel with my quest for acceptance. I desperately wanted to be in the Cool Gang, and be invited to the party; to be asked out by the captain of the football team; I yearned to be seated in the middle of the girly lunchtime huddle, and not perched perilously on the outskirts. I wanted to be Sandy from *Grease* when she revamps her square Little Miss Prim image, and dons her circulation-stopping leather trousers. I wanted to make an about-turn on my insanely provocative stilettoes, and invite a panting Danny to 'Tell me about it, stud!' Yes! That's what I wanted! ALL of that.

Like Sandy, I *had* revamped my hair; I *had* shrunk and poured myself into my very own painted-on leather pants; I *had* attracted the attention of the T-Birds who began to swoop and circle around me as if I were a recent kill. The Cool Girls *had* invited me to the party. And I went ... but it was shit.

All of it was shit. The promise of acceptance and validation held as much water as a leaky bucket. It filled me with fear and unease. *What if I put a stone back on and don't fit into my size eight trousers any more? Will I still be invited to the party then?* I wasn't convinced. *What if I don't want to be blonde, and I decide to grow back my heavy fringe? Do I suddenly become invisible?* Again, I feared that I knew the answer.

I felt trapped in a dichotomy between *wanting* to be invited to the party by the Cool Gang, but at the same time wanting nothing whatsoever to do with it. I may have earned the invitation to their party, but I knew that I never really belonged there. Or even wanted to go.

September 2015

Some races are just over way before the finish line. I had one of those today. I turned up and I tried to race, but my body wasn't having any of it. My gut feeling has been one of fighting an underlying infection for a good week or so now.

Perhaps the definition of stupidity is turning up expecting to be able to race knowing full well I'm not right, but even more stupid would have been to ignore my body's screams to stop, and carry on pushing it regardless. For once, I listened.

Every time I took a breath, my throat felt like it was closing up. Gut feelings go a long way, and at the very least I listened to mine today. I'm trying to deal with my feelings of disappointment and frustration that on this occasion, my body just wouldn't perform as I've asked it to. And there is literally nothing I could do about it.

I guess from a 'learning experience' and a more holistic point of view, I've been trying to think about what I can take from today. What can I learn from it? What are the positives? It reminds me that there are times when it really is OK to just get off the bus.

I thought back to the decision I made to step off my degree course, with the same feelings of disappointment and frustration.

There is a right and a wrong time to race ... I'll have my time another day.

So, my university years were a runaway emotional roller-coaster. Turning up all wet behind the ears on day one at my new student house in a very average street in Hull, I could never have predicted the 'me' that would emerge, somewhat battered and bruised – not to mention scarred – two years later.

I was spent. The previous years of inner turmoil had left me without any will or desire to complete my degree. I just didn't care any more. I felt broken and exhausted. The endless study, lectures and seminars, not to mention my more recent emotional baggage, had all but destroyed me: I simply needed to stop the bus and get off for a while – even if just to stretch my legs and have a loo break. Every ounce of my being told me that if I didn't, I would either flunk my degree or – even worse, and far more likely – have a complete breakdown. I'd kept so many secrets to myself that I was at serious risk of imploding: inside my own head was the loneliest place on earth.

Dad was heartbroken at my decision to step off the law degree, especially in such sudden, dramatic style. My fall from grace must have been shocking, on top of all the upset surrounding my 'drastic' weight loss and breast operation only months before. I can fully understand why. *How could it have gone so wrong?* He'd invested in me. He'd seen my academic achievements build year on year, and he saw my prestigious law degree as the hope for his youngest girl's future. But that was his hope, not mine. It was where my potential existed in *his* world – not in mine. *How could I have come so far down the road, only to fall at the last hurdle? How could I throw in the towel when the finish line was right around the corner? Where had his girl gone?*

He didn't realise that my bus was going to crash.

'But, Dad, this isn't the end for me,' I frustratingly tried to explain. 'Honestly, you need to trust me on this one, Dad. I don't plan on wasting the past two years to come away with absolutely nothing.'

I willed him to believe that I wasn't a quitter or a *'nearly girl'*. I simply needed time out to save myself from breaking down. But I could see in his eyes that he didn't believe me, not for a second. This was a particularly deep disappointment, because I was supposed to be the one from our family – his family – who *'did well for themselves'*. It was often quoted in jest that Dad's only qualification was his cycling proficiency. He'd built his own successful business regardless, but he saw my qualifications as the golden ticket to a brighter, happier, more successful future.

His daughter, the lawyer: *oh yes – that sounds wonderful!* I imagined the conversations with his work colleagues down the pub: *'My youngest, Rachel, she's at university studying for a law degree. Oh for sure, Bob – we're all VERY proud of her. She's always been a clever girl. Naturally studious. She must get it from her mother – it's certainly not from me!'* (Cue raucous laughter.)

Instead, he got:

'Yes, well, our Rachel has, erm, she's had a mini – well, actually quite a major – meltdown whilst at university … (embarrassed cough). She's had some (ahem) personal issues to deal with which have pushed her into a kind of depression, and it's sort of gone downhill from there …' (Cue awkward silence and swift change of conversation.)

I felt like the worst daughter in the world for robbing my dad of the far preferable first option for his pub-night conversation, and replacing it with the toe-curling, real-life alternative. I absorbed his despondency, but deep down I knew I wasn't done with my law degree. I fully believed I would finish it somehow, some way – but not like this, and not whilst I was broken and in need of repair.

Overriding everything was the need to get myself well. No qualification in the world would help whilst I was a person on the edge of not being able to get out of bed in the morning and function. Interviewers tend to pick up on these things. Just like the guy on the desk at the university campus gym: I could have been a qualified NASA flight technician, but he wouldn't have given me a job mopping up the gym floor given the space cadet he saw in front of him that day.

I made my arrangements with the university, and I walked away from there, knowing that even if one day I resumed my studies, I would never go back to that particular institution. Not ever. I knew I wouldn't see any of the friends I'd made there again. I made a very clinical decision to move forward with my life, and never look back.

My dad would have to deal with his own issues around the general pessimism and concerns about my future. Yes, it was '*a shame*' that I'd apparently fallen at the last hurdle, but he wasn't to know that around the corner, I would find the strength to get back on the horse …

My race wasn't over yet.

PART 4

GROWING UP

AGED 21

July 1999

God, what a relief! I almost feel — dare I even say it? — normal! Yes: NORMAL! That most elusive of states I've been relentlessly chasing for what seems like an eternity. I've been mulling it over — why and how do I feel 'normal' now?

- I felt 'normal' wearing my new fitted grey work suit today — like a shiny pin, in fact. I even got wolf-whistled as I was walking along the main road to the office (cringe!).
- My new suit fits in all the right places, and I didn't buy two sizes too big just to try and hide or disguise myself in some way (plus, I am wearing a NORMAL BRA underneath it. WOO HOO!).
- Nobody knows me here. It's a new start, with new people, in a new job, and I've got a brand-new blank canvas ...
- I feel like a grown-up. I'm earning my own income, and not stuck in some bloody lecture theatre sucking up all kinds of

> bullshit philosophising about criminology
> (although it was mostly policies and
> procedures today, and various other
> induction-related bollocks so ...).
> - I also feel like I'm part of the world, now, and
>   not just pretending to be.
>
> This is light years away from where I was just a
> few months ago. God forbid I ever go back to that
> dark place. Perhaps this is the dawning of a new
> era for me ... Fingers crossed!

Having jumped off the Runaway Nervous Breakdown Bus, I was utterly relieved to leave my recent miseries behind me and focus on putting my life back together. My quest for normality got off to a good start.

I found myself a job temping at the Halifax building society's head office in Leeds, and I felt like an adult for the first time. It was the change I so desperately needed, and the chance to start again. Nobody knew me. Nobody needed to know the mess I'd just escaped from, or how only months earlier I felt like the saddest, loneliest girl in the world, stuck in my prison university bedroom in Hull, wishing I could be transported to another place. This *was* that new place: the new start I'd been gifted. I could meet new people, and introduce them to the new, improved Rachel who'd discarded the shackles of the past and created a whole new 'me' ... again.

Welcome then the more traditional, stereotypical early twenties melting pot of work, overly frequent post-work vodka-bar drinking binges, and darting around town in my Peugeot 205. *This is what other people are doing! This is what real life consists of. Phew! Maybe I can be 'normal' after all.*

As I began to move on from my troubles, and as time helped distance me from the painful memories, things settled down. At the very least I knew I looked good in my tailored work suit: the weight had stayed off, and my new boobs remained firmly in place (literally – they did). My newly high-lighted hair flattered me, and I entered my new chapter every bit the shiny pin – albeit a fragile one.

All the outer work I'd done on fixing my sub-standard, delinquent body had gone some way to restoring my belief that I could feel normal, and fit in. And I did carry it off with some degree of success (I may even have been picked for position of Centre at netball, with a bit of work on the screeching). But the well-rehearsed outer air of confidence I now exuded masked completely the inner doubts and insecurities that continued to plague me. I was told by a new work colleague that on first meeting I initially came across as being 'rather aloof with an air of superiority'. I laughed, knowing the insecure reality that bubbled behind the glossy veneer (we subsequently became good friends).

And so, problems were lurking just around the corner. Despite all the recent aesthetic mouldings, shaping, trimming and fixings – *still* no repair had taken place to the inner me. She was as vulnerable as ever; maybe even more so, as now the risk of being absolutely misunderstood was at its greatest. The distance between the real me, and the polished version of myself I now portrayed, was vast.

As I settled into my new commuting groove, all that I could have hoped for began to become a reality: I was steadily beginning to make a life for myself. But I had mistakenly attached my self-worth on the glossy veneer – on the things that really didn't matter: what I looked like on the label meant more to me than what was inside the bottle. It didn't cross my mind that I would be better placed trying to fix the inner me, as opposed to focusing on how I looked in a power suit.

Eventually, I would be made to face this glaring omission.

RUNNING: YOU'RE DUMPED

My train journey over to Leeds of a morning and back again at the end of the day was proving to be a particular highlight. I met a colourful character called Tom who worked in our office. I'd spot his amazing dreadlocks bouncing along the Leeds station platform from a thousand paces. I looked out for him every morning, and again at night. Before long we travelled into work together and back home again, locating each other like homing pigeons amongst the swarm of daily commuters. As we gradually began spending more and more time together, we soon started dating, eventually becoming like a pair of self-absorbed kids who didn't want to play with anyone else in the playground. It didn't matter what scars I had, what my insecurities were, or what either of us had been through. I could be myself with Tom. There were no staged conversations; no stilted moments when conscious thought had to step in and spare us an awkward silence. We just were. And that was enough … or it should have been.

This was the year that I dumped running. Sadly, it has happened since – and I've paid a high price every single time. I was fully consumed with the other self-absorbed melodramas in my life, and perhaps I thought I didn't need running any more. *I can easily fit into my tailored power suit now, so surely that's job done?*

Maybe I mistakenly believed I'd already been saved.

I hadn't.

Remember my relationship with my wanker boyfriend when I was seventeen? I hadn't learned my lesson, and so I was made to go through hell for a second time.

There was a stud in our office – let's call him 'Mr T'. He was a good few years older than me, being a mature, worldly-wise twenty-six to my naive twenty-one. He was also considered to be the Hugh Grant eligible bachelor of our open-plan, corporate floor: The Catch.

Whether I was tempted by the lure of being the girl to bag this paper-pushing Adonis, I can't be sure. However, just like a desperate teen to a pop idol, my ego was attracted by the possibility of attaching myself to said Mr T. With his maturity and sophistication, not to mention his purported good looks and single status, it was all too much for my fragile ego to resist.

One day, close to Christmas time, I looked over at his desk and saw that he'd put silver tinsel up around his PC monitor. Before my brain could step in and press ABORT, my fingers set about tapping out an email. It simply said:

EMAIL TO: Mr T
SUBJECT: Nice Tinsel

And that was it. With those two words, I made the leap into flirtation cyberspace with Mr T, and at that very moment, I turned my back on Tom.

I couldn't see the impact of my silly, fragile ego hard at work. I ended things with Tom, and – of course – he was heartbroken. He looked as sad as anyone I'd ever seen.

Mr T was, well, bland. He was Mr Average: pleasant, yet lacking in any sparkle. Decent looking, but on closer inspection, he looked tired and sallow. He wasn't particularly funny either. I didn't enjoy his company at all, if truth be told. And I'm pretty sure he felt equally as underwhelmed about me: I didn't rock his world either.

Without even realising it, I had entered the tumbleweed land of Relationship Desolation once again. I tolerated, accepted and condoned. I 'made do'. *WHY HADN'T I LEARNED MY LESSON?* Because I was still firmly in the vice-like grip of the cripplingly low self-esteem that had engulfed me for so long.

Being in a relationship validated my existence. My fragile ego needed to prove that I was 'good enough' or 'attractive enough' or '(whatever) enough' to bag myself not just any old boyfriend, but our very own small-town Office Stud. That validation never came from myself. Not ever.

I would have to kiss a lot of frogs, stomach a generous helping of heartache and come to the realisation over the next fifteen years that I could – and would – only ever be able to legitimise myself. I had no idea what I was searching for back then. How ironic that the only place I didn't think of looking was inside of myself.

Worse still, a strange neediness had engulfed me since my faux companionship with Mr T. I became afraid to leave his side. I feared building and enjoying my own life independently of him and risking abandonment. I rarely ran. I rarely did

anything either by or for myself. It was more than my fragile
self could bear. If I went for even a half-hour run, would he be
there when I got back? I have only one recollection of going
for a run during this godforsaken time. Even that was done
purely out of abject fear of becoming invisible again.

But perhaps I could sense it already happening ...

October 2015

I'm persistently reminded of my past, of my
'fatness', and my insecurities. I'm haunted by the
fear of regressing into being That Person again: the
one who shudders at the memories of those sad, lost
and lonely years more than logic could possibly
explain. The one who didn't know running: who
couldn't run very well, or fast, or barely at all; the
one who struggled to drag her sorry self around
even the lowliest of routes and distances for so
many of her 'prime' years. The one for whom
running began merely as a begrudging weight-
loss tool, and yet ended up saving her sanity.

Maybe I'm being reminded that I am not That
Person any more – that I need to move past this
point of being driven by fear. By now, surely I
should be motivated by progression and success
... Haven't I earned that, at least?

Perhaps it's also a lesson for me to appreciate
what my body and my bloody-mindedness

have done for me: what I've proven time and time again I'm capable of, and to appreciate experiencing what I never believed could be mine.

It's also a timely reminder for me to be grateful for when my running flows – when it feels effortless, and I feel free and alive: a gentle reminder of the importance of gratitude.

More, more, more, further, faster, harder, better, lighter, thinner – when does it end? When is enough ever enough? Today brings it back to these – gratitude, freedom and joy. Without all these things, I shouldn't be running at all, let alone racing.

I have to remind myself: look how far you've come, Rach! You're not 'That Person' any more.

Mr T wasn't a deliberately cruel person. He hadn't locked me in the house or stolen my car keys – he hadn't burnt my trainers either. But I knew that I stifled him with my intense, unrelenting ever-presence. One day, as if to assert that I had once, previously, had a life, I picked up my trainers. I tried hard to remember the person I was before I'd lost myself – again.

'Do you mind if I go for a bit of a run?' I ventured, as if I were making some outlandish proposal.

'No, not at all. Ben's coming round shortly and we're going to play on the PlayStation, anyway.'

I knew he genuinely didn't mind if I went out. In fact, I sensed that he WILLED me to go and leave him alone, even just for a short while.

Anyway, I hated the fucking PlayStation and the smoking, beer-swilling layabouts who came round and polluted the air with their fag breath, endless bags of stinking onion rings and their ban on daylight. And I hated myself even more for putting up with it.

'I don't know when I'll be back,' I said, heading out the door as if about to depart for a Himalayan trekking adventure.

He grunted some half-acknowledgement which, in reality, meant *'Oh just fuck off out, Rachel – can't you see I'm playing* Grand Theft Auto?'

I'd barely put my trainers on since getting together with Mr T. They felt uncomfortable and weird. I took my time shutting the door behind me. *Shit. It's a long time since I did this.*

My brain was overloaded with choice. It spun me into a panic. *Which direction do I head off in? Which route shall I take? Hang on, I don't know any routes … Fucking hell, all the roads and side streets look the same. Where do I go, what do I do?*

In the short time I'd been with Mr T, I'd lost running, I'd lost confidence and I'd lost myself. I hadn't seen it coming. I hadn't felt my confidence slowly erode, like the edges of a cliff waiting to fall into the sea. It was overwhelming. I literally didn't know which direction to turn, or what to do. I didn't even realise how utterly lost I'd become.

I ran up one tatty urban side street, and back down another – also lined from top to bottom with grim-looking wheelie-bins. *Am I running around in circles?* I had no idea. I just wanted to stop and collapse on the floor. My neediness was suddenly in overdrive. I was on a main road, and saw a phone box. I made a beeline for it.

'Hi, it's me. I'm – erm, I'm lost. I don't know where I am or how to get back to yours. Can you come and pick me up?' I said, weakly. I knew I sounded as pathetic as I felt – perhaps even more so. At least I'd been out of the house though: that was something.

'Jesus, Rachel. You've haven't been gone for ten minutes!' he replied, sounding irritated. I didn't blame him. 'What can you see from where you are?'

'Yeah … well, I'm sorry. There's a big Esso garage straight opposite. I'm on a main road, if that helps?' I said sheepishly. I was becoming increasingly frustrated with my own pitiful self, but was simply unable to shake myself out of it.

'For fuck's sake, Rachel. You're only about two minutes away from the house!' he snarled down the phone. I heard him take a long drag of his Marlboro to stem his exasperation.

'Turn around and come all the way back up the same street you're standing on, and you'll see my car.'

There was no warmth in his voice. No shared comedy value in my weak directional misgivings. This wouldn't be one to tell the grandkids. I felt pathetic and useless.

I'd run around in circles for all of about two miles – if that – and *even then* I couldn't find my way home. And it wasn't my home anyway – it was somebody else's; somebody who I was clinging on to whilst desperately trying to keep myself from falling into the reject bin … again.

I couldn't hang on for much longer.

If ever I needed to find my running again, it was now. If I needed to rediscover some semblance of self-worth, which I'd successfully managed to erode throughout this whole debacle, then this was that time. Instead, I clung on to the threads of a soulless relationship, and even allowed myself to feel convinced that I needed it more and more.

I couldn't walk away and be on my own. That would be awful. Inconceivable.

And so, I clung to Mr T with the strength of a limpet on a rock face, despite knowing in the deepest crevasses of my being that it was wrong, and that we were ultimately doomed. Denial can be a spectacular thing.

One large wave would be all it took to dislodge me from the rock, as painful as it felt at the time.

December 2015

Well, it's fine poring over the 'miraculous properties' of running and its ability to cure manic depression, sleep deprivation, grumpiness, and a whole host of other unwelcome mental-health afflictions. But today's run painted a very different picture. It didn't feel like therapy; I wasn't overcome with any kind of 'spiritual healing'; I didn't have an epiphany. It was just bloody hard – fourteen miles of hard.

How can running do that to me? It teases me, and plays with my mind. Just when I begin to think I've 'seen the light', it changes the game: It becomes hard again. I have to dig deep again. I wonder why the hell I bother – again. I wonder when it will be over … again.

And so it was today. It didn't flow. I didn't float along the canal towpath bedazzled by the beauty of nature. I trudged, chugged and heaved myself along – slowly ticking off the miles. How could they go so slowly? So painfully slowly.

And then, just as I turned around at the halfway point (still miffed that I had to drag my sorry arse all the way back along the never-ending canal towpath, but grateful at least to be heading in the direction of home), an elderly gent came walking towards me.

'See you in the next Olympics!' he said, with a wry smile as he pushed his grandson along in a pushchair.

'Yeah – keep an eye out for me, won't you?' I replied, dryly.

I couldn't work out if I was actually rather offended by his quip and subsequent chuckle, or whether I was just being overly sensitive. Was he being friendly, or was he mocking me? Either way, I was too tired to care. And with seven miles still to go, I wished I could click my ruby slippers together and be transported instantly back to my car. Unfortunately, I had to settle for the harder, less comfortable one-foot-in-front-of-the-other option.

Some runs are just hard. That is all.

The harder I clung on to the rock face, the weaker my grip became. It didn't take long before he dumped me. It was Wanker Josh scenario all over again! Only worse, because I *should* have been fixed; I *should* have learned my lesson. I'd been given the chance of a clean slate, and instead of creating a happy future, I'd repeated all of the sad, insecure, desperate mistakes that had led me to flounder in that place called Lostness before. And to add insult to injury, I'd met – and lost – someone who I genuinely *did* care about, and I'd let him go because of my silly egotistical need to prove some pointless, invisible nothingness to some pointless, invisible nobody.

I went for a run from my mum's house. Tears stung my eyes, and snot snaked its way from my nostrils like competing slug trails, whilst the rain doused me through to the bone. *'Even the fucking weather is pitying me!'* I thought, allowing myself to wallow briefly in my own pathetic misfortune.

But at the same time, the relentless rain was cleansing me; stunning me into a sudden realisation. *I can still do this! I haven't been running lately – for ages, in fact – but I can STILL put my trainers on, and run. I can run, and I am free. That's it … I'M FREE!*

And then. Out of all the mess, the destruction and complete blur that was my life, I began to open my eyes. As I squinted through my rolling, salty tears and the heavy, swollen raindrops, I could just about see the makings of some clarity forming.

I could vaguely make out a future that could still be mine. If I tried *really* hard, I could make the blurry image bigger and brighter, stronger and clearer. My law degree was two-thirds complete: I could finish it and give myself options.

Whilst still running face-first into the relentless, lashing rain, I repeated the words to myself over and over again. *I'M FREE!* I had no Wanker Boyfriend, no shackles, and nothing to stop me from dusting off the cobwebs and picking up from where I'd dived off the bus as it made its emergency stop. All of this became clear to me in that magical running, rainy 'pathetic fallacy' moment. Running had reminded me that I had freedom and choices, and whilst I had those, I would be brave and trust in my ability to make the right one. I needed – and desperately wanted – a new start. As some small comfort, I knew I'd done the whole 'starting again' thing before. *Surely I'd make a better fist of it this time around?*

I'd always planned on crossing the finishing line.

And so I got back in the saddle of my semi-abandoned law degree. Once I was up and galloping again, things progressed quite nicely.

My Inner Geek rejoiced as it was reunited with learning and study. *YESSSS! I'M HOME! I CAN DO THIS!* It breathed a sigh of relief as I immersed myself in legal statutes, theories and dissertations. My brain was given such a monumental task in finally achieving my nearly flunked law degree that I barely had the time or inclination to be sucked into the downward spiral of yet more self-absorbed angst. That goal was my only focus, and thankfully, my fear of failure allowed me to be temporarily freed from any competing, ugly agenda.

I was also alone again. I had joined a new university rather than go back to my old one which held too many painful memories. *Who jumps on to a three-year degree course, at a strange university, in the last year, knowing nobody?* I did.

All of my focus was on achieving my qualification. I couldn't even comprehend an alternative after all I'd been through.

I did finally complete my law degree … and I opted for the most obvious route possible: a legal career beckoned. Still absolutely bamboozled with – well – life really, and with no particular ambition, thoughts of my dad's new conversations with his work mates down the pub echoed in my mind. He could *still* boast about his daughter, The Lawyer. I had given him back his dream.

It was simply the most obvious thing to do, in the absence of any better ideas. It wasn't *my* dream, but following his was better than none.

THE DAILY CHORE

AGED 22

November 2000

At least it's flat over here in York. I've found a new route from my house. I run into the city centre after law college a couple of times a week. It's only a four-mile round trip, but I've found a way of making it enjoyable. I've picked up a (very) dodgy habit of calling into this 'health food shop' and buying a big bag of yoghurt-coated bananas as a reward for my efforts. I think I'm getting addicted to the bloody things! I've been wondering why my weight is slowly creeping back up, and then today I shocked myself: there's more saturated fat, sugar and calories in a bag of those bloody yoghurt bananas than in a Mars bar! Jesus. I've been on a diet equivalent to about eight friggin' Mars bars a week, and I fell for it, thinking I was being 'healthy'! God, I feel so stupid, but I'm going to have to find a new, less damaging 'fix'.

    I need to up my game with running too: I know I'm only ticking a box and going through the motions at the moment — probably so I can ease

> *my guilt over some of the frequent indulgences I've been tucking into. I know I'm putting weight back on, but it's hard not to when I'm dating a guy who thinks nothing of eating a bucket full of pasta whilst watching Pop Idol ... AS A SNACK!*

My renewed focus on study helped me to get a grip on the ever-present threat of the Black Mist descending, as I fell comfortably back into my default 'academic' box once more.

Following the trauma of recent years, I had sought help to manage the darkness which could – and did so frequently – inhabit my mind, and I was prescribed antidepressants. Undoubtedly, the Prozac helped. It numbed the harsh, painful edges, and I did feel strangely calmer and more able to cope with the waves continually threatening to bash me from the rock face.

However, I'm convinced that the daily pill-induced semi-numbness also opened the door to a new place for me: a place called 'complacency'. I slumped into mediocrity. A sloppy, limp, half-arsed laziness engulfed me, and made itself at home. I went through the motions, making token gestures to continue managing my weight, and my running dribbled off into a mere trickle – mainly courtesy of my yoghurt-coated banana running routine, where I frequently took in many more sugar-coated calories than I expended.

My weight had stabilised, albeit on the heavier side, and running was still a necessary evil. My laboured four-mile jog to the banana shop enabled me to fasten my jeans (although they weren't 'skinny' ones any more) but it was damage limitation at best. Running was only a bit part in my (once again) qualification-driven life. I was firmly back on the education bandwagon, and felt some comfort in this familiar place.

Running also began to diminish as a distracting, listless relationship sucked me back into a lifestyle of booze and bagels, films and takeaways. I put on some of the weight I'd lost prior to the op, but my hair remained blonde, and my relationship – however uninspiring it was – gave me the confidence I needed to carry the extra carb-induced stones. Talk about setting the bar low; I learned how to limbo.

A clear pattern was emerging: but at least I wasn't limbo-ing alone.

'Hi Rach, it's Penny,' she said, sounding her usual bright, unburdened self. *Does she worry about ANYTHING, ever?*

'Oh hi, Pen. How are you doing? You up to much?' I replied, trying too hard to mirror the carefree, chirpy tone on the other end of the phone, whilst seated on my boyfriend Kevin's Sofa for Resident Sloths munching on a foot-long Subway. He was doing the same.

'Yeah, uni's going well. Oh and – it's a bit of a random one – but I've entered into the Great North Run for September. May as well, seeing as though it's on my doorstep. You fancy it?'

'Oh. Crikey – I, erm haven't been...' I trailed off, slightly stunned by the suggestion, before eventually replying, 'Let me think about it.'

I looked over at my boyfriend, Kev, on the opposite sofa, as he took yet another enormous mouthful of his unnecessarily large foot-long Sub. He tried to mutter something inconsequential, but instead of words, he produced a spray of damp crumbs whilst some melted cheese dribbled down his chin. I was momentarily sickened.

'Actually, Pen,' I said, interrupting her mid-sentence. 'Yes – I'll do it. I'm in.'

When faced with the option of Half Marathon Challenge vs Sofa Residence and as my confidence slowly began to increase, aided by my daily Prozac pill, there was only one choice for me to make.

I couldn't bring myself to make excuses and dig around for every reason under the sun as to why I *couldn't* join Penny in her first half marathon. How could I face the prospect of sitting on the sofa whilst my friend had been brave enough to challenge herself? *DO IT, RACH. MAKE THE RIGHT CHOICE!*

It was 2001. This would be my very first half marathon. I'd never run that far, for that long, or even entered a race before. It was a bold move for a 'non-sporty' girl like me. I had no idea where to start, or what I was doing, but I didn't care. *And anyway, surely I could eat as many yoghurt-coated bananas as I liked with a half marathon as my goal?*

That was motivation enough for me.

THE MEDAL

AGED 23

September 2001

I did it! I bloody did it! I ran my very first half marathon today, and it nearly killed me. Obviously, my only goal was to complete the 13.1 miles and come away unscathed. I feel utterly broken. I can't walk down stairs, or sit on the loo without wincing in pain. I've never known leg aches like it. How on earth am I going to get into work tomorrow? I can hardly bloody walk!

The whole thing was unbelievable. The start was like an endless sea of people in all directions. They swarmed around every single square inch of Newcastle, it seemed, meandering in and out of portaloos or taking a piss wherever they could — mainly up and down the grass bankings lining the starting pens. Loads of runners wore black dustbin liners with head and armholes cut out. I didn't really know why, as it was already hot just by virtue of body heat alone. I was sweating just standing in my pen, but I'm sure some of that was pure nerves.

Hundreds upon hundreds of people lined the streets to support us. There were kids standing in clumps on pavements holding out tins of jelly babies, and mothers with plates of cut-up oranges. Honestly, it was like the world's longest All You Can Eat buffet!

Penny ran with me for the first six miles or so, then she left me as I started to struggle and found the hills of the GNR course too demanding. I walked a bit, then ran when I could. I was pissed off at having to walk, but I honestly did do my best to keep with Penny for as long as I possibly could.

Coming into the home straight was incredible. People stood ten-deep lining the route, hollering and cheering so loudly that I could feel the adrenalin surge through my thoroughly knackered body. I hung on to the end and crawled over the finish line in two hours twenty-five minutes, barely able to take another step.

I wonder how on earth those other 'superhumans' can even contemplate running a full marathon. How the hell do they do that? Just the thought of turning around and running back the whole way makes me shudder with horror!

The morning after my first half marathon was a difficult one. Physically, I struggled to bend at the knees, walk down stairs or lower myself onto the toilet without wincing. My quads ached so badly, they screamed with every sudden, un-choreographed movement. Shooting, searing pains would dart down my limbs, catching me off guard whenever I momentarily forgot that I was broken. Trying to carry out my normal morning routine was a deliberate and painstaking task.

But that very first race medal was my pride and joy. It was enormous and shiny, and it hung proudly from a bright blue ribbon. I didn't care that another 40,000 people had one. This one was mine – it would *always* be mine. I'd earned it. I took it to work, and I wore it around the office. I looked like a dickhead, but I didn't care. That medal symbolised everything to me. The overwhelming sense of achievement was beyond anything I'd ever experienced. It meant more to me than any exam result, any qualification or commendation: it symbolised everything that I thought I could never achieve.

In the context of my isolated, sedentary adolescence and my absolute lack of belief in my sporting ability, this was huge. It allowed me to challenge the version of myself I'd cursed in the mirror for all those years. My medal was my new prized possession and I wanted to wear it for the next week to show the world: '*Look! No one thought I could even run for one mile without stopping for an iced finger, let alone complete a half marathon!*' More than that, I wanted to wear it to remind myself that I was capable of so much more than I'd ever allowed myself to believe. This was the start of the long climb out of the hole in which I'd found myself towards the end of my teenage years, right through into early adulthood.

The non-sporty, invisible girl who'd successfully avoided exercise for so long had now managed to coerce her body into running 13.1 miles, having been unable to manage ten minutes of steady running on a treadmill only a few years earlier.

I still hadn't extricated myself from my listless boyfriend, but I was growing in confidence and strength. I looked at my medal and I felt brave. I'd chosen to step up to the challenge instead of resigning myself to the Sofa of Mediocrity. Running had helped me to believe that I could do so much more; I could be so much more. The end was nigh for me and Subway ... and my sofa-based relationship.

I wanted more medals.

PART 5

WHEELIE BINS

This story *should* end here. It *should* conclude that I'd discovered running, found my self-esteem, got myself back on track with my promising legal career, and skipped off into the sunset. Oh, and my 'happy ending' should also include a walk-in wardrobe full of size ten skinny jeans, an entire room set aside to house my ever-expanding collection of race medals, with photos adorning the walls of me crossing the finish line of yet another marathon, my perfectly blonde hair blowing in the breeze as my dad looks on, weeping with pride.

Needless to say, it doesn't.

That first half marathon was so symbolic for me in a million different ways, and yet soon enough, it drifted back into being just a memory of a special day: a moment in time. The grand, shiny medal with the proud blue ribbon was put away into a box. It wasn't taken out again for years.

I'd proven to myself that I could challenge my own warped perception of who I was: I could achieve small things that I never dared to believe were within my grasp – completing a half marathon being one such tiny example. I'd ticked off No. 7 from my list of 'Things I can't do now but would like to learn how' aged 18½ – 'To be able to run, even just a little bit' – and in the process, I'd also nudged closer to my 'fantasy want' No. 6: 'To like myself', with the same caveat, 'even just a little bit'.

I felt proud. Proud of my decision to enter the race in the first place – it would have been *far* easier to stay on Kev's couch inhaling carbs; proud of my commitment to train for it; proud of standing on the start line, along with the other 40,000 brave souls, all of whom had their own special stories. I was proud of running the first six miles with my friend Penny, and for continuing by myself, even though I had to jog-walk for the last few miles. It didn't matter. I'd crossed the finishing line, and I'd earned my medal – just like everybody else. Rachel at school couldn't have *dreamt* of doing that; Rachel a few years ago couldn't have done that. And yet, *this* Rachel *had* done that.

But wait! Let's get real, Rach! Don't risk appearing delusional and mentally unbalanced with grand ambitions of achieving sporting (or any) greatness. Don't be so ridiculous. Remember who you are!

My whirring mind continued: *You've completed ONE half marathon, and you struggled with even that. You couldn't run all of it, and maybe it was just one of those things you do once to tell the grandkids, and bring the medal out of its dusty old box at some indeterminate future moment in time. It's a fluke. It's not really 'you', Rach, is it? You're no runner. You dragged yourself through this, but it's hardly opened the floodgates to some 'running epiphany', has it? Best stop before you make a fool of yourself. You'll only be disappointed.*

And so I retreated from Delusionville, and my Satnav recalculated the route, avoiding any diversions through Aspiration City.

Perhaps I didn't have the confidence to believe that I could create my own reality, and not simply live in the shadows of my old self. Admittedly, I felt safer in the shadows.

Throughout all of my searching up to this point, I'd hankered after one thing: normality. I thoroughly and entirely wanted to be normal – whatever that looked like; whatever it was. I'd wanted a normal body, with normal boobs; normal friends and normal hobbies. I wanted to wear normal bras, to be asked out by normal boys, and to live in a normal house with a normal garden.

But the truth is that I had absolutely *no idea* what I wanted. My head spun with the never-ending battle between different versions of myself, and somewhere along the way, I simply lost sight of who I was. *Am I the blonde imposter? Is that me, now? What would SHE want to do?* I pondered. *Or am I still the chubby geek with a heavy fringe? Who is she, and what does SHE want me to do now?* My mind was a clear half marathon distance back down the road, lagging way behind the Rachel who had recently crossed the Great North Run finishing line. It had a long way to go to catch her up. And so, normality became my goal. It was a default setting, in the absence of my own clear direction. And I achieved it.

I settled down. I secured a training contract with a large commercial law firm. I got myself a mortgage, a lawn mower and four cats. And finally, I stopped messing about with silly small-fry relationships, and went for the full mashings: I bagged myself a stunning, lovely, gorgeous, beautiful, kind, genuine and successful man. Enter stage left, Captain Sensible, a.k.a. Tim.

There was just one small problem: it was all based on lies.

COPING ...
WELL, KIND OF

AGED 24

July 2002

I went to the Yorkshire Lawyer Awards last night. Bloody hell, what a disaster! We were greeted with champagne flutes on arrival. 'Ahhh! A couple of these should ease the nerves,' I stupidly thought, and so I quickly necked two (not clever on an empty stomach and Happy Pills combo!).

Once my initial anxious palpitations had abated — aided by bottled confidence — I settled down. As the evening wore on and the endless supply of wine continued to flow, my booze-fuelled self-assurance grew.

In the plush old room full of rich lawyers, there literally was money to burn. As the evening's charity auction lots became grander and more extravagant — and in my increasingly pissed state — I flirted outrageously with one of the (much older) senior partners on my table. I can remember howling at his crap jokes, and

encouraging his heavily innuendo-based 'banter'.
God knows what I must have looked like. I'm SO
embarrassed.

My evening got a whole lot worse as my boss
had to drive me home, and I then polished off the
evening's spectaculars by projectile vomiting all
over myself ... in his car! I am dreading going
into work on Monday.

I'm thoroughly ashamed of myself, and I can't
believe I've made such a monumental fuck-up.

I need to stop drinking.

Drinking had become my coping mechanism for my unequivocal mess of a life. After work, I would head straight to the pub if others were going, or else I'd make a beeline to the fridge on arriving home. *Ahhh, that's better – a chilled glass of white ... And another. Phew. What a relief!*

Fed up of having to call at the corner shop to buy another bottle of Blue Nun day after day, I'd long since progressed onto buying boxes: boxes of wine.

My behaviour was reprehensible too. To some degree, schmoozing with managing partners and hobnobbing with the legal movers and shakers was all in my job description, but I took it to another level. It was all part of the Big City living, which I didn't particularly enjoy and which certainly didn't suit me. The Prozac/booze combo was proving to be a very effective – if potent – one. I was even beginning to convince myself that I was a fully fledged Corporate Wanker: I was acting like one, anyway.

I somehow survived my two-year training contract and emerged on the other side a commercial litigation solicitor. I've no idea how. I'm pretty sure that sheer belligerency took a hold and wouldn't let go, in spite of the fact I hated most of it, and was ticking days off as if I was in a lengthy custodial sentence. I still can't watch old episodes of *LA Law* for the swell of bitterness I feel inside at the misrepresentation of a legal career.

I sold my house and, together with my four cats, moved in with the lovely Captain Sensible. We did very British, delightful things and explored far-flung places together. Dad was impressed.

'Oh yes, Dad, we're having a MARVELLOUS time! Just arrived in Kyoto – we got the bullet train from Shinjuku station, don't you know?! Yeah, we're off to Minami Alps later in the week – going to climb Mount Fuji. See you in a week or so!'

Having 'settled down' with Mr Sensible, we dabbled in a bit of fun running together. I call it 'fun running' because we had no idea what we were doing, or why. Besides which, we couldn't see much beyond the constant head fuzz of our stroke-inducing lifestyles: we were an equally unhealthy mix of clueless and careless.

But we were *entirely* normal.

AGED 25

April 2004
Oh. My. God. I'm just getting over the shock of today's run. It was bloody awful! The worst run I can remember for a long, long time. All of it felt wrong,

the entire way round. I felt physically drained and mentally shattered right from the start. Maybe a lot of things have caught up with me.

I feel a general kind of sadness today and I can't work out why. I know I'm disappointed with today's run. It felt like I was running carrying a rucksack full of rocks. I've got all sorts of things weighing heavy on my mind, and all of it is energy sapping. Anyway, I'm just tucking into a wedge of gorgeous homemade pie, washed down with way too much Prosecco ... I'll pay for it in the morning!

I've booked in to see Dr Sheppard later this week to have a chat about the tablets I'm on. I've had Prozac on repeat prescription for a good few years now, but every six months I'm told I need to come in for a review. Maybe it's stopped working? Or is too much booze negating its effect? Either way, I need to speak to him because something isn't right.

Anyway, I'm going to the cinema with Ness at the weekend. She's got a right tale to tell — they bloody sectioned her recently, and she's only just back home! I don't even know what that means, but I spoke to her on the phone and she was laughing about it, saying how stupid it all was. I've no idea what that's about, but it'll be good to see her on Friday. God knows what she'd make of my fuck-up of a life — if she ever knew, that is!

It was the summer of 2004, and the lovely, kind, responsible, successful Captain Sensible whisked me away to a posh Italian villa. I knew what was coming.

I didn't rejoice at his proposal: my heart didn't miss a beat, or even flutter. I feigned understated, grown-up excitement. I didn't want to get married. I didn't want to get married to him, anyway. I just felt a deep and nauseating sadness, which echoed around every corner of my being. I knew it wasn't supposed to feel like this.

But, of course, I said yes. *YES! YES! I'D <u>LOVE</u> TO MARRY YOU, TIM! OH MY GOD! WE'LL HAVE TO TELL EVERYONE!* The lies were steadily growing. *How could I let so many people down, and stamp all over their dreams?* I couldn't. We'd even embroiled Debenhams into our plans for feigned future happiness.

The pretence was ever-present. I imagined the office gossips behind our backs. *'Poor Tim. Does he know what he's getting himself into?'* And they were right. At times I felt angry that he couldn't – or wouldn't – stop me from destroying myself, and breaking him in the process. It would never happen like that. He placated, understood, rationalised, reasoned, excused and tolerated. He allowed me to behave like a complete twat, when all along he deserved better: I *willed* him to challenge my behaviour. He never did. If I pushed hard enough, behaved badly enough, then maybe I wouldn't have to be the one destroying his and other people's dreams: I was looking to him to provide the get-out clause.

He wouldn't.

In my lostness, I attempted to fit into a life that I honestly believed I could shoehorn myself into. But I didn't want any of it. I just wanted to run away.

So instead, I carried on, and I pretended.

I drank. A lot. It helped me to fake it: to relax, unwind, portray confidence, appear to be 'having fun' at corporate bullshit parties; it helped me to bury the truth so deep inside that I couldn't even begin to uncover it, and come face to face with my own sadness. It wasn't as though just one small part of my life was a lie – *ALL* of it was. Like an apple with a rotten core, none of it was spared. Not one aspect was free from rot.

And worse still was the guilt I felt for hating my life. *Surely I should be happy? How bloody ungrateful can you be, Rachel? To be here, feeling utterly empty, cold and lonely, with all of this.* I would frequently berate myself. '*LOOK AT ALL THAT YOU HAVE! WHAT MORE COULD YOU POSSIBLY WANT, YOU UNGRATEFUL EXCUSE FOR A HUMAN BEING?*'

And it was true: I did have the lot. I had normality. But it was stifling me.

I met up with my friend, Ness, one Friday night. I'd heard about her having recently been 'sectioned', and it sounded terrifying. *Has she gone mad?* It sounded like such a brutal, involuntary, passive thing to be done *to* you, whether you like it or not. I was concerned about her, and I genuinely didn't know what the hell it all meant. *Could they section ME?* I wondered. *Surely they can. I'm mad! My life is entirely mad. Shit! What if they do?* I figured I'd best stay quiet – just in case.

We arranged to go to the cinema. I had no idea what to expect when I saw her. *Will she look bonkers? Deranged? Different? Will she wear weird, oddball clothes and have matted, unkempt hair? Will she cry randomly, or all the time? Will I know what to say, if she does?*

When we met, she looked entirely … normal. Yes, that word again. *Oh. Right.* I was shocked at the lack of visible evidence of any mental struggle. Even more confusing was that she *seemed* her normal, jokey self.

'What happened then, Ness?' I ventured, not wanting to turn the evening into anything too heavy – I was quite sure that's the last thing she would either want or need.

'Oh that!' she belly-laughed in response. 'It was bloody crazy, Rach. Honestly. Look at me! I'm absolutely fine!' she continued, laughing about the whole thing as if it were some debacle in a comedy farce that had gone too far.

I didn't press the issue. She seemed like her 'normal' self, and we had a nice evening. Mine and Ness's friendship wasn't based on deep, heartfelt discussions. We didn't cry on each other's shoulders and talk about our 'struggles'. I guess we buried them deep inside ourselves, and tried to laugh them off, instead.

I went home somewhat relieved, thinking, 'Well, thankfully she seems all right. Good old Ness.'

So, I carried on. But that word – 'normality' – came back to haunt me. I understand completely what had led to my being swept away along on a tidal wave of other people's desires for how my life might turn out. I was a product – and equally a victim – of the inherent pressures to:

Have a …

Be a ...
Marry a ...
Live in a ...
Buy a ...
Drive a ...
Own a ...

These messages were swarming, buzzing, circling around me every waking moment of every single day. It takes a brave person to say, *'STOP THE BUS – I WANT TO GET OFF.'*

I simply wasn't that brave.

And so, Tim and I began putting our wedding plans together. We lived in suburban bliss. He wheeled the bins out on a Tuesday. We went round to the in-laws for Sunday dinners.

I bought a lot of self-help books.

And I tried. I really, honestly tried.

A REALITY CHECK

January 2016

I ran from work today. I never imagined I'd know this place. It's close to our old school, and near to where she lived.

The graveyard is somewhere I'd never noticed. I didn't even know it was there before.

As I ran up the road towards the windmills, I thought of Ness. I wondered why, as I always do, and I wondered why I didn't know. I wondered if, from wherever she is, she could see me, running. Giggling to herself that I'm still the goofy old Rach who couldn't be cool if she tried.

I miss her.

She's been with me today, and so many times – helping me through more painful miles than she could ever know.

I was hovering around the kitchen with the door wide open watching our cats playing outside on our oversized suburban lawn when I answered the phone.

'Rach? Is that you?'

'Yeah. Yeah – of course it's me! Hey, Pen! How's tricks?'
The sunshine made me feel bouncy and light.

'It's ...'

Silence.

'Penny? What's up? I'm here. What's wrong?' I could hear
the silence getting louder. 'Are you still there? What on earth's
happened?' I stopped smiling.

'It's Ness, Rach. Her mum found her.'

There was a bit more detail, but I couldn't hear any more.
My body slumped to the floor, my legs drained of every single
ounce of energy. I let out a wail. It was a sound that I didn't
know my body could make. My overwhelming sadness, grief
and pain were interwoven with guilt.

Yes, guilt.

In my confused, hypocritical mess of a life, amidst all
the lies and the webs of feigned happiness I had woven, I'd
lost sight of her. I'd become so caught up in my own self-
absorbed, Prozac-managed, booze-numbed bullshit world
that I'd failed to spot that she was suffering. Maybe she'd
been trying – pretending – to be normal, too, just like me.

I was so desperate to hide my own sadness, my insecurities, and the reality hiding behind my sham of a life because
I was too ashamed to admit what a fucking mess it all was –
and equally what a bigger mess I was.

What if I'd been brave enough to admit it? What if I'd
opened up to Ness and told her that the picture-perfect life I
portrayed was riddled with lies? What if I'd told her about my
endless inner turmoil, about my antidepressants? The wonky
boobs? The place called Lostness? What if she'd known about
my dependency on alcohol to feign confidence, and my affairs

to circumvent the need to discover my own self-worth? What if she'd known about the stifling loneliness, which engulfed me day after day? How could she have known that I was even dreading my own wedding day?

Would it have helped her to know any of this? That whatever she was going through, however bad it was, there were plenty of us just like her fighting our own sorry little battles – even those of us who professed outwardly to be 'normal' and to 'have it all'.

That question haunted me: *what if she'd known?* Would it have saved her? I'll never know.

She had always been so full of fun, cheek and mischief. Right from the early days of senior school, we all flocked to her because she was – well, she was just cool. She thought I was hilarious, enjoying both laughing with me and at me in equal measure. Three of us went on a girls' holiday to Kos. Ness and Kate had far more of the genuine party-animal in them than I did. One night, they planned on heading out into the town to down copious vodka shots in their skimpy skirts and crop tops.

'Are you sure you're not coming out, Rach?' Ness asked me for the fifteenth time.

'Yeah – I'm sure. I'm happy staying here tonight,' I replied, knowing full well I would spend my evening penning a love letter to Andy, our fit pool attendant, instead.

'OK, if you're sure!' she replied, whilst I munched on Pringles and gazed at Kate hopping about with her tanned, effortless ironing board of a stomach.

'Ness, come over here and stand by the balcony wall. I'll take a picture of you before you go out,' I offered. She looked beautiful, as did Kate with her inverted, mahogany abs. Ness did a silly pose, but I was (thankfully) a fraction too late and caught her laughing naturally, instead. *CLICK!*

Later the following morning – or more like early afternoon – they eventually stirred. Bleary-eyed following one Jägerbomb too many, Ness tried to mop up her hangover the best way she could. I told her the tale. 'You did what, you idiot?' she spluttered, as I hid behind our balcony, which unfortunately faced out on to the pool. She bent over double with laughter as I told her about my evening, and my love letter to Andy the Fit Pool Attendant.

Crouched down behind the drying, sandy towels, I explained my logic. 'But I really like him, Ness – he seems nice. I thought he might want to keep in touch with me when he comes back to the UK. You never know, he may need some legal advice?'

She rolled around with laughter, clutching her aching abdominals, whilst peering over the balcony. Being a true friend, she updated me on Andy's movements.

'Well, he's looking up here and smiling, so you must have written something good in that letter! Maybe he does need some legal advice after all!'

Following another good belly laugh, the two of them headed down to the pool. I stayed rooted to the balcony, refusing to move an inch closer to the big blue gates, or to Andy the Fit Pool Attendant.

Only a few years later, that photo – the one I'd taken of beautiful Ness, full of life and mischief standing by the balcony wall – sat perfectly still on her coffin. I saw her smiling, laughing at me down the camera lens. But she was in the box instead. *What if she'd known?* I sat, staring at her beautiful, smiling face, now on top of the box – and I howled beside my lovely, unfortunate husband-to-be. *What if she'd known?*

I missed her throughout all of those desolate Captain Sensible years, when I'd been so lost and alone.

She wouldn't be there, at my wedding. I wish she'd known the truth. Perhaps the only real difference between us was the web of lies I'd managed to weave.

WINE, CHOCOLATE, PROZAC

AGED 26

February 2005

I went out running with the ladies from the Wakefield Harriers running club for the first time last night. It was REALLY tough, but I just about managed to stick with them. A lovely older lady called Pat took me under her wing, and although I struggled to keep up with her, I did manage to keep some conversation flowing in amongst my hyperventilated breaths.

I've no idea how she ran so well, plus — dare I say it — she was old enough to be my mum. Talk about an inspiration! She had a permanent smile on her face, and looked as happy as anyone I've ever seen. I want some of what she's having, please (I bet it's not Prozac, either).

We were <u>supposed</u> to be doing a gentle four miles, but that was a load of old bollocks because we ended up doing six! One of the other ladies *said to me at the end, 'Oh, you'll have to get used to that, love. Pat always tells us how far we're running, and then we end up taking an extended detour. For future reference, always add a couple of miles onto whatever she tells you. You won't be far off, then.'*

When I got home I was buzzing — and also starving. I ate far too much tea, drank about half a bottle of rosé, and inhaled a Boost chocolate bar.

'Hey! You're not going to believe it,' I shouted up the stairs to Tim. 'We only ended up doing six bloody miles! It was brilliant, but I am absolutely wrecked now!'

'Wow! You'll kick my arse at the Sheffield Half!' he replied.

Secretly, I hope he's right ... I'm sure that running with the Harriers will be great for my training. It was nerve-wracking, but so much fun! If I can stick to running with them on a Tuesday night, then I should be in half-decent shape for the Sheffield half marathon ... not to mention our wedding in a few months' time!

My own motivation to run was waning, as my repressive reality sucked what energy I did have from my body, and so I made some tentative enquiries about joining a local running club. I knew I was seriously struggling with motivation, and limping along without any real focus was doing me no favours at all. Plus, I had a wedding dress to fit into! Maybe this was the first hint of my building up enough confidence to believe I wouldn't disgrace myself entirely amidst the other 'real' runners, and my reaching out to gain more support. And as I became increasingly sucked into the booze, bagels and bullshit of my ill-fitting corporate lifestyle, this was perhaps *some* attempt to mitigate further damage.

'Oh, just come along, love. You'll be fine!' a kind, elderly-sounding gentleman said on the phone. I felt sick with nerves whilst trying to silence my ranting mind: *'You won't be able to keep up, Rach. Not a chance! They'll ALL be faster than you. You'll make a complete fool of yourself. Remember – you're not a runner, Rach!'*

As I sat in my car, a good half-hour too early, the temptation was to turn on the car engine and drive straight back home again. No one would know! But I remembered the Great North Run vs Sofa crossroads a few years earlier. I got out of my car.

As I began chatting with Pat, our group leader, she uncovered my motivation for joining.

'Ahhh, you're getting married are you, love? What an exciting time for you!' she said, trotting alongside me and apparently breathing without effort whilst I tried to shorten my laboured replies.

'Yes [gasp] … and we've got the Sheffield half marathon next month, too,' I said, hoping she'd launch into a lengthy reply, so I wouldn't have to speak again.

'Brilliant!' she said, excitedly. 'We'll get you into shape for those, Rachel. Don't you worry, my love!' she assured me as she increased the pace, whilst I was utterly relieved to see the car park come into view up ahead.

I liked Pat. She was happiness on legs. I enjoyed running and chatting with her on Tuesday evenings, and this became my new routine. My confidence steadily grew as, week in, week out, I would turn up and join lovely Pat and her small group of running friends. We would run four miles one week, then five the next. I was amazed when we ventured slightly further afield and managed six, even seven miles, and I felt my pride and my self-esteem grow with every outing. It wasn't a miraculous, sudden realisation, but a slow burner: running was steadily making its way back into my life, at a time when – again – I needed it the most, and in a gentle, unassuming way. Those tiny, incremental endorphin hits, together with the mini confidence boosts, kept me buoyant whilst I was still on very choppy waters.

It's also exactly what I needed at that time to enable me to pour myself into my power suit trousers, and – of course – my size twelve wedding dress.

My mind was in a permanent state of abject denial, and the wedding itself seemed such a long way off. *A whole year is an eternity!* I would reassure myself. Such delusional thoughts gave me some temporary reprieve, and I could carry on in my complete refusal to acknowledge the Big Day ever arriving. Head buried firmly in sand, I did my very best to shun reality.

Running was slowly making its way back to me, but wine, chocolate and Prozac still had my heart.

May 2005

Wowsers, I'm wrecked! We did the Sheffield half marathon today. I seriously struggled with the hills (just for a change), and my recent lack of energy felt to have caught up with me. I wish I'd started going to those Tuesday-night training runs with Pat down at the Harriers sooner. I was doing so well with those, but I have also been sidetracked by other small energy-sapping matters ... like our wedding!

We set off quite fast, and flew along for the first few miles. Tim turned to me and said, 'Bloody hell, Rach. We're doing 8:30 min/miles, here!'

I looked down at my watch and couldn't believe it, either. 'We'd best slow it down otherwise we'll blow up,' he suggested, and so I took my foot off the gas a bit. We would have been on for a ridiculously good time if we'd carried on at that pace — I've never run sub-1:50 for a half before. But he was right — we'd have died if we carried on at that silly pace.

My friend Amy did it, too. She's offensively fast, and finished in some insane time — I think it was somewhere in the 1:30s. How on earth does she run that fast? I've got more chance of flying a one-manned vessel to the moon!

Anyway, I desperately need to get back on track now we're back from our honeymoon. I've let my training with the Harriers slide recently,

> and I've been feeling slow and heavy again. And
> — I guess — sadder, if that makes sense? I'm sure
> it shouldn't have felt so tough today. I even had
> to stop and walk a bit, which frustrated the hell
> out of me.
>
> When we got back home, Tim and I were
> chatting about the race. I mentioned Amy, and
> how fast she is. Tim said innocently, 'Neither
> of us are built like runners, Rach. We're never
> going to be.' I wonder what he means by that?
> He's 6' 2" and has a podgy belly. I'm 5' 9" and I
> guess I have one too, thanks to my questionable
> diet. Either way, it didn't make me feel great
> about myself.
>
> It's pissed me off, though. Why couldn't I be a
> half-decent runner? What's stopping me?

I woke up and we were married. It had happened. My head hurt. *Shit. What time is it?* I could barely muster the energy to roll over. Everything felt worse than bad.

'I can't come downstairs, Tim,' I drawled, my mouth feeling like a sand pit and tasting like a public toilet. 'I just can't face anyone. I think, er I'm—' I leapt out of bed and dashed to the beautiful ceramic bathroom suite where yet more of last night's duck à l'orange and Veuve Clicquot splattered into the exquisite white bowl.

I missed my own wedding breakfast. The guests must have wondered where the Cinderella Bride had disappeared to. Or maybe some of them had (correctly) guessed that I was in fact hanging over a bowl somewhere, holding my overly sprayed hair back, vomiting profusely.

I was finally smuggled out of the exclusive wedding venue mid-morning. Like a high-profile celebrity avoiding the paparazzi, I hid under unnecessary coats and Jackie O sunglasses. It was appropriately cloudy outside.

We dutifully called at my new in-laws to show our ecstatic faces after the Big Day. Mine was varying shades of green. Sitting around their apparently revolving kitchen table, my head was still spinning: partly the incessant hangover, but mostly just shock, as my internal compass was stuck on permanent search for a GPS signal. *Where am I? What the hell am I doing? How do I escape from this place?*

And then, at possibly the worst conceivable moment, my new mother-in-law turned to me and said excitedly, 'I'll keep the top tier of the wedding cake safe for when we hear the patter of tiny feet, then!'

SEARCHING FOR SANITY, FINDING FITNESS

AGED 27

April 2006

I don't belong here. I know I'm in the wrong place, in the wrong job, in the wrong life. I feel trapped but I don't know how to escape.

I'm just about clinging on to some sanity courtesy of my Tuesday-night runs with lovely Pat and the Harriers' ladies, and I've joined the plush Hilton gym opposite work. It costs a fortune, but who cares? I'm sure it's helping me to cope with these feelings of lostness. It's precisely that: I feel lost and trapped, and like I've shoehorned myself into a life that doesn't fit me. Going to the gym and running is my only escape.

Do I break my dad's heart — not least because he stumped up a good few grand to help pay for the Wedding of the Year — by telling him it was (yet another) 'mistake'?

Or do I confide in my mum, knowing that she's permanently teetering on a knife-edge of sanity herself, and any slight nudge from me may tip her over the edge? She hates to think of me being lost. She wants me to be 'settled' and not to have to ride the same turbulent path that she has.

But I'm living a lie, and I know it.

I've just taken on a personal trainer at the gym, called Fiona. She's an international heptathlete who's out of competition for a while due to injury. I'm thinking she can help me to put some focus into my daily lunchtime gym visits, and make them more interesting/intensive/purposeful. I love going to the gym (it's the most enjoyable part of my otherwise depressingly dull day), but I feel like I need some fresh ideas as to what to do to add a bit of variety, otherwise I'll fall into the trap of doing the same old boring, steady treadmill plod I always do. I'm scared to death of weights — I wouldn't know where to start!

I'll give it a go and see what happens ... who knows, it might be the dawning of a new me!

Most days, when the clock struck twelve, I leapt from the confines of my office incarceration and made a dash straight for the gym. I'd frequently stay there long after my lunch break had expired, and I tried in vain to shuffle my way back to my life-sapping desk without being noticed: not easy when panting like a dog, with wet hair, wearing no make-up and carrying a gym bag the size of a golf buggy.

But my daily visits to the gym were helping me: I had something – *one little thing* – to look forward to in my otherwise thoroughly miserable day. I'd accidentally found myself turning to fitness again, largely to try and cling on to some sanity whilst my life lacked any kind of direction at all. I didn't know *why* it helped me: I just knew I felt better, somehow. Now, I realise it was a magical concoction of fleetingly escaping the confines of my sterile office, the simple act of moving my body, and the exercise-induced endorphins that made my lunchtime hour the most enjoyable of my entire day.

Not wanting to run out of mojo with my increasingly lacklustre training routine, I took on a personal trainer. I saw Fiona once, maybe twice a week, and I would go to the gym myself most other days.

It helped knowing I had someone else to plan my training schedule for me, so I didn't have to think for myself. As the stress hormone cortisol flooded my veins from the morning's workload, my head struggled with choice. I could barely string a sentence together, let alone consider reps, sets and training cycles. My training with Fiona wasn't intensive arse-kicking. It was fluffy, supportive, expensive hand-holding.

One lunchtime, I turned up to the gym for my usual session.

'Hey, Rach! Right! Let's get started. Warm up on the bike then we're messing about in the studio upstairs with some new plyometric stuff!' she said, sounding far too enthusiastic in stark contrast to my heavily burdensome lethargy.

'I'm so sorry, Fi,' I blurted. 'I just can't do this. I can't [sob]. I don't know what to do [sob].'

I broke down and wept. My fake life had zapped every single ounce of energy from my body. I knew I was careering down a runaway track completely out of control.

'Hey, hey, Rach. It's OK. It's really OK. Listen. We'll call it a day for today. Come on, it can't be that bad,' she said, looking stunned and bemused.

I could see the panicked thoughts flash across her face: *Shit. I'm a personal trainer, not a bloody therapist!* Her internal cogs struggled to locate the right words with which to soothe me, and I felt bad for her – she wasn't paid to listen to my shit. I had to sort that out for myself.

To be fair, I was making some efforts to unscramble my mess of a life. I invested heavily in self-help books – the local bookshop fast becoming my oasis in the desert. *I'll read and study my way out of this hole I'm in!* I would follow the blueprint for other people's escape plans, and piggy-back their get-out-of-jail-free cards.

My list of purchases was endless. I read about Healing my Life, and how to Write It Down and Make It Happen; I learned to Stop Worrying and Start Living, and I pondered on Who'd Moved my Cheese. I studied Success Principles, and all about the Power of Now. I bought scrapbooks and started cutting bits out of magazines, creating 'vision boards' for a future life: one that didn't in any way resemble my current reality. And boy, did I take the book-bound encouragement to 'Think Big' to a whole new level.

'I think we should emigrate, Tim. Somewhere completely new, and start again,' I randomly declared one day, whilst spooning a foil cat-food packet into one of the four colour-co-ordinated empty bowls. 'Canada! What about Canada? We'd *love* it over there! The freedom and the outdoors; we'd have loads of space and the chance to start afresh.'

The thing is, I wasn't even joking. I was deadly serious.

'British Columbia sounds *right* up our street,' I went on. 'I've been researching it, and it's got everything we'd love. They have distinct seasons, instead of this incessant grey modge we have over here, and we could even ski on weekends! How amazing would that be?'

Tim stood in the kitchen, his head spinning with bemusement at the suggestion that we should pack up and fuck off to another place far, far away. But at least he hadn't eliminated it as a possibility. The door was nudged open, and I was ready to push on it with all my might. I wanted to run away.

Dream BIG, Rach. Think BIG. All the books told me so. I had to do everything *BIG* and *LARGE* and *GRAND*. *Kick this current, sad little bullshit life out of the ball park and into another, BIGGER, BETTER one! YES! That's the plan! Simply pack up and move.* I didn't know it at the time, but I wanted to run away from my life. And from myself.

One day, I happened across a small, self-published book sitting tucked away on a Borders bookshelf. It was a tiny, modest-looking publication that pulled me in because it looked like someone had printed it in their own front room. *How has this even got onto the shelves in here?* I wondered. *Has the author just come and placed a few copies in an appropriate section, in the hope that someone will pick them up?* If so, it had worked (and it wasn't far off the truth).

This small, unassuming publication grabbed me. Titled *Believe You Can!*, it was the raw and unpolished story of a very ordinary man who had taken on the extraordinary challenge of running the Marathon des Sables. This, I went on to read, is one of the world's most gruelling races: a 156-mile race across the desert, in 120-degree heat, carrying *everything* you would need with you (including water) for the entire six days. I bought it, and read it from cover to cover in under an hour. And then I read it again.

The story touched a raw nerve inside me. It told of a man who had also struggled with the demons of depression. He had battled with them, and won. His race across the desert was the epitome of that gladiatorial battle.

Inside the front cover, I noticed that the author, Clive Gott, had an email and website address. He actively invited readers to make direct contact with him, to both share their own experiences and draw inspiration from his. I checked out his website, which heralded him as a highly acclaimed 'inspirational speaker'. *WOW! I WANT SOME OF WHAT HE'S GOT!* Remembering that one of the 'Things I can't do now but would like to learn how' goals I'd set myself aged 18½ was to 'learn to run – even just a little bit' and another was to 'write a book (and have the patience to finish it)', Clive had ticked off *both* of those boxes, in some style, and against the odds. I wanted to meet him. He was based in Tadcaster, only a short driving distance from my Yorkshire home. I wondered if I could get in contact with Mr Gott, and possibly even arrange to meet him. His book said he wanted to! On the presumption that this was a genuine invitation then, that is exactly what I did.

Over endless cups of coffee, he spoke with passion about his Marathon des Sables experiences, and I listened and lapped up his enthusiasm like it was oxygen in finite supply. I looked up at the beautifully framed race photos hanging proudly on the walls of his lovely home, and I tried to comprehend the enormity of the challenge he'd faced. Standing before me was a 6'3" ex-firefighter, of heavy build, who was many years older than me.

But Clive's message to me was that his race *wasn't* physical. Yes, of course he had to undertake a mammoth training schedule in preparation for the monumental task – but he assured me that 99 per cent of this race was *mental*. 'It's all about conquering the mental limits we impose on ourselves, Rach,' he said, passionately.

Over the following weeks, something struck me about Clive's message, and I replayed it over and over in my mind. *It's about the mental limits we impose on ourselves ...* The voice of my inner coach began to shout louder: *Right, Rach. It's time to set some BIG goals. This is it. Break through the mental limits you've imposed on yourself. DO IT NOW! Maybe you can't run hundreds of miles across a desert; that's a step too far just now – or ever – but ...*

My mind raced back to Amanda's mum and her foil blanket, and it flirted with the idea that I may be able to obtain my very own. Had this dream been lying dormant inside me for all these years? Was all this because, aged nine, I'd pictured Amanda's mum running past the palace and waving at the Queen? Throughout even my most intensely solitary, crushingly depressing telly-addict teenage years, I'd sat and watched the entire London Marathon race on its annual Sunday-morning BBC slot, and I'd marvelled at the spectacle. It contained more drama and emotion, pain and euphoria than even the most outlandish *Neighbours* plot line (yes – including Scott and Charlene's wedding).

It was *ALL* of life within one race.

Maybe I could run 26.2 miles? Maybe I could run a marathon? That's it! I'll run a marathon!

My Google searching had impulsively led me to select New York as my marathon of choice (remember, my goal had to be 'BIG'), and within days, I'd entered both myself and Tim through an international sports tours company, at not insignificant expense.

I was still only running once a week with the Wakefield Harriers by this time, doing five or six miles at a very steady pace with lovely Pat and her (older) ladies. I also dabbled in a bit of steady treadmill work at the gym, but nothing even close to either the type or quantity of training required to prepare me for any marathon. Not one in under three months' time, anyway.

The following week, I opened up the conversation with Fiona, my personal trainer. It went something like this:

'Fi – I know this is a complete curve ball, but I've entered into the New York Marathon for November.'

'What? Really? *This* November? As in – a few months' time? Oh right, well, erm, OK. I guess we'd better get some training plans sorted out for you pretty bloody quickly, then.'

There was a stunned, pregnant pause, followed by a more than reasonable request to confirm what she thought she'd just heard. 'Are you *sure* you're ready for this, Rach? I mean, are you *really* sure?'

'Yeah! Definitely – I'm up for it. I want to do it,' I said glibly. 'And anyway, it's booked, now!' I added, like I'd sealed the deal by throwing money at it – which I had.

'What's your weekly mileage like at the moment, Rach? Just remind me ...'

'Erm, about ten miles.' I didn't even sound ironic.

She was polite and somehow managed to contain her primal instinct to laugh out loud. 'Oh. You'll have to give me a few days, I'll have a think ...'

'Cheers, Fi.'

Inspired by my new author friend, Clive, and true to my own impulsive, 'act now – think later' nature (remembering my 18½-year-old self's list of 'Qualities I believe I lack' including both 'thinking of consequences' and 'rationality'), I naively entered into the New York Marathon 2006.

MISSION: ESCAPE

AGED 28

July 2006

I think my colleague Jonathan finally thinks I've gone insane. He leaned over and looked at my PC this morning and, noticing that I wasn't preparing for our conference with counsel, he said inquisitively, 'What are you looking at there, Rach? Looks interesting.'

'Oh, you know — just daydreaming, I guess. I'm pretending I'm a rich eighteen-year-old with my whole life ahead of me, planning a no-expense-spared gap year! Ha ha!'

'That looks ace! Is it a safari or something?' he asked, peering closer at my screen. He's lovely, but so bloody nosy.

'Yeah, pretty much. It's a conservation project that offers work placements on a game reserve in South Africa. It's either that or a monkey sanctuary in Uganda, but I'm worried that they'd never let me out!'

'I'm dreaming of opening a sandwich shop just over there,' he said, pointing to the stone-arched business units on the other side of the canal towpath opposite our offices.

'Really? Would you honestly love to do that? To own a sandwich shop?' I asked, wondering if he was bluffing, and just being polite joining in the Fantasy Life conversation.

'Yeah! I'd do it in a heartbeat,' he said, his voice sounding softer with a tinge of sadness.

'What's stopping you, then?' I asked, already knowing the answer.

He turned to look at my face, as if to sniff out any sarcasm before replying, 'Are you joking, Rach? I'm fifty years old with a wife and two kids, and I'm being paid £60k a year to shuffle paper around. I'm not getting out of here any time soon.'

Jesus. Are we sitting in a workplace here, or a prison? Or is it both? I couldn't help but wonder.

A few minutes later, he piped up, 'Rach, are you ready for that telephone conference with Counsel? Oh, and one more thing,' he said, putting his hand gently on my arm, 'keep daydreaming, Rach. Don't turn into me.'

And with that, I knew he'd just given me every reason to continue with my research as to possible escape routes. Monkey sanctuary or not.

Perhaps my work colleague thought I was joking, but I was deadly serious. My life had to change, and I was prepared to throw all my balls into the air to make that happen. I'd spoken to Tim about emigrating to Canada – we'd even completed all of the application paperwork, plus I'd naively entered us into the New York Marathon.

But I wasn't done yet (*I know – poor Tim*).

That lunchtime, whilst hanging on for the right moment to finally cut myself free from the soul-destroying legal world, and still enthused with self-help BIG THINKING ideas, my frantic Googling opened up a whole world of possibilities. '*It's about the mental limits we impose on ourselves …*'

My random searching for Getting a New Life included:

- Working abroad
- Volunteering abroad
- Sabbaticals abroad
- Doing *ANYTHING* abroad
- Escaping from my current life (although I don't think this came up with many helpful options)

Meanwhile, Fiona did her optimistic best to put together a crash course of Marathon Training Programme for Dummies for me to follow, but it was all in vain. I wasn't ready to take on any marathon. I looked at her proposed training schedule, and my new 'Big Thinking' self crumbled. It didn't make any sense to me. *How can I possibly run for 26.2 miles?* I hadn't even considered it.

In truth, I know exactly what kiboshed my grand New York Marathon plans for 2006: I didn't yet *believe* that I could. I'd jumped in both feet first, with my over-enthusiastic, kick-ass goal-setting, courtesy of my self-help home library. But iron-ically, the very title of Mr Gott's own book *Believe You Can!* – the one that had inspired me to take such monumental steps

– still eluded me. Quite clearly, I didn't believe that I could. I was still sufficiently exhausted by my own life. But denial is a wonderful thing, and I'd had plenty of experience of that.

So, my own painfully limiting beliefs were about to pull me out of my false start marathon pipe dream before it had even begun, but at least it showed me that running a marathon was on my radar, and that maybe I'd tackle it … one day.

And anyway, my plan to run the New York Marathon now seemed small-fry in comparison to a complete redesign of my life.

I started thinking about what I wanted to do and what would matter to me in my new BIG THINKING life. I thought about how finding fitness, and running – even at a very modest level – had given me the first glimmer of confidence and inner strength. From enabling me to escape from my sad old self, and launch a new and 'improved' version, to helping me deal with the stress and pressures of my more recent, ill-fitting corporate life: finding fitness had helped me in some magical, mystical way, and I wanted to pass it on – to pay it forward. Besides, I also hated the confines of a daily office incarceration, and I wanted freedom.

Fiona had been my personal trainer and my fitness guru throughout my most recent painful, turbulent months, but I could offer someone – *just like me* – a deeper understanding about their *real* motivations for change. I wasn't an international athlete like Fiona, but I was a real person who had struggled with overweight invisibility, fitness levels that belied my young years, and crippling body image. Finding my place in the world was a constant and evolving battle, but it was undoubtedly being aided with the help of my own journey

in discovering fitness. I was, therefore, a person who understood intricately why somebody *just like me* may possibly
want to create a brand-new 'them'; I would understand why
taking home a big, shiny medal from a half-marathon race,
just like I'd done those years earlier, could be the beginning of
somebody else's very own personal journey. My experiences
had gifted me that much.

So, in possibly the most ridiculous of career choices for
someone with my background, fitness levels and body-image
issues, I decided to retrain as a personal trainer.

Once my mind was made up, I booked onto an intensive training course to start in January 2007. But my decision
to shake things up a bit didn't stop there. All of my Google
searches had one consistent theme running throughout: I
still wanted to run away. Somewhere; *anywhere.* I wanted
to be elsewhere. Anywhere away from the wheelie bins on
a Tuesday and car washing on a Sunday; away from the
colour-coordinated cat bowls and the garden with room
for a pony. I wanted out of the corporate cul-de-sac and the
bedroom overlooking our neighbour's sensible family saloon.
All of them felt to be smothering me – suffocating me in a
choking fog, and in a life that I didn't want to be mine.

My 'stumbling across' options for volunteering abroad
online had churned up a crazy idea in my mind of working
on a game reserve in South Africa for a few months before
commencing my new life back home. *What would Clive say?*
Oh yeah, *THINK BIG, RACH. THINK BIG.*

Then there was the issue of my marriage. It was at best
built on quicksand, and we were sinking fast. Perhaps if we
both caught on with this BIG THINKING, self-help stuff, we

might work out what to do to get out of this unholy mess. *Surely that will be easier if we're thousands of miles away from the cat bowls, in-laws and wheelie bins?*

I went home and mooted the idea. 'Erm, I've been looking online today, Tim, and I've seen a volunteering programme over in South Africa, working on a game reserve,' I said, trying hard to swallow the nervous cough rising from the pit of my stomach. 'I've printed out some information. It's not just for eighteen-year-olds with rich dads either. They cater for all ages, even oldies like us!' I laughed, nervously. 'What do you reckon?'

It sounded ridiculous, crazy, random, unfeasible, expensive ... but at the same time exciting, unique, challenging and fulfilling. All of a sudden, it seemed like the sanest, most obvious plan in the world.

I cashed in what savings I had, and booked two places for us to work as volunteers on the Shamwari game reserve in South Africa for three months. On the back end of the work placement, we planned to travel down the Garden Route to Cape Town. It would be a journey of discovery regardless of the outcome, and I knew that there was a new life for me on our return.

I had found a purpose again, and with my new lease of life a sense that things were possible, and that I was only ever one decision away from steering my life back on track, avoiding being swept along the relentless Normality Rapids.

I was fully committed to the ride.

A NEW PATH

May 2015

Today was a very lovely reminder of the special moments in races. Fleeting 'blink and you'll miss them' moments that will never happen again, with people you are likely to never meet again. It happened a few times today. My eyes would catch someone else's and they communicated exactly the right thing, at just the right time. And it really mattered to me.

In the final mile, I was losing strength and motivation to just keep motoring on to the finish line. I knew I was so close to my goal for a dream half-marathon result. A girl ran alongside me and saw me struggling. She said, 'Come on, lassie, don't let me pass you!' as I ached and hurt and willed for it all to end.

Could I keep my legs motoring on at a sub-7 minute-mile pace for the last mile? I repeated it to myself, 'Come on, Rach — JUST ONE LAST MILE. There will be no more after this one, I promise.'

I turned and gave her a tired, thankful smile. She dragged me on and helped me to keep pace for another half-mile. I was so grateful for her warmth and her selfless encouragement. She could have seen me weaken, and used that to push herself forward: she chose to be kind, and to reach out to me instead.

Today's race was fantastic: hard work, fast, fun, exciting, in a beautiful part of the world. The scenery was incredible.

We took selfies; we looked out onto the rolling sapphire sea; we had an adventure on the Edinburgh buses, and we even got PB's in spite of a ridiculous headwind on the way back in! Happy days.

AGED 28½

November 2006

My new personal commitments are:

- Using my experiences to help others
- Living my life — actually living it for ME — and not on somebody else's terms (I've a way to go on this one, but this is at least a step in the right direction)
- Refusing to be controlled by fear. I've seen fear of the unknown kill so many dreams. I want to believe in what _is_ possible, and not be consumed by what, theoretically, could go

wrong. If I fail, I'll be far happier knowing I've at least had the balls to try in the first place

I opened up the conversations with Ma and Pa last night. Here's how it went:

Me: 'Mum, I've decided that I'm going to retrain as a personal trainer. I've been giving it a lot of thought, and it's something I absolutely want to do. I know it's a huge change, but it honestly feels right for me to do this.'

Mum: 'That's wonderful, Rach! Just so long as you're happy.'

Me: 'Thanks, Mum.'

Me: 'Dad, I've decided that I'm going to retrain as a personal trainer. I've been giving it a lot of thought, and it's something I absolutely want to do. I know it's a huge change, but it honestly feels right for me to do this.'

Dad: 'You're going to do what? What on earth for? ... [awkward silence] What about your legal career? ... [another awkward silence] And how much will that cost?'

Me: [silence]

Bit of a difference in reactions then, but I refer to my new personal commitments above, and more notably point (2). On that basis, I can't allow myself to give a damn what they — or anyone else — say.

So, with the certainty of at least two enormous, life-changing plans around the corner, I duly handed in my notice at said law firm with my absolute pleasure. I couldn't wait to be free.

There was a lot to do in preparation for our travels abroad and for my retraining and planned future career. Strangely, none of it seemed overly daunting, which made me even more convinced that it was the right path for me to take. What I hadn't quite bargained for were the views of others when I informed them of my impending career change. Most frequently I was met with shocked gasps of 'You're doing what? Leaving your well-paid legal job to become a personal trainer?! Hmmppff. What about all those wasted years of education and training? And the salary? Are you REALLY going to throw all that away, Rach?'

The fact that I felt like my life was being flushed down the toilet was virtually never of any interest or relevance. The status and money that I was apparently 'throwing away' were the only notable headlines.

I became familiar with having to swallow my own horse pill of disappointment, and delivering a considered, rational response which went something like this: 'I'm pretty excited about it all really, and my legal training will always come in handy. I'm sure it certainly won't go to waste! Anyway, here's to the next chapter!'

Given that my marriage had run aground on the rocks some while back, it was quite a feat for Tim and I to drag this dead weight with us to South Africa – but it was our last chance saloon.

Even then, I knew there was only one way it would ulti-mately be resolved, but at the very least we would support

each other at the start of a new journey, and a new life –
whatever that consisted of.

December 2006
South Africa

Ahhh, it's SOOOO good to be back running! But
how the HELL did I do that? It seemed like a good
idea at the time! Unsurprisingly, I haven't done
much running at all since I've been over here, but
I needed to justify bringing my trainers all this
way, so I ran into Alicedale this morning. My plan
was to head for the one oasis in the desert: there's
nothing much in Alicedale other than a small shop
with a healthy supply of cheap alcohol, crisps and
chocolate — but that's enough motivation for me!

It's around 13km (thirteen bloody kilometres!),
which is the furthest I've run in a long time.
The weather hasn't been spectacular over here
recently, but boy, did the sun come out today.
There is one single, dusty track from the game
reserve into Alicedale. It weaves and winds its
way through sprawling, rolling clumps of dense
greenery amongst the hills. When the sun shines,
it heats up the dirt track and dries it out to
become a paler, dusty red. When it rains, it turns
a deeper, burnt clay colour.

And so, I set off. My trainers kicked up dust
with every step. A couple of bashed-up old cars

drove past me and the drivers looked at me quizzically as if to say, 'What the hell are you doing running out here by yourself, lady?'

I soaked up the sunshine and the peace. It was bliss having time to get away from everybody else — Tim included — and to have time to think. I thought about lots, and I thought about nothing at the same time. I could only hear my own dusty footsteps for most of the way, and noticed all the pot holes and craters in the road. No wonder the ride into town is such a bumpy one and all the old cars are completely battered. A van drove past me with an entirely smashed windscreen, and a bonnet that wouldn't close. It looked like it had lost a fight with one of the bull elephants on the reserve: it probably had!

Today reminded me why I run; it reminded me what I miss when I don't run, and why I need to make time and space in my life to get my 'fix'.

Maybe my sanity has depended on it far more than I realised? Today was a special day: it was a reminder of the why.

ME? A PERSONAL TRAINER? DON'T BE DAFT!

On our return to the UK, the stories and memories from our South African adventures saw Tim and I through Christmas, and before we knew it, a new year was underway. There was a new start for me, with my challenge of retraining, and a new legal role lined up for Tim. In a strange dichotomy, our South African trip had brought us closer together, whilst at the same time cementing our demise. It was too much to comprehend at that time, with our new, separate paths unfolding. But, my internal GPS had finally picked up a signal: I knew that this was the start of a brand-new life for me: it was Game On. In the meantime, we settled back into our new routines, and we did so supporting each other as best we could.

Now, it is worth bearing in mind a couple of factors here:

I didn't know any of the 'hows' – and there were plenty of those chomping at the bit. *How the hell am I going to do this? What am I supposed to do? Where do I even start?*

Whilst it is true to say that I had maintained some basic level of fitness over the previous years, my running and training commitments were all very modest to say the least. And whilst I'd been able to manage my weight with some success since my late teens, I had fallen into a comfort zone of 'minimal effort' required to maintain what I would now describe as minimal standards.

Only in retrospect do I see very clearly how much more I could have achieved. I can only presume that my internal limited-belief system had kicked in to remind me that this was as good as I could get: my weight had stabilised, and I continued to run with the Tuesday-night Wakefield Harriers group. We did our usual five or six miles at our usual ten min/mile chatty pace; I could run a half marathon in around two hours by now, and I never even imagined myself going to another level of fitness, or dreamt of achieving more.

Running alongside the above (excuse the pun) was the ever-present monkey on my back ... my absolutely crippling relationship with my own body, and my distorted body image. I'd already been through so many changes, it was hard to keep a tab on exactly what I saw when I looked in the mirror. Still driven by a fear of regressing into the teenage me of yesteryear, I couldn't let go of that person, and even begin to focus on who and what I could potentially become.

Seeking the approval of others was a continuing theme, and one which I hadn't yet been able to identify, let alone address.

My newly chosen career path would challenge me to tackle this head on.

February 2016

I went to the gym this morning to do some cross-training. My injured calf won't allow me to run at the moment, so I guess a slightly different cardio workout and a strength class is better than nothing.

After my reluctant bike session, I crept into the main studio and joined the regular Lycra-clad class groupies. I saw one lady I recognised who seems to do almost all of the classes any day, at any time. I ambled over to have a word.

'Excuse me, I wonder if you know whether there is much high-impact work in this class?' I asked. 'It's just that I can't do any impact training at all right now, as I've strained my calf,' I said, pointing to my swollen left leg.

'Oh, yeah no problem – you should be fine. Are you a runner?' she asked, smiling whilst taking out her earphones. 'You look like a runner.'

I heard those words, and wondered to myself, 'Do I? Really? Me? I look like a runner? And what exactly does "a runner" look like?'

'Erm, yeah. Yes – I am. I don't do many classes at all, to be honest. And today I've got to be really careful. Maybe I'll just have a word with the teacher when she comes in,' I chuntered on, still pondering how and when I actually began to 'look like a runner'.

We exchanged a few pleasantries, and I headed off to collect a pair of baby dumbbells for us sparrow-armed runners.

I wonder if I ever 'looked like' a personal trainer? Hmmmm...

February 2007

I visited a gym in Halifax on Wednesday evening to see the fitness manager bloke and discuss the possibility of me working as a PT over there once I'm qualified. He was a right wanker. I know it's good to challenge yourself, but I honestly felt so insanely far outside my comfort zone, I'm amazed I didn't turn around and leg it straight out the door.

I kept hearing a voice inside my head jibing at me, whispering, 'How can you be a personal trainer, Rach? Look at you! Why would people want to be trained by you? Who on earth would _pay_ to be trained by you?! You're having a laugh!'

I'll just have to deal with those horrible, crippling thoughts, because they're nothing new, and I can't allow them to hold me back. I've come too far, and I have to believe that I can do this. I _can_ do this!

Plus, I keep having major confidence crises about my body, and whether I'm up to being a PT (that wanker gym manager certainly didn't help matters). I worry that I won't be any good at designing training programmes — what do I know?! And I worry that I'm not 'skinny' or 'ripped' or 'fake tanned' enough. Will people eye me up and down and judge me? The reality is that they probably will. And I'm going to have to be OK with that. Shit! Will I be OK? Will my fragile ego be able to cope?

These aren't new or even recent issues — I've been paranoid about my body for as long as I can remember. How ironic then, that I'm now going into the fitness industry! Am I a complete fraud, or what?

I sometimes wonder if I'll ever be totally happy with myself — but I guess I've come a long way from, say, ten years ago. It seems like that was another person!

Who knows where I'll be another ten years from now ...

So, by virtue of my relatively low fitness levels, combined with my rampant body dysmorphia, deciding to become a personal trainer was arguably one of the most ridiculous career choices in the world for me. Perhaps akin to Daniel walking blindly into the lion's den, or an alcoholic taking a position pulling pints behind Dublin's busiest bar. I was about to put myself on show as someone who exuded body confidence and had taken control of her fitness, her health and her life. Brave? Or stupid? Or both?

My intentions were good: I naively wanted to help other women who were maybe experiencing similar issues to me – to help them see that they were capable of being so much more, and of regaining control of themselves, and their lives. And yet, with the best of intentions, I barely had a handle on my own. I was also lining myself up to be judged, assessed, critiqued – even criticised – for my own physical shortcomings, my less-than-impressive fitness levels, and the unequivocal absence of a mahogany ironing board stomach (it was still No. 4 on my list of 'fantasy wants – no matter how ridiculous').

How ironic then, that I actively invited that attention upon myself, and onto my greatest vulnerabilities. How on earth could I do that, with my own levels of raging insecurity and body dysmorphia? I still have no idea.

During the personal training qualification itself, I was so (ahem) 'busy' commuting and studying, that – absurdly enough – I spent very little time actually training myself. I would learn all the theory behind different methods of training, the *hows* and the *whys*, but in terms of physically experiencing a shift in gear myself, it never came.

I was the equivalent of the morbidly obese GP who smokes, or the teacher who can't stand children. I was the psychotherapist with OCD and the lawyer with a drink-driving conviction. *The personal trainer who barely trains – have you heard of that one?*

I look back now and I see a raft of well-worn excuses.

I didn't have time! Yes. I did. I could have made time.

I trained alongside my clients. Sometimes that was true, but it was *their* training, not mine. *I did a few walking lunges today with a fifty-eight-year-old who wants to tone her legs.* So what? That's not *my* training, for me. It's a convenient tick-box exercise: an excuse not to try harder.

Running was lost. It fell between the treadmills at my gym, and off a cliff of purported busyness. I wasn't around to run with the Wakefield Harriers any more. But why didn't I join a Halifax-based running club? I have no answer.

Whatever the reasons (or excuses), I was very aware of my weight starting to creep back up.

The truth of the matter is that I was becoming lazy and unfit again – an irony so ludicrously comical that I could have written the script.

THE CHICKEN SHED FITNESS STUDIO

March 2007

The wanker gym manager took hold of his shitty instant camera, and stood up motioning for me to follow him. 'Right, Rach. We're going to need a photo of you for the main board in the gym reception. You know, to go next to the "Meet Your New Personal Trainer" blurb,' he spouted.

I felt awkward and uncomfortable, and feigned a relaxed smile.

He laughed meanly as I squirmed in front of the cheap Kodak lens. 'Bloody hell, you're certainly no model, are you, Rach! Ha ha ha.'

I tried to laugh along with him light-heartedly, but his words had hit me like bullets from his loaded camera-gun: MAN DOWN!

I knew with some certainty that my time working in the godforsaken gym with Wanker Fitness Manager was only for the short term: I was simply there to gain experience, observe the good, the bad and the ugly – and to learn. I wanted to train people on *my* terms, and in *my* way. I would have empathy and understanding; I would listen to them, and look past all of the obvious goals a client may have set for themselves. I would try to identify their *real* motivation for change. Granted: some people don't have a Bag for Life full of 'issues'. They may literally just want to tone up so they can kick ass at the forthcoming office party, and pull the new bloke from Accounts. *Easy!* No head mess to contend with. But – as I would discover – those people were few and far between.

Once I settled into a semi-regular routine with a few clients of my own and some vaguely forming working patterns, things began to fall into place. The gym was based in Halifax, whereas our suburban-bliss marital home was in Wakefield. For those without the benefit of local geographical knowledge, this meant a sixty-mile round trip to work and back: it would actually cost me far more in petrol to get to work than I would earn, but in reality, the potential makings of a new life was an unexpected benefit of this otherwise completely illogical arrangement.

It also felt a bit like coming home, to a place I knew and felt safe. Like a child running back to its mother with a grazed knee, I gravitated to my mum's house, and stayed over in my old, time-frozen bedroom more and more frequently. It became a convenient excuse not to tackle the M62 on the dreaded thirty-mile trek back to our neatly trimmed lawn.

It was an interesting place, the gym, and I kept my ear to the ground. One day I heard of some potentially suitable business units from a canny old chap who regularly eyed up the scantily clad totty whilst purportedly training down there.

'The rent would be a lot cheaper than what you're paying to work here, love,' he said, with a knowing look in his eye. *How does he even know that?* I mused.

'You know, our business park is in a lovely rural setting,' he continued. 'I've got one particular unit in mind which may just suit your needs.'

I barely slept with excitement. *Maybe my dream of opening my own personal training studio could become a reality?*

I set off to go and take a look the very next day. As the journey became more and more – ahem – 'rural', I did wonder where the hell this supposedly 'perfect setting' for my very own fitness studio was. *A bunker, hidden down a dirt track in the middle of a field, perhaps?* Never mind about that for now, though … my excitement grew as I neared the end destination.

'Hi, it's Rachel. I'm coming to see the business unit we spoke about? Yeah, I'm just wondering where you are from here.' I thought I'd better give him a call to check directions rather than become wedged up some narrow country track with a burned-out clutch. 'What can I see? Oh, erm – fields. Lots of fields, a very long hedge shaped to look like – is it a crocodile or a dragon or something? And a big old farmhouse with lots of plant and machinery outside … Am I anywhere near?'

A couple of short telephone calls later, and there it was … an old chicken shed. It had no windows, and no door to speak of, other than a wide corrugated metal shutter that rolled to one side, complete with a mini ramp walkway –

which I could only presume was for the convenience of the chickens who once resided there. It was quite simply the furthest removed thing from a fitness studio that I could possibly conceive of.

But I rallied my sinking heart, and looked again. My eyes saw something very different. *What if I put windows along the entire length of the shed?* We would look out onto the most beautiful, rolling countryside. *What if it had a real door, and a real floor, and a little shower/changing room area?* Possibly even a small kitchen unit and a few comfy chairs for a waiting area? What if rather than view the chicken shed as being 'in the middle of nowhere' and 'out on a limb', I saw it as being 'exclusive'? It might be perfectly feasible for people to come out of their way to train somewhere like this – so beautiful and quiet, and away from all of life's hustle and bustle. This could become an idyllic place, where clients wouldn't be overlooked, viewed or judged. I was beginning to learn how to turn obstacles into opportunities. Through the dark, dirty, derelict shell of an old chicken shed – complete with chicken filth and matted feathers all over the dirt floor – I could see the makings of *my* fitness studio.

I was sold.

All of my waking (and sleeping) hours were consumed by my efforts to transform said chicken shed into my own 'exclusive' fitness studio, and of course establishing a feasible business, which would keep a roof over my head and food (albeit predominantly Soreen) in my belly. Disappointingly, the bank had turned me down for a business loan with which I had planned on revamping the place from (non-existent) floor to ceiling. It was early 2008, and the financial world was just about grinding to a halt. With many businesses teetering on the brink of collapse, my unrelenting enthusiasm for the creation of an 'exclusive' fitness studio from a derelict old chicken shed fell on deaf ears. They apparently couldn't take the risk. However, I had also been busy beavering away trying to convince some local business support teams of my plans. Luckily, I won the favour of a few key decision makers, and my dogged determination to see my vision become a reality had made an impact. I was awarded a small start-up grant, and so set about planning the transformation. I frequently woke in the middle of the night with random, inspired marketing ideas – anything from logos to PR opportunities. A local paper covered my story, and a 'Women in Business' networking group asked me to go along and deliver a talk about my chicken shed transformation project. My plan was working!

Before long, I was attracting plenty of regular PT clients – mostly women – just as I'd hoped. And, also as I'd predicted, the majority of them had personal issues that I could relate to. Leading up to the opening of my new studio, I would train them outside in the fresh air, until my new revamped chicken shed set-up was complete. I loved the feeling of freedom: I was unshackled, at last.

I considered my job to be far more than personal training in a purely fitness sense: I understood first-hand how intricate the relationship between physical and mental health was – the two being inextricably interwoven, as I'd experienced time and again for myself. I couldn't believe how much personal fulfilment I got from helping to support others, even if my role was only a tiny part of their journey.

I seemed to have an in-built sixth sense for the *real* reason every single one of my clients first walked through the door. I could smell low self-esteem at a thousand paces; I could sense a 'quick-fix-seeker' within a millisecond. Some were recovering from broken hearts, disguising unnecessary extra pounds in tatty, oversized hoodies; others were simply lonely, and wanted to unburden their problems on a trusting, friendly ear. Some wanted me to do the work for them; others wanted me to work them to the bone. I knew virtually instantly which type they were, and got it right (almost) every time.

Establishing a base level of fitness towards the latter end of my teenage years had rewarded me with the first glint of self-esteem and confidence through a fog of self-doubt. It may have only been for short periods of time initially, but it was a start.

'Yes, I can manage my weight …

Yes, I can run, even just a little bit…

In fact, I can run for longer than ten minutes…

As it happens, I can complete a half marathon…'

These were all small, incremental steps but I'm absolutely convinced that by gradually building up a base of mini-victories in the context of my running, it enabled me to believe that I could make bigger, braver choices in other areas of my life – choices that were based on *my* wants, desires and aspirations. I could punch my way out of the paper bag in which I'd been packaged; the insecure, academic, non-sporty, invisible girl could rewrite the label she'd been given.

Eventually, I dared to believe that I could make other changes. *Maybe I AM brave enough to leave the pseudo-safety of a soulless legal career; maybe I CAN succeed in setting up a business that fulfils me; perhaps I AM strong enough to walk away from my hopeless marriage and start all over again.*

None of these may have been conceivable had I never dug my trainers out from underneath the battered old sledge and taken those first reluctant steps out of my mum's front door all those years earlier.

MAKING
THE BREAK

It was an unusually bright day in late April. We both got an ice cream and sat on our oversized, suburban lawn, silent tears streaming down our faces.

'It's over, isn't it? We're done.' I was only voicing what we both knew. Tim nodded his head slowly, his eyes tired and bloodshot – finally resigned to the inevitable.

'Yes, Rach. I think we are.' He'd never admitted defeat before. At last, it had dawned on him.

There were no arguments and no raised voices: there was no blame. Here we were, sitting on 'our' lawn: the picture-perfect lawn that was meant to be part of the fairytale, but the fairytale didn't exist. Instead, there was just empty sadness and reluctant acceptance. He didn't fight for me or for us, and he was right not to. His heartbreak was quiet, gentle and dignified. If I could have loved him, I would have done so in a second – I willed myself to, in fact. As it was, we had nothing to fight for.

This was our accepting failure. A series of flawed and flunked decisions had led us both to this place – to our silent tears in our sun-filled garden. But was it *really* failure? Failure in what context? In our 'bad' decision to get married, and the failure to stop the runaway vehicle before it crashed? Failure to be honest, and brave, and get off the bus sooner? Was it *my* failure for not realising that I couldn't fix myself by misguided box-ticking? Was it *his* failure for being blinded to that, and allowing me to sweep him along my path of self-destruction? Maybe it was all of the above. But right then, on the suburban lawn, we made a decision that – as hard as it was – would sever the diseased limb of all the previous 'failings' and allow us to start again.

Surely an even bigger failure would have been to carry on, knowing it was all based on lies. We couldn't allow that to happen.

And so, we parted, and we never looked back.

Following the initial aftershock, I returned to damage-limitation mode yet again, with a steely focus on putting my life back together … again. My own running and training regressed, having been pushed further and further down the pecking order behind Mission: Survival. I was living back at my mum's, earning barely enough to feed myself, having walked away from my marriage and dumped my misconceived legal career – and with it, the safety and comfort of a 'successful' corporate lifestyle. I was now without a lawn of any description, and entirely void of room for a pony.

To many, it seemed like complete madness. Having apparently 'had it all', I had actively chosen to turn my back on the lot. This wasn't some passive thing that had happened to me. Circumstance hadn't robbed me of the trappings; misfortune hadn't conspired to knock me off my comfortable, corporate perch. But I'd lived with the daily stench of emptiness for such a long time that just to feel free again was like raindrops falling onto parched earth; to discover a sense of purpose felt like oxygen at altitude. I needed the raindrops and the oxygen regardless how long or difficult the road ahead appeared to be.

The uncertainty didn't worry me. My deep, pulsating inner belief had to see me through other people's negativity about the direction of my life, including those who could only express fear at what may lie ahead for me – and there were plenty of those. *Freedom and purpose; raindrops and oxygen.* Sometimes it's the very things we can't see or don't even notice that are keeping us alive.

But I also felt like a cat with nine lives. *We've been here before, Rach, haven't we?* My ever-doubting Bastard Inner Chimp would bleat. *We've 'started again' before, haven't we?* It cackled, cruelly. *What next, Rach? What's the next calamity?* I began to doubt my own ability to get onto the right path. I listened to the Bastard Chimp, and I was terrified that he was right. *What if I do jump straight into another disaster? What then, Rach?* I had no answer. *Raindrops and oxygen. Just focus on raindrops and oxygen. That's enough for now.*

PODGE

A year or so into running my Chicken Shed fitness studio, and a new kind of problem was emerging: me ... again.

I'd invested so much time and energy into training other people and running my business, that by the time it came to training myself, I was spent. It may sound like an excuse – and to a (very) large degree it probably was – but more often than not I came away from sessions with clients feeling completely drained.

I was oblivious at the time, but a pattern had emerged which threatened to undo all of my hard work, and take me back to the very place I started out all those years before, as that unhealthy, overweight, insecure teen. The pattern was this: *wake up, train folk, feel exhausted, miss a meal having run over-schedule at the studio, inhale a loaf of Soreen and down an energy drink (feel free to gasp in horror), train some more folk, miss another meal as a client would typically be running late, eat whatever I can get my hands on, get home late, crack open the rosé wine, fall asleep, wake up, feel lethargic ... and go again.*

Granted – it's hardly an ideal lifestyle for a purported fitness trainer, but the business of helping others had engulfed me, and I put my clients' needs far higher up the pecking order than I did my own. This was fundamental error number one:

I was failing to practise what I preached, or live by the same standards I was advocating to others.

My training should have been about me, and specifically for me. I didn't see it at the time – how my tunnel vision on keeping my clients happy and the business profitable meant that my own health was suffering.

Yet again, it was as though I didn't think enough of myself to make *me* a priority. Ironic, to say the least. There would be consequences for such a lackadaisical approach to my own health, and my own fitness.

My weight had crept up, and I turned into a kind of hypocritical martyr with my own purported busyness. But whatever the reasons or the excuses, my standards – as I see them now – were far too low. And my clients noticed too.

'Hey, Rach, what's this? You're getting a bit podgy around your middle, aren't you!' one particularly ignorant male client said as he placed his hands on the exact spongy area around my midriff which he 'kindly' brought to my attention.

I stood there, stunned into silence. *What could I say?* I took a deep breath, and I held it there in some kind of shocked, automatic non-breathing response. This was a client. Somebody who wasn't close to me. He wasn't a partner, or a relative, or a friend (it would still have been inexcusable even if he was!). And yet he believed he had the right to put his hands onto *my body*, and tell me that I was 'getting podgy'. *Who on earth does that?!* I couldn't believe that a person could be so out of order, not to mention insensitive and cruel. I went home, poured myself an extra large glass of rosé wine, looked in the mirror, and I cried.

Did being 'a bit podgy' make me any less of a personal trainer? Nope. Did it mean I didn't know my subject, or create excellent training programmes for my clients? No, it didn't. It simply meant that I had lost sight of myself in my desire to help and understand them. And, as predicted, I had put myself into the bear pit to be judged on how I looked: the one place I was perhaps most ill-equipped to be.

One of my regular female clients frequently eyed me up and down as if to scan me for faults. I knew she was doing it, as an unspoken elephant hovered blatantly in the room – or the fitness studio in this case. I dreaded taking her session every single week. *How will she hurt me without even saying a single word THIS time?*

I could feel my anxiety levels rise to almost a state of panic, as I regressed – yet again – to my sixteen-year-old self, who had hated everything about herself and her delinquent body. And yet here I was, aged thirty, trying my very best to pretend otherwise: feigning self-confidence, when inside I was still crippled with self-loathing.

How many times will I have to be lost, and find my way back home again? What will it take for me to finally, FINALLY prioritise my own fitness, and my own needs?

My greatest fear: pregnancy. That's what it would take.

PART 6

MY GREATEST CHALLENGE: PREGNANCY

I met Tilly's dad, Chris, in the summer of 2009. We met, and we hiked all around the glorious Yorkshire fields in blissful innocence for a good few happy, summer months. We laughed as I baked apple pies in frying pans; we skipped through fields full of daisies on sunshiny walks to village pubs, and we genuinely believed that we had a future together. So much so that we got engaged, and planned to start a family. All the stars lined up, and we had 'The Conversation'.

Why am I so fearful? What exactly is it that I'm afraid of?

Oh, erm … only absolutely *everything*!

The thought terrified me. In fact, it wasn't even on my radar throughout my chaotic twenties, right through into my early thirties. I simply wasn't one of those girls who'd dreamt of growing up, getting married in a floating-island meringue dress and having 2.4 kids (or even 1.0 kids, for that matter). It just didn't seem relevant to me. Plus, babies didn't appear to do much other than puke, shit, and scream. I hadn't considered any of those to be particularly strong selling points.

It was also the strangest dichotomy: I hit my early thirties, and whilst settled in a 'good, stable relationship' – whatever the hell *that* means – I suddenly, *desperately* wanted to become a mum, whilst at the same time, *not wanting it at all*. Is that even comprehensible?

My fear of pregnancy and becoming a mother was real, and it consumed me. I was scared to death, and yet somehow believed I was strong enough to face the fear. I had an understanding, supportive partner, and yet knowing the conflicting duality warring within me was both confusing and frightening. *Can I do this? SHOULD I do this? What if I CAN'T do this?* The questions played on constant repeat in my mind, like the warped tape of *Best Christmas Songs* that droned on endlessly as I stacked Woolworths shelves with early Boxing Day sale tat back in 1992.

I was afraid on many counts: firstly, *what will pregnancy do to my body?* Having gone through the myriad struggles and physical metamorphoses – both good and bad – over the previous fifteen years, *how will my body cope with pregnancy?* It was a given that my body would become unrecognisable. I vowed that I would remain as active as I possibly could throughout my pregnancy and would learn everything I could about how to keep fit whilst growing a baby.

How will I cope mentally with the changes? It was a fact that I'd suffered badly from serious bouts of depression, body dysmorphia and disordered eating. I'd spent years popping my daily Happy Pills, and quite clearly, this pushed me into a 'high risk' category of suffering from post-natal depression. That was just a fact, and it scared me to death. *SHIT! DR. SHEPPARD HAS TOLD ME THAT I CAN'T*

TAKE MY HAPPY PILLS WHILST I'M PREGNANT. WHAT AM I GOING TO DO?! I felt like a crack addict being given the final ultimatum of going Cold Turkey. *Will I sweat and shiver in a cold, lonely bed, crying into my pillow with the Samaritans' helpline number on speed dial? Will body dysmorphia run riot once more? And will I simply see myself as 'getting fat', despite understanding logically that isn't the case?* I knew that this would require a certain level of logical comprehension; one which body dysmorphia tramples on as though it were a vat of grapes being reduced to pulp in the pre-fermentation stage. *I don't know if I'm even capable of being that rational, or logical, or both.*

How will my boobs cope? And will the pain be manageable? I didn't know if the operation I'd had aged nineteen would even allow me to breastfeed, such was the violation of my milk ducts and related pipe-work. *Will the pain be unbearable? Will they ever shrink back and fit into the safety of my fully scaffolded sports bra again?*

How will I deal with my changing physique in this line of work – within this aesthetically judgemental, entirely visible bear pit? Will my clients see me 'blossom' with a perfectly neat bump, or will they witness the spread of spongy, undefined flesh along with an accompanying waddle, complete with the departure of any hint of tone and definition? If it all fell apart, and I emerged the other side of pregnancy a hefty, wobbling, milk-making machine, what success would I have working in the fitness industry then? Even my livelihood was on the line.

What about the undeniable fact that I'm inherently selfish? After all, I'd been entirely consumed with my own personal soap opera of a life for well over two decades. Everything was about *my* drama: I realised and accepted this about myself. Although believing myself to be a very caring, giving, not to mention *sensitive* person, the thought of putting someone else's needs before my own terrified me. Especially a tiny, crying, kicking, shitting ball of flesh who would be entirely dependent on my sanity and decision-making skills – my track record not being particularly strong on either count. *I'm barely able to look after myself, so what superhuman powers will I be able to muster to look after, let alone priori- tise, another little life?* I knew that I couldn't permit myself to be a 'bad mother' in any sense (perfectionism doesn't tolerate corner-cutting), but equally, I wouldn't allow myself to be placed on suicide watch either.

It was all truly terrifying.

Despite all of these real, pulsating fears, Mother Nature is an incredible thing, and my desire – *our* desire – to have a child quite literally overrode every single one. Nothing was insurmountable. I felt happy, settled and supported in my relationship, and I would do whatever it took to adapt, cope and survive the choppy waters of pregnancy and the rough ride into motherhood.

For whatever mystical reason, and with oodles of support behind me, I felt strong enough to tackle my fears.

It was *GAME ON*.

And it all happened rather quickly. We discovered I was pregnant immediately after a New Year's skiing holiday, during which I'd displayed every possible symptom in the book, including:

- Feeling nauseous at the faintest smell of coffee (and I *love* coffee) or – bizarrely – any kind of cured meats … of which there are plenty, in Lech …
- An insane and endless craving for fruit-flavoured iced lollies (we're talking about a Raynaud's sufferer … in winter)
- Crying inexplicably in random places, including at the top of otherwise perfectly manageable red ski runs
- A constantly metallic taste in my mouth, as if I'd been obsessively licking tin foil
- My boobs swelling painfully to the size of the very same beach balls I'd chosen to avoid all those years earlier

This was it. It was happening. My greatest fear on earth was pregnancy, and here I was, about to go head to head with it.

AGED 31, AND NEWLY PREGNANT

> January 2010
> I've put things in place to make the coming nine months bearable. Arguably, big changes are required if my business is to adapt and survive, but I know that clinging on to my sanity is the most important outcome: it's on this that everything else depends. To keep myself occupied, I've set the following plates spinning:

1) I've introduced a new personal trainer to my business, and slowly set about handing over my clients, holding their hand whilst someone other than me stands in my usual place. Some clients are happy with it; some aren't.

2) I've undertaken a pre- and post-pregnancy fitness training qualification on the basis that 'knowledge is power' (also being the completely self-absorbed control freak that I am).

3) I'm rethinking my business offer, and planning on bringing my impending motherhood into the mix. My plan is to set up 'mums and babies' group training sessions when my daughter-to-be is a few weeks old.

4) I'm designing a new marketing strategy to reflect the changing nature of my business — it will take on a 'new mums' training focus. Arguably, it will be designed more with my own refashioned obligations in mind than as any feasible long-term business strategy, but it's survival for now.

5) I'm continuing to take some one-to-one personal training sessions — a few clients vehemently object to somebody else standing in my place, even though I'm now officially a Weeble.

6) I'm looking into childcare options: I don't have the luxury of maternity leave, so will have to get back to work as soon as possible if my business is to survive. Plus, it'll be good for my sanity. All being well, my new baby girl can work alongside me for some of the madcap plans I've concocted, but at least one day of paid childcare per week will be required if I'm going to pay the bills.

7) I'm moving to a larger fitness studio — mainly due to the revamped plans at point number (3) above. We'll need space for several prams, a million baby changing bags packed full of overanxious New Mum Essentials, and space for x number of neurotic new mums, together with their gurgling, squirming, offspring ... and my own, of course. I can't wait (GULP!).

8) We've just moved to a larger house — just because there isn't enough going on already (oh, and we need room for a sports buggy the size of a Reliant Robin).

9) I'm beginning to plan my post-pregnancy comeback. Hmmmm. This is a big one ...

What helped me massively was the mental focus of preparing for the inevitable changes to my business. Most of my clients had become insanely attached to having me as their sole source of support and hand-holding, insisting on my personal delivery of their training sessions. Dodgy puns aside, there is an obvious analogy to an umbilical cord here – and it's not far off how it felt. However, when faced with no other choice – once I was officially a Space Hopper, and no longer able to demonstrate a squat or go ten minutes without needing a wee – most of my clients understood the new remit, and they generally adapted well.

Most of my clients were lovely and supportive, making great efforts to work around my need to attend antenatal classes, or break off and dash to the loo at short notice. Many grew excited at the prospect of my impending motherhood, and we frequently mooted potential baby names whilst stacking up the dumbbells. One of my more insensitive clients, on the other hand, prodded at the flesh on the back of my arms. 'You're losing a bit of tone on your arms, aren't you, Rach?'

I wanted to crawl into a hole, under a rock – anywhere to escape the surreal, humiliating conversation.

'Erm, I guess I'm losing some muscle tone, but I am twenty-eight weeks pregnant, so I think I'll cut myself some slack,' I responded, dryly. *I AM TWENTY-EIGHT WEEKS BLOODY PREGNANT!* I thought to myself, welling up with tired rage at her opportunistic humiliation of me. *I'M ALLOWED TO FEEL FUCKING HEAVY AND TIRED, YOU STUPID COW!* I gulped the words down and swallowed hard so they didn't spew uncontrollably out of my mouth.

She looked at me with a particularly unwelcome smirk on her face, and simply replied, 'Hmmm.'

JESUS. How long will I have to endure her energy-sap-ping, negative presence in my own personal space? I mused, once I'd managed to steer the excruciating conversation away from my newly proclaimed bat-wing arms, and force my fake, painted smile back on. *Fifty-five minutes and counting ...*

I walked everywhere, and absolutely anywhere: far more so than I ever did pre-pregnancy – inexcusably. Up hills and down dale. *A walk to the shop two miles away to pick up a pint of milk and back again? No problem.* I didn't know why, but I simply had to move in order to stay sane. I power-walked up our particularly steep hill at least four times a day, trekking to and from my studio, again, and again ... if only to try and remember what my gluteal muscles felt like, and the reassurance of my heart pumping hard in my chest.

I made a conscious decision to stop running early on in my pregnancy. Now, I would hate to give the impression that I was any kind of mile-chasing, endurance-running freak who was familiar with clocking up relentless miles pounding the streets prior to my pregnancy. As I'm sure you can gather, that simply wasn't the case. As small-fry and as modest as my running was pre-pregnancy, I chose nonetheless to leave it well alone until I was safely through to the other side. *Why?* I knew rationally – and with a plethora of medical research and evidence to back it up – that running during pregnancy *is* perfectly safe, but I doubted my own body's ability to handle that on top of all the other modifications. *'If anything goes wrong with this pregnancy, Rach, anything at all – YOU will be ENTIRELY to blame.'* I listened to my worrying thoughts, and I couldn't shut them up. I felt unable to risk any further self-hatred should the desired outcome for a happy, healthy baby not end up being the entirely random cards we were dealt. I knew I would never have forgiven myself, even if it were proven to be something completely beyond my control. Having already experienced what stinging self-hatred felt like, I needed to minimise any further damage.

And so, the very last race I took part in was the Brass Monkey Half Marathon, when I paced my sister around the course whilst only a few weeks pregnant.

1 MONTH PREGNANT

January 2010

Phew! Am I glad that's over! I stupidly offered to pace Jane around the Brass Monkey Half Marathon today over in York. She's no runner at the best of times — and I'm in the early weeks of pregnancy — but bloody hell, she made hard work of it. The comedy started in the first mile when she looked over at me pathetically and said, 'I'm having my energy gel now, Rach. I'm knackered!' We'd only gone one friggin' mile!

'Bloody hell, sis, we've only just set off! You've got another thirteen miles to go yet, petal!' I replied, half-laughing whilst also genuinely perturbed by the prospect that she might not make it to the end.

I gave her my (only) gel, and told her to save hers for mile nine when she'd need to refuel

> again. I'm certainly no speed demon at the moment myself, but she was running so slowly I had to virtually run backwards to make sure I didn't fly off ahead. I stuck with her throughout her entire 13.1-mile ordeal, and we eventually passed the finish line in something around two hours and thirty minutes.
>
> Bless her. I think she'll stick with swimming.
>
> How times have changed. Who'd have thought that I would be pacing my Swan Princess sister around a half-marathon race — let alone whilst newly pregnant!

If I do say so myself, I exhibited a surprising amount of patience throughout my pregnancy. My body was changing, hormones were surging, and I was morphing into an unrecognisable baby-growing vehicle. All of it felt frightening and alien to me.

I was fully prepared to be a walking, talking incubator for nine months, and to face my own fears of how pregnancy might ravish me. *Get my business in order?* Check. *Studio move planned?* Check. *House move sorted?* Check.

What I was *not* prepared to do was to lose myself at the other end of that process, and to drift into a lost version of my former self.

I needed a plan: a plan to survive it.

THE PLAN

FOUR MONTHS PREGNANT

April 2010

I'm sitting at my table in the coffee shop with a bump that is already the size of Bournemouth, and two cantaloupe melons for boobs. I'm trying to read — trying to plan. A new mum walks in, with her freshly baked offspring.

'Ahhh. Isn't she cute! She's just _adorable!_' an old lady coos at the gurgling ball of flesh kicking the air in the latest model buggy which costs more than a small car.

My boobs feel swollen and sore. And I'm trying to plan.

'How old is she? And doesn't she have a pretty little face!' The old lady is clearly a baby person. (Perhaps most old ladies are. Is it a rite of passage for getting a bus pass?)

The mum looks radiant. Her face is healthy and plump with pink cheeks, and she seems totally at peace with her little kicking ball of flesh. She smiles sweetly at the old lady.

'She's just two weeks old,' she beams. 'We're going to our first Mums and Babies coffee morning soon, aren't we, Abigail? Yes, we ARE!'

> Is she expecting a response from the fleshy ball named Abigail? I can't tell.
>
> I feel my bump boot me from the inside. Again. What will she be like? I know she's a she. Shit! What if she's like me? What will I do then? And how will I cope, trying to make chit-chat with a tiny, kicking, shitting, ball of mini-me — however 'cute' she is?
>
> I try to ignore their friendly, fluffy exchange, and focus on my planning.
>
> I'm desperate for a plan.

I needed a goal to eclipse all goals in order to come out of my pregnancy unscathed. I had to believe that I would regain my fitness, and reclaim my body – not to mention my sanity.

Therefore, I set about to finding a challenge bigger and better than anything I'd ever undertaken before: something to give me an absolute reason to fight for and reclaim my identity.

I sat down at my office desk, the cogs whirring, spinning around in my mind. If it were possible to hear someone's brain clang, churn and clatter whilst merely *thinking*, then my thoughts were surely audible. I thought about my need for a plan. But it was more than that: it was an intense and burning desire, as if my entire future survival depended on it. I felt it pulsating inside me with such force that I mistook it for my (then) foetus restlessly squirming around in my abdomen. This desire was relentless. It had a life and a pulse all of its own. It would be born – just like my baby would.

My mind flashed back to postcards of my previous, pre-natal life: to Amanda and her mum's space blanket; to the fun Tuesday-night runs with Pat and the lovely Harriers' ladies; to the medal I kept in my special box – the one from my very first Great North Run; to the time when Tim said to me, 'We're not *built* like runners, Rach,' and how I felt my insides twist; to the Sheffield Half Marathon when I'd fallen over a cone waiting for Shaz to catch me up; and – more recently – to the Brass Monkey Half Marathon, the race I'd completed only a few weeks before, when I'd struggled to run slowly enough to stick with my non-pregnant, non-runner older sister. I thought about my running, and how I missed it. I thought back to my dream of the New York Marathon, and the place that had been mine, but wasn't meant to be.

THAT'S IT! I felt a pang of unfinished business as the thought flashed across my buzzing mind and made my heart leap with adrenalin. I suddenly knew that *this* was my plan.

I'll enter into the ballot for the Virgin London Marathon 2011!

Race day would be an estimated six and a half months from the moment my bun came out of my (very accommodating) oven.

This felt different to *all* of the plans that had gone before. It was bigger than the *entirety* of the goals I'd set in my life up to this point. It was far grander than achieving my law degree, or any subsequent professional qualifications; it was more ambitious than retraining and changing career. This felt vaster than the task of transforming a shitty old chicken shed into an 'exclusive' fitness studio – and far more ludicrous.

How on earth will I get from the delivery room to the start line of the London Marathon in under seven months? I had no idea.

But it also felt to be a goal – a plan – that was *so* real, because it cemented my love of and my belief in running. It was as if I *knew* that running could save me: like it had done before, and so it could do again. I'd missed running like I hadn't imagined I could, or I would.

This felt to be in stark contrast to my pipe dream of running the New York Marathon just a few years before. That *hadn't* felt real. It hadn't gripped at my heart and made it leap as though my very existence depended on it. Back then, my own sadness was all-consuming as I stared down a void of what had been my life.

Now, there was no void. Instead, there was an epic challenge ahead – an enormous beast of a mountain to climb. But it wouldn't be insurmountable. This time, I needed to climb that mountain, to tackle the beast. *Why?* Because my very sanity – the belief I had in myself to face my fears head on – depended on it.

Maybe all of the postcards from my previous life had been leading up to this point. *What if that were the case?* I couldn't help but wonder.

I had an insane and overwhelming conviction that firstly, I would secure a place in the 2011 Virgin London Marathon by hook or by crook, and secondly, I would be on that start line. What's more, I knew that I would complete every single 26.2 miles of it. I would run, walk, or crawl over the finish line.

It would be the biggest achievement of my life. Not only in the context of it being my first ever full marathon, which scared me half to death, but in proving to myself that I could complete it only seven months after conquering my greatest fear on earth – becoming a mum.

I needed to set myself the kind of challenge that made me question whether I had *seriously* bitten off more than I could chew. I'd set myself a goal of epic proportions to greet me on the other side of motherhood, and I needed sheer terror to motivate me: nothing else would do.

So, I applied online for a place in the Virgin London Marathon public ballot for 2011. In fact, I applied for myself … and for Tilly's dad, Chris (unbeknownst to him) … and for my older sister (she had no clue). Oh, and also for my mother – a then 68-year-old. My theory was that if any one of the above were lucky enough to obtain a place, then I would take it as my own. This was both stupid and naive, as I hadn't factored in the identification verification process at registration. I simply had no idea! (That said, if I *had* been required to turn up pretending to be my 68-year-old non-running mother, I would have given it a shot for a place on the start line.)

Months passed, and then they started arriving. Two 'Sorry! You've been unsuccessful…' London Marathon rejection magazines arrived through the post, together with ridiculously oversized consolation running jackets. *Ahhh shit.* Chris was relieved; my mum and sister were none the wiser.

Although my chances of securing a place were now reduced by 50 per cent, I kept focused on the possibility that maybe – *just maybe* – I'd slip through the net. Blind hope, I believe it's fair to say. *Look what happened to Charlie Bucket, even when he thought that ALL the Golden Tickets had been found!* I clung on to the vague possibility.

'Any post today?' I asked Chris, trying to sound convincingly nonchalant.

'Nope. Just a few bits for me, and a Yorkshire Water bill,' he replied, knowing full well what I was anchoring after.

We went through the same deflating routine for a good week or so, and then it arrived. I was the first down the stairs. Through the cellophane, I could clearly make out the letters 'CONGRATU ...' They were all I needed to see.

'HA HA, SHIT! Look here! You're not going to believe it. Aaaarrgggghhh! Shit shit SHIT! I can't believe it! I'm in! I've got a bloody place! I'M IN!' I screamed, running – or more like waddling – around the living room, kitchen, and both up and down the stairs in no discernible direction.

My dad – always a big fan of clichés – always said that 'fortune favours the brave', and so fate had apparently conspired to support me with my ridiculous, ambitious plan. Just like it had with my chicken shed conversion, a few years earlier.

I couldn't believe it – I had my place in the London Marathon. Chris was firstly stunned and, dare I say it, perhaps even mildly horrified that my wish had been granted. My epic goal – the one that would require my time, commitment, energy and focus – was now a reality: this was happening.

I took my 'CONGRATULATIONS! You're in!' magazine, and I read it from cover to cover ... fifty times.

SUPERWOMAN ...?

AGED 32, TWO WEEKS INTO MOTHERHOOD

October 2010

Getting through the pregnancy has seemed like enduring an endless long-haul flight (without any snacks or in-flight entertainment), but we finally got there, and on 22 September 2010 at 9.10 p.m. our Tilly was born.

It's given me a brand-new perspective on the pressures of being a new mum, having (already) unrealistic expectations of my own body, and adapting to a totally new way of life. I'm experiencing new responsibilities, and I have a new focus. This will be a ridiculously high mountain to climb to get myself back from pregnancy, and back to being 'me' again. Right now, it all seems like a very daunting task.

My little girl is now only a few weeks old, and my challenge has only just begun, only this time I want to be fitter, faster and stronger than I was before.

Why should being a new mum mean that I have to compromise on my fitness, my running, my body and my confidence?

I refuse to accept that it does.

Tilly ended up needing a significant amount of coaxing out of me, her mobile incubator. In fact, she was forcefully evicted when it came to it. Following a four-day mini-break in the local maternity ward (it was that or the asylum) we were finally allowed home on good behaviour – although I was still tagged. I'd continued managing my business, only stopping physically taking training sessions at thirty-eight weeks pregnant. I would be back at work six weeks later.

Thank God! I've been released. I'm free! I was prescribed a plethora of antibiotics, a cocktail of painkillers, and told to 'rest' (I still hate that word). My nether regions had swollen up to the size of a generous corner sofa. I couldn't imagine that they would ever return to normal, or that I'd be able to walk without my legs being a clear half-metre apart, ever again.

Having been incarcerated within my own body for what seemed like an eternity, I confidently announced that I was going out for a walk – our first walk. *Liberation was mine!*

I hollered up the stairs, my foot already half outside the front door, 'Right, Chris, I'm off out. I'm taking her for a walk. Won't be long.'

Chris peered over the balcony from his third-floor office. 'Are you sure you're up for this, Rach? Really? You've not been back home a day, and you're already on about hiking up the hillside with her in a heavy pram? You can hardly walk!'

'Yep! Of course I am! Honestly, we'll be fine!' I said, my voice sounding an octave too high to be convincing. The reality was that if I didn't get out of the front door, I'd be receiving a visit from the men in white coats – he'd be better off worrying about *that* as a distinct possibility.

'If you say so,' he replied distantly, as he drifted back upstairs to his precious child-free zone.

We lived at the top of a very steep hill, overlooking fields and the rural business park on which I had my chicken shed fitness studio. With my gurgling bundle fully mummified in layers of swaddling, I headed out the door. Together, we happily trundled off down the unquestionably steep drive, and in search of sanity.

I knew I was walking fast. The pram felt to weigh a ton as I tried to control the speed going downhill, but it felt so intensely good to move again – to be free at last. I couldn't even consider going home, back to my incarceration, and so I just kept on walking. The drugs must have been good, because although I could barely walk in a straight line, I didn't feel any (significant) pain at all. Or maybe I did, but the combined euphoria of freedom and movement was a particularly effective analgesic.

We did a short loop of the business park, and I made an about turn to push the sturdy pram back up the same impossibly steep hillside. Puffing like a steam train, I made my way up the sharpest incline. Head down, I locked out my arms and pushed through my legs. I could feel the sweat trickling down the back of my neck. It felt like ridiculously hard work, but I didn't care. It was a small price to pay for my freedom.

That night, I awoke in agony. I'd ruptured the stitches, aggravated my entire 'corner-sofa' area, and now I'd managed to bring on a secondary infection.

'It's your own stupid bloody fault!' an exhausted Chris said, as we trundled off back to hospital for yet more antibiotics, and more painkillers. I wept in desperation as the three of us sat once again in the miserable hospital ward, only hours after my earlier release. He had a point. This time it was entirely self-induced.

I winced as the doctor examined my wound. I could barely bring myself to tell her what I'd done to cause myself to be in such a state: she'd only patched me up a matter of hours earlier when she'd first come on shift, just before my release.

Around 2 a.m., once I was fully stitched and drugged up again, we lumbered sleepily back out of the hospital.

'STOP! We haven't fastened Tilly's car seat in!' I suddenly screeched, jolted by the realisation that Tilly was rocking and rolling around in her tiny newborn car seat that hadn't been clicked into its Watchdog Quality-Assessed safety moorings. Chris pulled over and we wrestled with the infuriating seat-belts, before driving back home and up the offending hillside in uncomfortable silence. I stepped wearily out of the car and wondered, *Can I behave myself this time?*

I didn't even know if I could trust myself to give an honest answer.

I had just short of seven months to transform myself from post-baby physical wreck to marathon-ready, and I was hellbent on making the start line of the London Marathon in April 2011, come what may.

I'd already adapted my business to incorporate mums and babies training sessions, and early in the pregnancy I'd started putting together my sanity/marathon training plans. I invited a local journalist to come to my studio and talk about the impending changes to my business, thinking that this was kind of a relaunch, and it would be good to get my 'new offer' out there.

She pulled up outside my studio and opened the door of her newly valeted hi-spec Range Rover.

'Hi Rachel! Great to meet you! Wow, what an amazing place you have here!' she beamed, scanning the studio and gazing at the stunning views.

She didn't know I'd been hoovering and polishing, cleaning mirrors and plumping cushions for an entire week in preparation for her visit. We sat down in the two freshly plumped comfy chairs, and we chatted. I told her about my weight problems as a youngster, and my subsequent cripplingly poor body image. She scribbled and nodded, underlining indecipherable scrawls as she laughed in all the appropriate places.

'Thank you *so* much for telling me your story, Rachel. It's been a real delight!' she gushed, leaning out of the open window of her pristine four-by-four. 'All being well, it'll be going in next Friday's paper, in the All Woman section. Bye for now!' And with that, she rolled away.

Crikey, what have I said? I mused to myself as my new journalist friend drove away from my 'exclusive' chicken shed fitness studio. *Surely I'm not all that interesting?*

Friday came, and I dashed out early to get my hands on a copy of the paper. A large photo of me and Tills jumped out at me from the front page. *The front bloody page!* I gulped hard as I wondered if I'd entirely missold myself, my business, and my capabilities.

I turned the pages frantically to the 'All Woman' section Journalist Lady had spoken of, and there it was: an entire centre double-page spread all about me. Little old me. Plastered with photos of me and my girl. One posed shot of me running whilst pushing Tills in a sports buggy; another doing tricep dips with her in a papoose; a random snap of me fake-running through some woods. *Me, me, frigging me. Bloody hell! What have I done?* I gulped again as I registered the headline that spanned across the entire double-page spread:

'SUPERWOMAN RUNS A TAILOR-MADE POST-NATAL TRAINING SERVICE WHILST ENJOYING FIRST-TIME MOTHERHOOD AND TRAINING FOR THE LONDON MARATHON!'

Shit! What have I done? I've painted a picture of someone I don't even recognise, here! What have I said?

I drove home and contemplated the words. *SUPER-WOMAN?! What's this reference to some flippin' Superwoman? Who on earth is that?*

I read the article over and over, trying to recognise any semblance of myself in it, and I tried hard to quash feeling like a narcissistic, egotistical dickhead. As it happened, she'd honed in on my background story, along with my commitment to run the London Marathon, far more than I'd anticipated she would.

Pride and embarrassment filled me in equal measure, but one thing was for certain – I was now fully committed to running this chuffing marathon: thanks to my new journalist friend, I'd made a public declaration of the fact. *Shit. There's no getting out of it now, Rach!* No excuses, and no way back. I had to deliver on my promise that I would be on that start line in London, April 2011, and what's more, that I would make it to the end.

It hadn't entered my head just *how* that might be possible, or what it would take to get there: I just knew that I would – whatever it took.

MOVEMENT, RUNNING, FREEDOM

It was a really, *really* hard winter. The snow fell, and it kept on falling. Fatter, heavier flakes descended and continued adding to the muted, disruptive wintery scene. We were soon marooned in our house on top of a hill. Some people would love the idea of being cosied-up at home with logs crackling on the fire, stuffing themselves with comforting carbs from their ever-bulging store cupboards, just waiting for nature to chill out a little and defrost. Not me. I'd only just completed my stint as a reluctant mobile baby-growing unit, and I *yearned* for my freedom. I ached to be outside, and my body craved movement. I also needed to train. Time was ticking by, and the countdown clock had well and truly begun. This marathon was coming, and I needed to be ready for it. No amount of snow-shovelling was going to help me on that day.

It felt as though nature was already against me. We had no water at home, as the pipes had frozen solid. I was cold, fed up and frustrated as the snow and ice made any suggestion of running anywhere almost laughable, and I'd barely even started my hotchpotch marathon training plan. Sessions at the studio were also being badly affected by the adverse weather, and with the build-up to the fitness world's Silly Season, aka Christmas, in full swing, I was spinning around in circles wondering how I could stop myself from freefalling at great speed into some dark, depressive abyss.

I felt the threat of my mental health demons looming as though waiting backstage for their cue to enter and hijack an otherwise enjoyable performance. At the core of my being, I *knew* that there were three things – and *only* three things – that could prevent the Bastard Chimp & Co from gatecrashing my stage, and wrecking the entire show: movement, running and freedom. They were inseparable, interchangeable, and all morphed seamlessly one into another. *Movement, running, freedom; movement, running, freedom.* I needed them like I needed air to breathe.

And I was coming down with a serious case of cabin fever. 'I just *have* to get out of this place. I'm going fucking insane stuck inside these four walls!' I wept theatrically to Chris, as I desperately searched inside myself for some logic, or even a smidgen of reasoning as to why I felt so utterly trapped. 'And how the hell am I ever going to train for a marathon in this fucking stuff?' I wailed, pointing to the apparently innocuous yet silently debilitating scene out of the window.

The question was posed more at myself than at him. I knew he didn't have any answers – and there was no reason why he should. It all seemed so utterly and completely overwhelming. *How on earth can I do this? I'm barely able to wade outside in snow boots, let alone trainers. When will it ever end?*

I bundled Tilly up in her cow-print blanket swaddling gear. 'Hey,' I shouted up the stairs. 'We're off down to the studio. I'm going to jump onto the treadmill for a bit. Tills is coming down with me – it's a change of scenery for her, anyway.'

I wasn't at all convinced that Tills was overly bothered about a change of scenery, what with her being only a few weeks old, but I figured she could at least shit and sleep somewhere with different coloured walls for an hour or so.

'But the car's snowed in. You can't get out!' Chris hollered back down the stairs from his third-floor attic office (which was – ironically enough – the one baby-free zone in the entire house). I knew he was happy up there: he could survive for days without any movement other than to reach for another gulp of real coffee. It's a kind of endurance, I guess.

'I've got legs. I'll walk,' I yelled back, jaded by yet more apparent obstacles.

We headed out into the snowy blizzard before he could descend all three flights of stairs to object, Tills and I fully kitted out as though we were off for a prolonged Arctic trek.

Once down in my chicken shed fitness studio, I powered up the treadmills, turned on the music and unswaddled Tills. She kicked and squirmed her way around one of the brightly coloured baby mats, gurgling happily whilst I tried to remind my body how to run …

AND I RAN. Everything started to feel much brighter. I wasn't cold any more. I began to put things into perspective as the endorphins worked their magic, and the Bastard Chimp and his hijack gang were silenced. Muted by the magical combination of movement, running and freedom. *Movement, running, freedom.*

'We can do this, Tills. WE CAN BLOODY DO THIS!' I shouted across to her, hollering above the iPod's overly loud mix of classic nineties dance tracks.

She gurgled back happily, and then messed her pants. Again.

I finished my treadmill session, and we headed back home up the steep, snowy hill to a heavenly, roaring fire. The world – *my* world – seemed like an infinitely happier place. I settled myself onto the sofa with our non-crying baby, flicked some goofy Chevy Chase Christmas movie onto the telly, and noticed the lights twinkling on the Christmas tree. I hadn't noticed them twinkling before.

'How was it? I was beginning to worry about you!' Chris said, as he slowly made his way down the flights of stairs from Mission Control at the top of the house. *Has he REALLY been up there all this time?* I couldn't understand how he hadn't gone completely insane.

'Ace, thanks!' I replied, sounding clearly brighter, and yet feeling frustrated that I couldn't quite express in words how much better I felt, or why. 'Tilly's been fine. She loved having a wriggle around on the mats in the studio. I think even she was getting beside herself being stuck in here!'

I knew he didn't understand. Why should he? I felt like I had found the key to a secret, happy place that he couldn't be a part of. And I couldn't *un*-know that place. Besides, I didn't want to. Already knowing this made me feel like a gap was forming between our two worlds, like ice masses shifting to form new continents. They could never be *un*-formed.

I made a mental note to myself. *When things start to get on top of you again, Rach, like they did this morning (and*

*they will), remember how easy it is to remedy: movement,
running, freedom.*

2011 Marathon Training Schedule

Dec 2010:
Race No. 1: Santa 5k
Race No. 2: Hot Toddy 10k

Jan 2011:
Race No. 3: The Preston 10k
Race No. 4: Fell Race 7 miles (hilly)

Feb 2011:
Race No. 5: Great North West Half Marathon
(13.1 miles)

Mar 2011:
Race No. 6: Trimpell 20 miles
Race No. 7: Kilomathon (26.2km/16 miles)
Race No. 8: Spen 20 miles

Apr 2011:
The Virgin London Marathon (26.2 miles)

RACE NO. 1:
THE SANTA SUIT

Early December 2010

Tills is ten weeks old now, and it's time to get
back on the horse and tackle my first race before
any more of this bastard snow descends.

Granted, a 5k Santa Dash is hardly the most
serious preparation for the London Marathon, but
this is the first organised event I've taken part
in since I ran that ridiculous half marathon with
my sister when I was just a few weeks pregnant
last winter.

It was hard work but great fun today.
I know it was only 5k, but it was the jolt I
needed. It also reminded me that I need to get
some *serious* training in if I'm going to achieve
the goal I set myself right at the start of this
pregnancy.

Hampered by my 'one-size-fits-all' felt
Santa suit (itchy as hell it was, too) and having
spent the entire race holding up the oversized
Santa pants and scratching my abrasive Santa
beard (!), I still finished in reasonable time. But

> more importantly, I beat Chris! Talk about a crushing defeat (for him — not me!).
>
> If that flippin' cheap felt suit hadn't swamped me, and without the oversized Santa pants threatening to collapse around my ankles on every step, I'm convinced I'd have been a good few minutes faster.
>
> Anyway, next stop is a 10k with no daft itchy pantomime costume to use as a convenient excuse for a poor performance. Bring it on!

I'd naively researched scheduled races during my pregnancy, and entered into those which I felt – based on having no clue whatsoever – would be helpful as part of my home-spun marathon training plan. Some were close to home, and others would require logistical manoeuvres akin to the first manned space flight, but I was fully committed to doing them regardless. My plan was riddled with jaw-dropping ignorance, and based on my own hair-brained training programme, but at least I had a plan ... of sorts. It was by no means the most advanced or watertight marathon-training plan in the world, but it was a start.

Racing: this would be my main motivator and schedule planner. It would give me plenty of mini-goals on the road to my very first marathon, and it would get me used to the racing scene, including everything from managing my battered nerves to learning about pre- and post-race nutrition and timing.

Taking part in regular races would keep the fear real enough for me to remain fully focused as the weeks and months passed by, not that there were too many of those to tick off. Plus, I knew that it was one of the best ways for me to train hard and to monitor my progress: I couldn't replicate the effort I put into a race in any other circumstance – and the same is still true today. In no other way could I dig deep enough or push myself to demand more of my body than in reality it lazily wanted to give: I knew that I needed the fear of a series of races to get me physically and mentally prepared for a marathon.

Blogging helped too: I decided to write a blog to follow my post-pregnancy marathon journey. The quite random and oddball series of races I'd signed up for over the coming months suggested there may be more than enough fodder for some light-hearted, comical musings. I had a complete mixed bag in there: nothing like any 'marathon-training plan' I've ever come across before, or since. It would be an interesting journey, and one that I could document and share with my clients, and anyone else who cared to read about it.

I wasn't a member of any running club at the time and I hadn't been for some years. This was *my* goal, and I would be solely responsible for making it achievable or not. Initially, that's how I wanted it. It felt like a solo trek that only I could make; a singular mission that depended entirely on my will and determination to get there. I knew that in the loneliest, hardest miles of the marathon it would be me – and me alone – who would have to find the means to get through.

Running was also my secret, happy place, and I didn't want to share it. It was the place I went to where I was tempo-rarily reprieved from my roles of New Mum, Business Owner, Someone's Partner, or Responsible Daughter. In becoming a mum, I'd been catapulted head first into responsibility. *Real, serious* responsibility, and it made my head spin around with questions for which I had no answers. The only time when my head stopped (or at least paused) with the incessant, tiring questioning, was when I was out running. I treasured that time as though it were sacred.

Ultimately, becoming a mum had changed everything. I needed to prove to myself that I could realise my goal of running the marathon in the same way that I needed to prove to myself that I could also be a mother. In doing one successfully, I would have some threads of evidence to suggest that I was up to the task of achieving the other. This boiled down to the very definition I had of myself. And so, I came to rely on running more and more.

ARMAGEDDON

Late December 2010

Very early this morning I wondered if I should just stay in bed with a bacon sarnie on fat doorstep wedges of white bloomer bread, and have a big Sunday morning cuddle with Tills. God knows, it was tempting.

Looking out of the bedroom window, my heart sank as I faced a scene from Armageddon at the top of our hill, with heavy, rolling grey clouds spewing out hard, unforgiving rain. It was also intent on blowing a furious gale, just for good measure.

Sounding embarrassingly like a dodgy self-help book, I knew that sticking to my plan — however disgusting it was outside — would easily outweigh any short-term fix of a bacon sarnie. So, right in that moment I knew that there was absolutely no contest.

I planned to tackle Cragg Road. It's on my doorstep and also happens to be the longest continuous gradient in England — rising 968 feet over five and a half miles. For the entire sodding climb I battled against an insane headwind, and within minutes I was soaked from head to foot. Just at the point where the wilderness hits and phone reception ends, I turned around and increased the pace all the way back home.

I'd spent the first five and a half desperate, uphill miles wondering what the hell I was doing, but then as I pelted back down the hill I realised that I felt AMAZING! My cheeks felt zingy and fresh, better than any ludicrously expensive facial I've ever had; my body felt alive and my skin was tingling all over from the pummelling wind and rain. Plus, I'd built up a genuine appetite for that bacon sarnie.

So, although I had plenty of moments asking myself 'WHY?' today, I did eventually realise that the sacrifice of my lie-in wasn't really a sacrifice at all.

Today — as hard as it was — I made the right call.

Oh, and the post-run bloomer-bread bacon sarnie was the most delicious thing in the entire world.

'What? You're going out in this? It's pissing it down out there and blowing a gale!' Chris said, sounding incredulous and looking at me with all the comprehension of a person staring at a three-headed beast. 'And it's Sunday morning, for God's sake. Just chill out and have a nice brekkie with us. I'll put some real coffee on. Go out another day. It's only a silly bloody run ...'

'Nope. I've got to do it. And anyway, I can't wimp out just 'coz of a few spots of rain,' I replied, trying to downplay the fact that he was right – there was actually a full-on deluge outside. 'And besides, what's to say it won't be like this on marathon day? I may have to run 26.2 miles in a monsoon, so best get used to it now!'

Maybe he just thought I'd gone mad. Maybe I *had* gone mad. I could see from his face that he simply couldn't comprehend why I would even consider stepping outside of the front door in those conditions. I didn't even know the answer myself. All I *did* know was that I was utterly committed to my goal. I knew I'd feel infinitely better once I'd ticked off my run, had my shot of endorphins, and earned my bacon sarnie. I also knew that sometimes – in fact, most times – the 'easy answer' was not the right answer. Maybe I was finally learning my lesson.

And besides having that as motivation enough, I knew that my now Prozac-free head needed it. This place I'd entered – the strange, new place called 'motherhood' – still felt like an alien planet on which I'd landed. It felt as though running had come to me right at the exact moment when I needed it the most. There was something about the movement, something mystical about the way it made things seem manageable to me, which had previously overwhelmed my constantly whirring mind. It eased my apprehension; it calmed my thoughts. It meant that when I was faced with the challenges innocently created by my tiny kicking ball of flesh, I didn't want to melt down and crawl on my hands and knees into the corner of a room and hide. It gave me a focus – a vent. It helped me to manage all of the mini frustrations which otherwise threatened to nudge me back towards my GP surgery and another Happy Pill prescription. It also steered me away from rosé wine, and prevented me from melting Mars bars against radiators.

And yet even I didn't understand why. *Why now? I've run before. I've been running on and off for years! Why has it suddenly become this 'thing' now? This crux on which my sanity – my mental health – hangs? It was never like this before.*

I didn't have an answer. It was here, and now: at this time. Perhaps there was no other explanation required. It was enough to know that I needed running more now than at any other time in my life. I'd played about with it before. I'd even managed to convince myself that I knew what running was, and all that it could offer me. I had no clue. Just as the giant meteor blasted the dinosaurs from the face of the earth, so pregnancy and motherhood was the seismic shift I needed to jolt me into realising what running was to me, and how much more it could become.

At the same time, I felt a genuine kind of sadness wash over me as I knew this was game-changing, and I could feel myself becoming a different person as a result. The partner Chris thought he'd found – the one he'd met only a year or so earlier – hadn't had any such epiphany back then. She was happy with her rosé wine and Soreen meal replacements; bacon sarnies and Sunday morning lie-ins. But she didn't exist any more – I wasn't her any more. It felt like a secret door had been opened that couldn't be shut. The tragedy was that I'd gone through the door by myself, whilst Chris had been left behind.

I was on my own.

Even though it was very early days in my post-pregnancy marathon journey, I already knew that these changes were irreversible. Along with the birth of my daughter, there had been a rebirth of myself, together with my newfound goals and aspirations. Perhaps the fact that I'd dared to take on and conquer motherhood lifted the lid on some other latent aspirations. *Why the hell can't I do this? Why can't I go out running in the cold, dark, wind, snow, hail or even a bloody monsoon? Why can't I tackle a race I've never done before, over a distance I've never imagined possible before? Why can't I face a marathon?*

And that's exactly what I did. I put challenges in my own way as part of my training plan – obstacles that I *knew* would push me so far outside my comfort zone that it would be blown to smithereens.

Next stop: a hilly 10k road race … skating on snow and ice.

RACE NO. 2: HOT STUFF

I woke up and didn't even know if the race would be going ahead. It was the post-Christmas, ironically named 'Hot Toddy' 10k road race. The first half is uphill (and a steep hill at that ... but then, they all seemed that way to me) with the second half skidding back down to the finish. Melting snow and stubborn ice covered the hillsides. The roads were drivable at least, and so for that reason alone, I begrudgingly committed to turning up regardless.

It was freezing cold. *What do I wear?* I hadn't a clue. *Best be safe and stay warm, then. Just in case.* And so, I layered up. Remember my first night out clubbing in Halifax's Cat's Bar? This was my racing equivalent. I was going for the 'more is more' approach to racing attire. It consisted of:

- Full-length thermal leggings: check
- Long-sleeved thermal top: check
- T-shirt over long-sleeved thermal top: check
- Waterproof jacket (it was too cold to rain) over T-shirt, over long-sleeved thermal top: check
- Mum's hand-knitted (non-runner's) woolly hat: check
- 2 x pairs gloves: check
- 2 x pairs thermal socks (making trainers feel too small): check

I stopped just short of a full-on Eskimo suit.

'Right then, I'm off,' I declared, waddling into the living room in my sub-zero Arctic attire.

'Hope it goes OK,' Chris said, barely giving me a second glance. 'Oh, and my folks will be over when you get back, so try not to be too long, won't you?'

I was happy for Chris and Tills to stay at home. Sometimes – in fact, most of the time – it felt easier that way. Would I have preferred that they'd come along to support me at races? That's a difficult one to answer. Over the coming weeks and months, I would experience both ends of the scale.

What I *didn't* want was to feel as though I were somehow imposing my training schedule on my recently proclaimed 'Running Widower' partner and our new baby daughter. I didn't want to feel the weight of his silent reluctance in dragging prams and changing bags around under the pretence of feigned support, and awkward 'Honestly, it's fine!' conversations, when in reality he would rather stay at home. To be fair, most people *would* choose a roaring log fire over the unnecessary logistical complications inherent in dragging a young baby out and about mid-winter.

The pair of them would join me for some of my later races, which proved to be an uncomfortable combination of on the one hand absolute joy at knowing my baby girl would be waiting for me at the end, juxtaposed with a feeling of unspoken, resentful inconvenience. It was a strained blend, and one that never balanced out into any kind of equilibrium.

What I also genuinely didn't need on this day was the added time pressure on my way out of the front door: I was crapping my pants enough at the prospect of putting myself in a race amidst real runners without inviting further unnecessary anxiety into the mix.

All the *real* runners had arrived at the Hot Toddy race well before me. *Where the hell have all these people come from?* Plus, worryingly, they looked exactly like that: *real runners.*

I dumped my car down a random back street, and – still adorned in my thermal layered insulation suit – had to leg it straight over to the race HQ to pick up my race number if I had any chance of making it to the start line in time.

Flying, panicked, through the door of the race HQ, I ran straight into one of the fitness trainers from my very own studio.

'Hi Rach! I didn't know you were racing today?'

'Hey Helen!' I replied, feigning excitement at our random meeting. 'Ohh, it was only a last-minute thing,' I lied. I simply hadn't told anyone I was doing the race, for the very reason that I wanted to *see* no one, bump into no one, and be made to converse with absolutely *nobody at all.* Being invisible would have been the best conceivable superpower at this point.

Helen smiled, looking understandably surprised, whilst kindly choosing to ignore my thermal running suit. Noticing that she was kitted out in (short) shorts and a skimpy vest whilst I sweated profusely under my mum's hand-knitted tea-cosy hat, I immediately turned a deep shade of crimson.

'Well, have a good one! Maybe see you at the end? Good luck!' she said, and headed out the door with her race number pinned neatly onto her slim-fitting club vest.

I looked around the room. No one else had a running fat suit on; no one else was wearing a hand-knitted woolly Aran hat, together with triple layer upper-body insulation.

I suddenly felt nauseatingly out of place. *I can't do this. I don't even know how to dress!* I panicked, feeling like a stray dog that had just been cornered by the Dog Catcher. *But it's FREEZING COLD!* I reassured myself. *There is still snow and ice on the ground, and it's bloody Arctic out there! What kind of people are these? I NEED my seventeen thermal layers ...*

Meanwhile, my Bastard Inner Chimp made himself comfortable and began chuntering away in my ear: *You should be faster; thinner; more 'PT-like' – whatever the hell that is. You're not a runner, Rach. Look around you! You're not even DRESSED like a runner! You're DIFFERENT to these 'real' running folk. What are you even DOING here?*

And then, before I could begin to wrestle with my Bastard Chimp, *BANG!* We were off, and almost immediately I felt my body begin to swelter under the repressive layers. Before long, we came to the hill. *Is there any possibility of me running up this? Any chance at all?* Not a hope. My slow trot soon turned into a frustrated trudge. *Maybe this is utterly beyond me. Look at me! I look fucking ridiculous – plodding up a semi-frozen street, dressed like a walking clothes horse.*

I was as exhausted by the incessant mantra of my Bastard Inner Chimp as I was by the hill itself.

As I eventually skidded and skated my way back into the finish, all the *real* skimpy vest-wearer runners had crossed the finish line hours ago. Or so my Bastard Chimp tried to convince me. They stood around in small, club-kit branded clusters, chewing the fat over PBs and the 'problematic ice on the roads'. 'Yeah, I'm sure it took at least fifteen seconds off my minute-mile pace,' one gangly, hollow-legged woman said to her nearest club mate, as I lumbered off back to my abandoned car. My head itched profusely under my sweaty, Aran wool hat.

I made a mental note to myself never to turn up to any race in my sumo suit again, regardless of the temperature. At least I could *pretend* to be like one of them: I'd risk hypothermia next time.

Once the embarrassment had subsided, relief engulfed me as my homing pigeon Mummy Radar kicked in. Within a millisecond, I couldn't care less about overheating in my seventeen layers: I simply wanted to be back home with my baby girl. I would become accustomed to this rapid jolt on my emotions.

I shot off in my car. Towards home, and away from any further humiliation.

'Hi, I'm back!' I called up the stairs as I dashed in the front door. 'It was a flippin' nightmare! They were all super-fast club runners in vests and shorts! You wouldn't believe how tough the route was, either!' I spewed, as though Chris were standing there, waiting eagerly to hear every detail about my ordeal.

He wasn't.

'Right,' he replied, dismissively. 'Tilly's been unsettled, and my folks are on their way over. They'll be here in the next fifteen minutes, so will you be ready?'

I looked down at my sweat-drenched thermal layers. 'Oh. Yep. I'll … erm … I won't bother with a shower, then. I'll just have a wash and quickly get changed,' I muttered, as though I were apologising for something, but I wasn't sure what.

It was a routine I would become disappointingly familiar with.

'Tills sounds settled now. What's been up?' I ventured, whilst trying to avoid the road sign ahead which was clearly marked 'Guilt Trip'.

'She's only just calmed down. I've had two hours from hell. The minute you walked out the door she started creating, and she hasn't stopped since. I'm bloody knackered!' he said, sounding as miserable as he looked.

Avoid 'Destination: Guilt Trip', Rach. Don't go there, I reassured myself, as I felt my mind hurtling towards the negative, self-berating cul-de-sac. *Avoid, avoid. Divert route. Change course.*

'Oh. Well, I'm back now, so I can take over from here,' I said, trying to sound infinitely jollier than I felt.

I couldn't stop the unwelcome feelings of guilt from permeating my head space and intermingling with the delayed-onset endorphins, together with the tiniest hint of smug satisfaction that I'd accomplished something.

'She seems fine to me,' I chirped, as Tilly continued happily experimenting to see how much of her entire fist she could fit into her mouth in one go. I took her in my arms, and began to tell her about the race. She gurgled and blew bubbles at me: it was some acknowledgement, at least.

Above all of the conflicting emotions, I felt pride wash over my heavily insulated self for just turning up to the start line and putting myself amongst the running club vest-wearers, when I could so easily have taken one look at them and driven off, straight back home.

And *at last* I felt to have commenced on my marathon journey, despite the harsh winter and the frustrations of being marooned in our house on top of a hill.

I looked at my diary and gulped. I could see the forth-coming races increase in both distance and gravity as the weeks drew ever closer to my dream: the London Marathon.

RACE NO. 3:
A COLD RECEPTION

'Preston? Why bloody Preston, of all places?' Chris grumbled.

'Erm, because that's where the race is!' I replied, bluntly.

It was Sunday again, which meant only one thing in our household ... Run Day – or increasingly, Mummy's Race Day. Once again my bacon sarnie was painfully sacrificed for the cause, and – leaving Tills with her dad in the warmth – I needed to set off to my race. This time it was over in Preston.

'So you're driving for over an hour to a bloody race which is shorter in distance than you could easily run from home, and then another hour's drive back afterwards? How on earth does that work, then?' he asked, clearly exasperated at my apparent lack of logic. I could sense this was going to be a losing battle.

'It's nothing to do with the *distance* of the race,' I said, exaggerating the bleedin' obvious. 'It's a *race*. That's totally different to me running from home, by myself.' I just about managed to stop myself wrapping up my already condescending response with a 'DUR!' But only just.

I wondered why he didn't understand. I felt selfish. *Am I selfish?* I asked myself, as I packed up my bag, and headed out of the door into the dark, eerily silent morning with only my flask of hot coffee for company. A heaviness accompanied me into the car, as I battled with feelings of motherly obligation and guilt. *Is this marathon a genuinely worthwhile pursuit, or simply a self-indulgent ego trip?* I was beginning to wonder myself.

Rocking up at random races by myself soon began to feel like second nature. My usual inner dialogue went something like this:

I'm shitting myself.

So what? That's normal.

But I don't know what to expect.

Again, so what? You never do.

What if I can't do it?

Well, you have the same chance as everyone else.

I don't know if I'm brave enough.

You always say that, but you turn up anyway. That's the deal.

Every single race was a completely different experience to the one before. I'd long since stopped pre-empting what I would face on a Sunday, from my navigational shortcomings to adverse weather conditions, unforgiving course profiles to unpredictable crowd turnout.

Chris had a valid point, though. I could easily have run the same distance (and more) from home, so why did I bother going on a ninety-mile round trip to Preston to run a race of relatively average distance? Quite a few reasons, actually.

Racing forced me to challenge myself. The field was always guaranteed to be fast, with many runners looking like they were old pros – most of them fully branded in their running club vests. How could I fail to be pulled along by these faster runners, and my desire to integrate with them under the promise of eventually being able to call myself a 'real runner'?

I dreamt of one day earning my stripes. I knew I would run *way* faster in a race than I would have done by myself on my own, familiar local route. This was an important aspect of my training for the London Marathon, and it was also great for my self-discipline.

Committing – and paying – to enter a race with an accurately measured distance, a fully marshalled course, lots of other entrants and a definite 'start' and 'finish' line was a brilliant motivator for me to up my game. Not only was it a commitment to myself to run the specified distance and not find some reason to bail out early (the promise of a bloomer-bread bacon sarnie being one such example), it's only human nature that I wanted to keep pace with other, faster runners around me, and so by default I had to push further and harder than I would if I were by myself. And it seemed to be working.

I became familiar with my solitary drives to races, and I grew to love them. It was *my* time. Time to think, process and ponder whilst sipping on my tepid coffee. I listened to the silence. Sometimes music, but mostly silence. How I loved the silence.

After each race, I felt to be building tiny, incremental steps in my plan going forward, and by sticking to it, I was more motivated than ever to reach my marathon goal with as much confidence and fitness as I possibly could.

But there was one commonality emerging. The end of each race was the beginning of a new one: the race back home. No sooner had I crossed the finish line than another clock started ticking – to get back home as soon as humanly possible and resume my motherly duties. I could feel myself being pulled back, like being permanently attached to a slingshot band.

As much as I couldn't wait to see my baby girl again, I resented the unnecessary, heavy pressure on me to return. As if I'd left behind some burden which I had to hurry back home to take care of. It began to add up to an ever-widening gulf between the apparent 'support' I was being given to train for my marathon, and the stark reality. A silent, unspoken elephant had moved into our house: it was Chris's increasing resentment towards my running. I could feel it hang in the air. It followed me through doorways and up and down the stairs.

The 'R' word was fast becoming a dirty word in our household. I tried to avoid using it wherever possible. Like a binge eater, I made huge efforts to keep it out of earshot, and out of sight. I had to mentally prepare myself to bring up dreaded conversations about 'the next race'. *How will he respond? What will he say? What will he NOT say?*

How self-centred will I be made to feel next time?

Running was changing me, and it was changing us. Like the effects of global warming on frozen terrain, our land masses were shifting. And just as I was learning to stand on top of my newly formed Prozac-free solid ground, I could feel the ice cracking beneath my feet.

RACE NO. 4: HILL HORRORS

I didn't want to get out of the car. 'What the hell am I *doing* here?' I said to myself, out loud. I looked around and saw the very same skinny vest-wearers I'd happened across only a few weeks before at the Hot Toddy road race. I may have been running in sub-zero temperatures back then, but at least we were running on a *road. WHAT THE HELL IS THIS?!*

I looked around, and I saw it. I'd never considered what the 'fell' part of a fell race would look like before. This was it: I stood face to face with a huge mound bulging from the earth. Bigger than a hill; smaller than a mountain. *Ahhh. That must be a fell, then.* Incredibly, I didn't run straight back into my car and hide.

I felt like a complete imposter, imagining the other runners looking over at me thinking, '*What the hell is SHE doing here? She's no fell runner! Look at her! I think she's turned up to the wrong bloody race!*'

This was, admittedly, quite bizarre training for the London Marathon, what with it being a couple of MASSIVE hill climbs along steep, muddy trails – where there *were* decipherable trails, that is. As far as I was aware, there wouldn't be too many steep, slippy, mud-drenched inclines in the London Marathon, but what did I know? I could yet be proved wrong. So why was this a part of my marathon training plan? That's simple. This was about challenging my fear. Fear that I *couldn't* do it; that it was beyond me. I had to prove to myself that it wasn't.

I was ridiculously nervous beforehand. I didn't know what to expect, other than a bloody big hill. *And what chance do I have of running up (and back down) a bloody big hill?* Admittedly, not much. I knew it would hurt. I knew it would challenge me in ways I would never have believed.

And I was right. It was relentless, and although breathtakingly beautiful, seemed to go on forever. The uphill climbs felt ridiculous, making my legs burn with a searing pain I'd never known, whilst on the downhill sections I turned into the Fearful Falling Fairy: worrying about slipping down the treacherous hillside and injuring myself ahead of my marathon dream. I took it very gingerly, hopping and tiptoeing down through the mud, clay and scree. I even pulled over to allow other 'real runners' room to fly confidently past me on the scarier downhill sections, but I (surprisingly) caught many of them up on the flat.

Fortunately, once we neared the bottom, the slope eased into a gentle farm track which we followed through to the finish. My terror finally eased as I found my feet and some confidence in my ability to remain upright. The end came, and I was thrilled: thrilled to have taken part; thrilled to have finished; and thrilled to have not come last.

I'd also successfully battled with the cruel, unhelpful mental chatter of my resident Bastard Chimp. At the very least I'd turned up, and I'd tried. *Surely I should give myself credit for that, if nothing else?* I'd created a scenario inside my head whereby every other person running today's race judged me as having turned up to a place where I didn't belong. However, that only happened inside my head. I wasn't the first over the finish line by any means, and equally I wasn't the last – but so what even if I was? I gave myself credit for facing my fear head on. *That* was the purpose behind today's race. Not the miles, or the terrain. It was all about battling my Chimp.

And as painful and horrid as it was at the time, I felt brilliant afterwards. I bounced home, buzzing that I'd done it. There was once a time that I didn't believe I'd be able to run up *any* hill – or even a slight incline – let alone complete a fell race.

I drove home singing badly with my music turned up too loud, endorphins swimming around my head and making me feel like I was floating high above my car seat. *I can do this. I CAN FUCKING DO THIS!* I couldn't contain my excitement as I felt my confidence surge. I was now fully geared up for the half marathon road race I would face next weekend. I knew that it would be an entirely different beast to a fell race, but I felt like I'd challenged myself in a new way today, and I'd come out victorious.

Rach: 1; Bastard Chimp: 0

That night, with my confidence still soaring, I ordered myself some brand-new, shiny fell-running shoes. *Who have I become?* I wondered, having successfully battered my Chimp back into its spiteful box.

Bring on the hills! (And the marathon …)

Next stop: Half Marathon Road Race.

RACE NO. 5: HEARTBREAK HALF MARATHON

We all piled into the car. 'Have you put a full change of clothes in for her?' I asked anybody who'd listen – primarily myself – 'and that warm cow-print onesie thing for her in case it's bloody freezing by the coast?'

I could barely think straight, as my internal New Mum's to-do list spiralled ridiculously out of control. *Oh yeah, and there's the small matter of this – the Great North West half marathon I'm running at 9:30 a.m. too,* I thought to myself. *I daren't mention that right now, though. Chris isn't exactly a morning person as it is.* The sun wasn't even up yet, and this may well have tipped him over the edge.

Cortisol must have been racing through my bloodstream as the stress was already starting to build. There was no shared excitement, or general chit-chat around my pre-race nerves. There was no reassuring talk about how far I'd come to even get to this point. I was silent in my apprehension, and my internalisation of all that this day and this race would mean to me. It felt like a biggie. This was the halfway point to my marathon. It would tell me all I needed to know about my chances for London, and put me in the picture regarding the next seven weeks. *Seven weeks!* That's all I had left, regardless of today's outcome. *Will I cross the finish line today full of positive mantra, telling myself, 'You've got this, Rach. You can do it'? Or will it send a warning signal to my ever-so-efficient internal risk-assessor: 'Nope, sorry, Rach. It's a bridge too far, this one. You've no chance of pulling it off, love.'*

I hadn't a clue.

The drive over to Blackpool was tiring. I tried to make small talk, but I wasn't listening to any of the banal responses. I made admirable efforts to appear calm and relaxed, whilst inside my head I was frantically screwing up pieces of paper and throwing them into a virtual waste bin: anything to distract me from the purpose of the journey. Eventually, he mentioned the race.

'Oh, the half marathon? I've barely even thought about it, to be honest,' I lied. 'I'll just do what I can. There's not much else I can do really, is there!'

Chris put his music on the car audio system. *Shit. It's jazz. I fucking hate jazz.*

I slumped down in my passenger seat in subdued silence, willing myself to some other place: somewhere I could be free to worry irrationally at will about the race ahead, and where I could grapple with my own anxiety without being forced into playing a cardboard cut-out version of myself that I couldn't quite carry off. It wasn't Chris's fault: he genuinely didn't understand.

We arrived at the coast, and no sooner had we parked up than I desperately wanted to leg it. I tried to telepathically communicate my urgent message to him: *this is where I need to leave my responsible parenting duties behind me just for a couple of hours, and get into pre-race anxiety-management mode.*

It didn't communicate as planned – it was never that simple. I saw other runners meandering around, looking relaxed. They'd already picked up their race numbers, having neatly pinned them to their T-shirts and slim-line vests. Some were carefully lining up energy gels around their midriffs like military cartridge belts. Granted – gels provide a much-needed glucose injection for longer runs and races, but *do they need fifteen gels for a half marathon?* I wondered with some degree of scepticism, before I was yet again sidetracked by my mothering duties. I needed to clock off.

Anxiety management was a big part of my training plan. I suffered badly with pre-race nerves, and often felt cornered by the virtual four walls within my own head, unsure how best to manage the internal warfare raging inside. Races were my way of submerging myself into the world of anxiety overload whilst learning how to ride the torrent and stay firmly in my small boat (more like dinghy) named *Sanity*. This was all part of the journey, and days like this would be vital to my own development and my ability to ride the rapids without the lifeline of Prozac to keep me afloat.

My marathon journey was proving to be every bit a mental as well as a physical one. Physically, it was hard enough after the ravages of pregnancy, but the mental training felt infinitely harder at times. Knowing that my body would be able to develop and catch up far sooner than my mind could adjust to the competing demands gave me some small comfort in my physical capabilities. Mentally, I wasn't anywhere near as confident.

'What will we do whilst you're running?' Chris asked, blankly, whilst Tills was peacefully nuzzling her fist, tucked up in her cosy cow-print onesie. I felt my heart sink just a little at the prospect of leaving them for the best part of two hours, whilst having to grapple with my own guilt for not providing adequate entertainment whilst I was 'otherwise engaged'. *Really – how hard could this be?*

Finally, as it became clear that all the other runners were gathering by the starting area, I had my cue to leave. 'Right. I'd better head off now,' I said, still trying to remain the picture of serenity whilst I paddled like mad under the surface. My adrenalin had already been exhausted some time ago. I left for the start, and tried to clear my head of the entire morning up to that point.

During the three whole minutes I had to myself before the gun went off, I wrestled my Bastard Chimp into submission and reminded myself of my half-marathon survival strategy: I would chop the forthcoming 13.1 miles into four lots of three-mile blocks. *Tick one block off, and move onto the next*, ending with one last mile to the finish. It sounded so easy. I've used the exact same game plan a thousand times since.

The first three-mile block came and went without issue. *Block one, done: begin block two.* But this one didn't go quite so well. As the route made us turn back on ourselves and into the most offensive coastal headwind, I felt my right hip flexor begin to grumble. It wasn't happy. Every time I lifted my right leg, a pain seared through what felt like an over-stretched elastic band being pulled just an inch too far. *For fuck's sake! As if this morning hasn't been difficult enough!* It felt like every single step was putting more and more pressure on my right, pre-weakened elastic band hip flexor. *Shit. I've only done four bloody miles! What on earth am I going to do now?*

Maths was never my strong point, but I knew that I had to eek out another nine miles, somehow. My thought process spiralled into despair: *this is only HALF a marathon. However bad this is, a full one will be infinitely worse.* My heart sank as I realised I would be battling both mentally *and* physically today far more than I'd bargained for.

'This isn't fair,' I protested to myself helplessly. 'It isn't meant to happen like this. This is not in my plan.' But I had to stop with the negative, unhelpful self-chatter. *How is that going to help me now?*

In the absence of any better ideas, I carried on putting one foot in front of the other. The miles seemed endless; the headwind felt cruel and spiteful. The crowds didn't know why I was struggling to continue moving forwards. I wanted to stop so badly, but I wouldn't allow myself the option.

I knew that if I didn't get myself over that finish line, I would be beaten seven weeks before I'd even arrived at the London marathon start line. This was now a battle of wills. Mine was stronger: I had to win.

The final mile came, and it felt like the longest mile of my life. After what seemed like an eternity, the finish line came nonchalantly into view. I could see the clock adding up the hours, minutes and seconds of my ordeal. I saw the numbers casually tick over the two-hour mark. As the digits rolled over to 2:00:00 on the computerised screen, it may as well have displayed a single digit – a middle finger. Perhaps I'd have felt marginally better about the whole thing if I'd crawled over the line just before the clock had brazenly displayed the two-hour mark. It may have given me the tiniest psychological boost. Instead, I felt utterly deflated. I'd dragged myself around the half marathon – in agony for most of it – only to be mocked by the offensive clock.

I ached. I was in pain. I was tired, and I felt broken. It was over, and I'd dragged myself across the line. Once I'd allowed myself the thirty seconds of sheer relief that I could finally stop running, my head was flooded with anxious, worrying thoughts. *That was bloody awful, and it was only a half marathon! How can I possibly run that all over again? How the hell am I going to do a full marathon in seven weeks' time? And what am I going to say to people if I simply can't do it? What if I just – what if I really – can't do this?* I broke down and sobbed as swollen, exhausted tears rolled lazily down my cheeks.

Through the crowds, I spotted the familiar cow-skin patterned onesie. There they were. I swallowed my salty tears, and darted straight over like a homing pigeon.

'It was too cold out here for Tills, so we headed inside a hotel for a coffee,' Chris said, not noticing either my limp or my tears. 'I didn't think it would be this cold,' he continued, 'and there's not much to do around here really, is there?' I wasn't sure if he was being serious.

He was.

'She's pretty tired now. It seemed like you were gone for ages! Oh, and well done,' he gifted me, blankly.

A few days after my half marathon ordeal, my diary entry read:

February 2011
Tilly aged 4 months; 7 weeks to Virgin London
Marathon 2011

Well, what should have been such an enjoyable
race along the coast in the sunshine was heart-
breaking, as the realisation has hit me that
physically all is not well. I'll need some serious
help — or more likely a miracle — if I'm going
to reach my goal of completing the rest of my
necessary training runs and, of course, to face
the marathon itself.

I've been prescribed anti-inflammatories,
and with the help of Chris's BUPA health
insurance I've booked some intensive
physiotherapy sessions. I'm doing all I can to
achieve my goal of running the London Marathon
injury-free in a few weeks' time. All I know is
that I am still utterly committed: this is just
another hurdle along the way, which I will (of
course) navigate my way through.

Fingers crossed for my first physio session on
Thursday morning, and then a decision will be
made about my first ever twenty-mile race this
coming weekend... Gulp!

RACE NO. 6: THE FAMILY OUTING

It was a full-on family outing to this one – the Trimpell twenty-mile road race, complete with Chris and our six-month-old baby girl. Once the car was fully loaded to the brim with prams, food, drinks, nappies and even chuffing picnic hampers, we headed on our way.

I'd never run twenty miles before … let alone in a race. And I was – understandably – nervous, not only because of the unknown, scary distance, but more so because of my demon hip flexors. That said, I'd taken some of the pressure off myself following the previous weekend's half marathon disaster – I had nothing left to lose. My hip flexors would either manage it, or they wouldn't. It was that simple.

I'd been religiously doing my mind-numbingly dull physio rehab exercises both day and night for the last week, popping anti-inflammatories like Smarties – and praying. *Surely this can't be the end of my marathon journey?*

This felt like a crucial race for me. Considering the problems in my right hip flexor, I was pretty much going against all advice to even consider running this race. But in all honesty, I was always going to do it regardless of any 'expert' advice. This would be my first time hitting the big twenty-mile marker in preparation for the London Marathon. I wanted – and needed – to be on the start line, today.

After all, there were only FIVE weeks to go now before the Big One ...

Thankfully, the sun was shining, which helped all our moods. The race HQ was a Lancastrian sports centre, with the race setting off from the accompanying athletics track. It was quite handy, as the spectators could watch us complete one lap of the track before we headed off along endless footpaths for the remaining 19.95 miles. This had the makings of a 'family-friendly' race. Granted, not much is particularly easy with a six-month-old baby and all the associated trappings. On this occasion, I had to give him his due: it may well be a more tiring morning for him than it would be for me. Perhaps I did have the easier job, today.

The gun fired and we set off, trotting steadily as a group around the track. I glanced over, smiled, and waved to my mini support crew as they watched me disappear around the corner and out of sight. They would be able to see me again around five miles in, when we would run back along the same stretch of cycle path and off into some other meandering, interwoven parts of Lancaster.

I reached mile thirteen and breathed a (small) sigh of relief. *Phew! I'm still running ... and I'm relatively pain-free!* I'd broken through the half-marathon distance miraculously without any of the sheer, stabbing pain of last weekend's race disaster. I could feel the early grumblings of tiredness in my already weakened hip flexors, but I was thankful for reaching the half-marathon milestone, at least.

Before long, the fluorescent yellow 'Fifteen Mile' sign came into view, and for the first time fatigue really began to kick in. I felt my pace slow down step by step, and I duly entered into the familiar 'grit your teeth and grind it out' mode. I looked ahead, and the footpath in front of me seemed to go on forever as my footsteps trickled to a snail's pace. *One step in front of the other, Rach. Just keep putting one step in front of the other.* My inner coach wouldn't let me fail now.

Finally, I recognised the bridge we'd crossed on the way out, and a more-than-welcome 'Nineteen Mile' sign came into view. *Bloody hell you're nearly home! Just keep going a bit further, Rach. You've got this!*

Suddenly, the spectators were back, clumped together around the entrance to the athletics track. Tilly's red pram complete with cow-skin buggy snuggle came into sight. It gave me a huge boost, and I hung on. One final bastard lap of the track, and I knew that would be the end: I could stop running.

I looked at my watch as I passed the finish line. *3:05. Shit! That's not too bad!* I had absolutely no idea what I might expect by way of a time for this race. I'd never even *run* twenty miles before, let alone raced it, so this was completely unknown territory for me.

And for the first time along my marathon journey I began to feel like a 'real' runner. *Perhaps these 'real' runners aren't an entirely different species to me, after all …?*

I'd felt like a comedy turn at the Hot Toddy 10k, and I'd gatecrashed a party at the Fell Race. I'd limped across the finish line of last weekend's half marathon, but today – *today* – I almost felt like I belonged. I didn't feel entirely out of place. I wasn't on some alien planet I didn't recognise, with species of an entirely different genetic make-up.

Granted, I had absolutely *no idea* what the last six miles of a marathon would feel like, and arguably I'd have struggled to run another single step over and above the twenty miles from today's race – but it was nice to have even the slightest glimmer of hope, especially in contrast with the thorough kicking I'd received from last weekend's ego-bashing.

I couldn't help thinking: *perhaps I've earned my stripes, at last?*

March 2011
Tilly aged 5 months; 4 weeks to Virgin London Marathon 2011

What is running to me now? What has this goal become for me? It's far bigger than the marathon, which is only four weeks away. This is changing me — it HAS changed me. What is running? Is it a hobby? Yes, but it's more than that. I could take or leave a hobby. It wouldn't feel like a feeding tube, sustaining my very existence.

I had no idea it would be like this. Running makes me feel alive; it is my medication and my meditation. It jolts me into life like defibrillators do on an emergency ward. It permeates my cells and makes my head spin with endorphins. Am I a running junkie? I know I need my regular 'fix' or I begin to wane like a tulip in a dry vase.

I couldn't have predicted this. I thought I knew what running was — I thought I knew who I was — but this marathon journey is turning me into a person I didn't know I could become.

How didn't I know?

It's hard. It's really, _really_ hard at times. But I am experiencing true joy. Juxtaposed with the aches, the frustrations and the tears are moments of elation.

This is by far the hardest thing I have ever done — combined with my newfound motherhood, of course — but I feel happy. I am heading towards that place, and it's a place free of Prozac or alcohol; affairs or binge eating. It is simply a place of hard effort, and one of sheer joy.

How didn't I know?

RACE NO. 7: WET TIGHTS

Off she goes to do another silly race in preparation for the London Marathon. Yawn …

With only a matter of weeks to go until my London Marathon dream, I wanted a break. The emotional rollercoaster was relentlessly shuttling me from moments of sheer elation to exhausted dread.

This race was one of those. The Kilomathon was sold as being a 'metric marathon'. We would run 26.2 kilometres – equivalent to 16.3 miles. It was horrible for so many reasons. I felt tired. I *was* tired. I was tired of the planning, the orchestrating, the logistics, the commitment, the travelling, the anxiety, not to mention the running itself! In fact, on this day, I was tired of *ALL* of it. For once, I had to remind myself why I was doing it at all.

The route felt like endless, interwoven loops around soulless industrial estates and car parks. And – quite fitting for this toilet of a race – I wet myself in the last 400 metres. Yep, I pissed in my pants. Even though the finishing line was in sight, I'd given up all attempts at saving face by then. In my defence, I'd stupidly worn running tights, despite it being a scorching hot day. As I unclenched my pelvic floor and felt the warm urine escaping down my second-skin leggings, I saw the finish line in sight, and I couldn't care less.

Standing there, utterly exhausted in my heavy, sodden, Lycra Skins, I thought only one thing: *when will this all end? I want it to end.*

It got me thinking. Do people *really* understand the commitment and sacrifice that goes into training for something like a marathon? Perhaps they think they do, but – just as I had been painfully ignorant/naive in my presumptions – this was *so* much harder than I ever thought it would be. Here is the stark reality of what is actually involved:

Travelling: Both time and expense. Organised races and events take place up and down the country, week in, week out. For me, they were an essential part of my training for the marathon. And yet for all the benefits the races bestowed, I've never spent so much money on diesel. I'm now familiar with every single service station between West Yorkshire and the east coast.

Cost: My marathon dream would cost a small fortune. All the 'other expenses' soon add up: race entries, hotel rooms, train tickets, eating out, petrol, take-out coffees from daylight-robbery service stations, sports gels, not to mention running kit. They all clock up to a princely sum. I wouldn't like to hazard a guess at how many hundreds of pounds were invisibly burned in the pursuit of my goal. And I *still* thoroughly object to paying a fiver for a post-race coffee – however desperate – on the journey home.

Impact on family: Unless you're single without kids, then training for a marathon is likely to impact heavily on family life. When I embarked on this journey, I kind of knew this would be the case, but I could never have predicted just how tough it would prove to be.

Most Tuesday and Thursday evenings were now dedicated to my running. It's simply not possible to just rock up on a weekend and expect to run twenty miles without doing some training during the week. This eats into family time, and it's another high price to be paid. Every weekend, there was some intricate, logistical plan to be concocted. *Will the entire brood commit to travelling with me to a race, or will I head off alone? Will Tilly's dad look after her for anything up to three hours whilst I run? And will I have merry hell to pay on my return?* None of these were easy to answer.

Sometimes the weather would be gorgeous, and sometimes it would be absolute pants. Some races would provide an amazing family-friendly spectacular, and other times, it would be a vast, underwhelming spectacle of nothingness. It was difficult to predict which races would fall into which category. As with life, often the least glamorous-looking events turned out to be the most thrilling. I'd long since stopped guessing.

Unforgiving small children: Tilly was – and is – an angel, but even she got entirely pissed off with motorway travel throughout her whistle-stop tour of Mummy's Race Schedule. There were times when her protesting screams at vehicular incarceration were enough to make us pull over and fall to our knees. Where that wasn't an option, we were stuck, car-bound, on motorways, with her ear-piercing shrieks for company.

Having a life: *Friends? What friends!* With so many demands on my time – predominantly with my training structured around my 'other obligations' – meeting friends for a coffee and a catch-up quickly fell by the wayside. That doesn't mean to say I became a *total* recluse, but not far off. Some friends were incredibly understanding of my commitments, others not so much. Again, it was all part of the price I was willing to pay. If they didn't understand, that was their problem, not mine.

Relationship: This was the biggie. It was where the irreparable cracks first appeared in the dam wall, and the water subsequently spewed out. Our 'weekends away' weren't romantic ones. Chris was busy putting up the *Krypton Factor* Challenge travel cot whilst I had ear plugs in preparing for my 6:30 a.m. start ... in my single bed: the same single bed I was tucked up in by 9 p.m. ... by myself. Not easy for any partner, but even harder for one who just couldn't for the life of him fathom the 'why'. He wasn't a runner. Hell, *I* wasn't even a runner when we'd met. *What had changed?*

Everything.

I wondered if he would ever understand me, and if we would ever find ourselves in a comfortable, mutually supportive place. *Would we ever accept each other's now diametrically opposed dreams?*

It was becoming increasingly clear that we wouldn't.

RACE NO. 8: OVERTAKEN

I knew I was pushing my luck entering this one. Looking at the course profile of the local, hilly Spen twenty-mile race, none of the route looked easy – or even manageable – but I committed to giving it a go regardless.

I'd proven to myself that I could survive a twenty-mile flat race. *How about trying twenty miles with undulating hills, climbing over 1100 feet?* Hmmm. This was a big ask: I was now at the very edge of my own physical and mental capability, and only a few weeks away from the marathon itself.

I looked around me. The field looked like semi-professional athletes, or at the very least running fanatics. I wasn't either. Yes, my love of running had taken firm root and was growing rapidly, but compared to 90 per cent of those taking part in the 'Spen 20' race, I clearly played about with it: once again I felt like an amateur who had gatecrashed the party. Only a week or so earlier, I'd foolishly considered that I *might* have earned my 'running stripes', but cruelly, this race took me back to a place where I'd strayed uninvited into the arena of the 'serious runner'.

I pulled over at mile ten and rang home. 'I can't do it,' I whimpered to Chris. 'I just can't do this. Honestly, it's too hard. The hills are killing me!' I wept at the side of the road whilst other 'real runners' ran past. My legs were screaming, whilst my hamstrings felt like they could pop, and my poor old hip flexors were doing well just to keep lifting one leg off the ground and placing it in front of the other.

'What do you want me to do? I'm here with Tilly. I can't exactly come and get you, can I?'

He was right. I'd phoned home in desperate search of a get-out-of-jail-free card – but there wasn't one. This particularly crushing mental wobble almost broke me. Unsurprisingly, Chris had no miracle answers on the other end of the phone. Ten miles done, thank God, but utterly horrifying was the prospect of ANOTHER TEN MILES STILL TO GO! *How can I manage another ten miles?* The climbs were torturing me with every single step. It all seemed too much, and I was totally on my own.

In the awful absence of any other options, I trudged slowly on. It felt like everyone was overtaking me. People were passing me on my left, and on my right. *Is there anyone left in this bastard race who hasn't gone past me? Any more takers?* I felt like a wounded animal being circled by vultures.

At mile thirteen, I glanced over my shoulder. I noticed a man who was slowly gaining on me. I looked again. He had a ridiculously heavy rucksack on his back, and was inching towards me, catching me up with every step. I couldn't believe my eyes. *How is he running carrying that?* And even more depressing, *how the HELL is he carrying that AND running faster than me?* It was the obvious question to ask him as he finally caught me up.

'Hey.' He could speak, at least. 'It's a toughie, isn't it?'

'Yeah, I'm struggling today,' I panted, glancing over at him pitifully.

'This is part of my training for the Marathon des Sables in three weeks' time,' he offered matter-of-factly. *Ahhhhh! That's the same race my self-published-book friend Clive Gott did!* I thought to myself, as I was reminded of this 150-mile race across the desert, in blistering heat, carrying *all* required kit across six days.

I suddenly felt weak and pathetic, being kindly cajoled along by this random, anonymous Superman. Jim and I jogged steadily together for a mile or so. He told me of the other feats that awaited him. They included the Canadian Iron Man, and the Brathay 'Ten Marathons in Ten Days' challenge. I gulped hard. After hearing about his gruelling race schedule, my pride wouldn't let me slow down any further. It would be thoroughly offensive to just stop and throw in the towel, although every single part of me wanted that to be the winning option.

Jim wasn't going fast, but the thing is that he *kept going*, which in turn kept me going. Over the next mile or so, he told me of his unlikely backstory to becoming this unassuming super-endurance runner.

'Oh, I'm no athlete!' he laughed, as I quizzed him further. 'There was a time when I couldn't run for a bus! I got bullied for being the Fat Lad at school. Setting myself only small goals initially then grew into bigger and bigger ones, which eventually led me here,' he said, looking over at me and smiling broadly.

I couldn't believe it. Just like me, Jim was no 'super athlete'. In fact, also very much like me, he was the chubby kid at school who didn't do sport.

I'd questioned my sanity and my motivation so many times during this race, but – thanks to Jim – I finished it. Today's madness brought about some interesting questions in my mind: *why am I doing this? Is it for attention? Praise? Self-glory? Is it even a healthy challenge for me, or does it venture into self-berating masochism?*

On this longest, toughest of races in preparation for my London Marathon dream, running alongside unassuming superman Jim was inspiring. He didn't have *any* superhuman powers other than just the ability to keep putting one foot in front of the other right up to the finishing line. This was one amazing yet very ordinary man who wanted to prove to himself that he could do far more than he ever thought he was capable of. I related to that feeling, and in that moment, I understood.

I kept putting one foot in front of the other, and I followed his lead. Suddenly, I *knew* my reasons for doing this. In that moment, it all became very simple, and very clear: *like Jim, I'm simply proving to myself that I can do what I never dreamt was possible for me.* So, my motivation wasn't quite as egotistical or masochistic as I feared. *What a relief!*

April 2011
Tilly aged 6 months; two weeks to Virgin London Marathon 2011

I'm not on Prozac, and I haven't been since before Tilly was born. For some reason, this fact has just hit me today. I don't feel like I need to go back on it, either, and I can't quite believe it.

Every morning, I used to wake up and pop my Happy Pill as a way of reassuring myself that on that day, I would be OK: the chemicals would make it so.

Before the pregnancy, I was terrified about the prospect of not having my daily dose of pseudo-sanity. Being only too aware of my own vulnerabilities, I had so many unanswerable questions.

How will I cope with nine months of hormonal warfare without my daily Happy Pill to make it OK? What about the aftermath, when all my fears of motherhood and newfound responsibilities may threaten to engulf me like an unwelcome parasite?

I had my list of endless, neurotic questions lined up for Mr Sheppard, my understanding GP: how quickly can I go back onto Prozac? How soon will it become effective again? When will it save me again?

My fears were real. Chris and I even had 'adult' conversations about it prior to the pregnancy. It's always difficult trying to explain depression to someone who hasn't experienced it, who is mulling over whether medication is _really_ necessary, or whether, with a brighter outlook, you could somehow 'make a better choice' to simply be happier.

How do you explain what depression feels like? It doesn't depend on circumstances. In fact, it often feels worse when everything should feel great, and juxtaposed emotions collide. Or, perhaps that's just my own personal experience. It isn't a choice. It wasn't my choice. And yet ... something strange has happened. Why don't I need my beloved Prozac any more? Why isn't it the first thing I think of in the morning? Why am I no longer afraid of not being on it? How am I surviving without my Happy Pills?

Why did I set myself the goal of running this marathon? It came into my head, and it appears to have challenged my own presumptions over my mental health, and my ability to manage it without the need for my beloved Prozac. How is that even possible? What has running done for me which nothing else could?

I'm so close to the marathon now. I'm two weeks away. I look back, and I can't quite believe how much I've already achieved. Even before I've reached the start line, I've done things I never believed were possible for me. I've challenged myself in ways I never dared to imagine. I've felt utterly defeated, and I've cried. I've turned up in thermal fat suits and felt foolish, but I've put myself on the start line again and again.

I've taken myself so far outside my sad old comfort zone that — happily — I don't know where it is any more. In fact, I've obliterated it. And it's worked wonders for my self-belief.

Who is this person I now see looking back at me in the mirror? I _like_ her: I'm proud of her, and I want her to keep going, regardless of how this marathon goes.

They say that the journey is more important than the destination. I'm not there yet, but I know what this marathon journey has done for me already. I am free: free from Happy Pills, and I am filled with a sense of achievement and satisfaction that I can't quite put into words.

Why didn't I discover this sooner? Why didn't I know?

Why is this only becoming clear to me now?

ALMOST THERE…

AGED 32

April 2011

The London Marathon

It's finally here. After all these months of build-up; after all those godforsaken races — the good, the bad and the downright bloody ugly.

I've done more running over these past six months than I've ever done in my entire life. Training for this marathon has forced me to take it seriously.

And now I'm here, on my way down to London for the conclusion of this marathon journey. I'm sitting in my seat on the train, surrounded by other runners and their entourage, wondering how it will go. What will happen? Will we each come away victorious in our own mini — and at the same time enormous — personal challenges? Or will it break us? I can tell we're all here, pondering on exactly the same thing: what will happen to us on Sunday?

I'm trying not to get too caught up in outcomes, and so my mind is flicking back through my memory scrapbook, and I'm realising that whatever happens on Sunday, I've won anyway.

Along this journey, and as a most unexpected by-product of my original marathon goal, running has saved me. It's enabled me to grapple with my fitness, and wrestle my body back from the grips of pregnancy and childbirth; it's unleashed a whole new range of armoury with which I can tame the Stormtroopers continually threatening to rampage through my mind, and wreck otherwise tranquil thoughts.

I've met a new breed of people — people just like me who understand my need to run. I've learned that other people do exist who would also choose a Sunday-morning ten-miler over a pain au chocolat and a 'real' coffee (or who would at least wait until afterwards before devouring them!).

I get it now. I understand the 'why'. Maybe my _real_ race was the journey to get here, and not the marathon itself.

So anyway, it's here. It's Friday now, and in two days' time it will all be over. I wonder what the next few days will bring ... I can't wait to find out.

We headed out of our front door and I began to speed walk, pulling my little wheelie suitcases behind me with purpose. Chris didn't seem in such a hurry. The sun shone brightly as we bounced along the small country lane, less than a mile down the hill to our village train station.

Planning Tilly's weekend away at her grandparents was akin to relocating a small army, and the pair of us quizzed each other about all the obvious essentials that may have fallen foul of those preparations.

'Can we just check the tickets one more time?' I asked within the first hundred yards of leaving the house. 'Phew! Yep. All there. We're in Coach C. Seats 23 and 24,' I reassured myself before we took another step. Chris didn't seem overly concerned. I scanned through a mental list of all my running essentials. *Shorts?* Yep. *Vest?* Yep. *Running belt?* Yep. *Gels?* Yep. *TRAINERS? Shit, did I pack my trainers?!* I stopped (again) to double check.

We could *finally* get on our way.

Once settled in our seats, I looked around the train carriage. *Who else is running the marathon on Sunday?* I wondered. I played a game in my head guessing who looked like a marathon runner and who was in supportive partner/running widow role. *Did the distant, nervous look indicate 'runner'?* Perhaps so. The chatter also gave plenty away. I felt like I'd strayed into another world; one with an entirely new language.

'Yeah, I've been foam rolling my hammies,' one tracksuit-top wearing man explained to his running companion. I noticed his top was from last year's marathon. He'd been through all this before. 'And I've been upping the fartlek sessions, increasing my weekly mileage right through to tapering, but my hammies have been giving me jip for most of the winter, to be honest,' he continued.

He'd been what? Foam rolling his hammies? Is he talking about slow roast pork? And fartlek sessions? I'd heard of them – being vaguely aware that it's a method of training that combines slow running with sprints – but I imagined someone making a sudden mad dash between lampposts and wondered how it fit into marathon training. *Surely you just build up your mileage?* I questioned myself. *Don't tell me I've missed something here.*

Thankfully, I'd heard about tapering: it was a most enjoyable part of my marathon training – two weeks without the apprehension of races, with no silly long runs either. Maybe I wasn't such a marathon gatecrasher after all ...

We arrived in London and the buzz was electric with pre-marathon anticipation. 'Right. Let's drop our bags at the hotel first, and then head off to the Expo. I've got to collect my number,' I said to Chris, sounding preoccupied and slightly agitated.

I had no experience of a marathon Expo. *Hmmm ... perhaps there are a few stalls selling a bit of VLM-branded running gear?* I mused, having given it precious little thought.

We meandered through the swarm of runners already clogging up the Docklands Light Railway platform, and finally hit the Expo. 'Bloody hell! This is insane!' I said a bit too loudly, inviting a couple of passing wry smiles. I couldn't believe the people. I couldn't believe the *size* of this thing. *It's a BEAST!*

Walking through the Expo doors, I knew how Charlie Bucket felt as he stepped foot inside Willy Wonka's chocolate factory for the very first time. It was a sensory bombardment of all things running-related. A poem titled 'All the Reasons Why' hung down from an inflatable, virtual finish line in enormous letters. It made the hairs on the back of my neck stand on end. *I'm a part of this.* I swallowed, hard. *I've earned my place, and I'm really a part of this!*

This year, I wouldn't be watching it on TV; I wouldn't be dipping my four-fingered Kit-Kat into a mug of steaming hot chocolate (with all the toppings), listening to Brendan Foster commentate on Ronnie the Running Rhino, or watching newbie *Blue Peter* presenters chasing after hapless celebrities who didn't know why they were there. This year, I was *in* it. *I'm here! I'm actually bloody here!*

People were everywhere. They carried their bright red, shiny VLM duffel bags, and – unlike me – darted around as if they knew what to do. *Where do I go? What do I do?* I had no idea.

I turned the corner and came face to face with an endless row of registration cubicles, all manned by efficient-looking staff.

'Good afternoon, young lady,' said a kind, elderly gentleman as he welcomed me to his cubicle.

'Oh, erm, hello,' I replied, suddenly feeling entirely overwhelmed.

'And do you have your ID to hand, please?' He smiled at me patiently. I was quite clearly a marathon virgin.

'Oh, yes. Of course,' I said, sounding naively surprised at his request, as I quickly began fumbling around for my passport and registration documents. *What did I expect him to ask me?* I had no clue.

'That's lovely, thank you,' he said warmly as he handed me my very own shiny, red VLM bag, with my very own race number – 9389. 'If you head across to the gentleman over there, he will give you your timing chip.' This would record precisely how many hours, minutes and seconds it would take for me to cross the finish line from the official start of the London Marathon. I gulped again. 'Have a fabulous time, and the very best of luck tomorrow!' he offered, smiling generously. I felt strangely reassured by his kindness.

Bloody hell. This is seriously well-orchestrated shit! My mind boggled at the memory of my naive ballot applications for various family members all those months earlier. I suddenly felt stupid, imagining the scene turning up at the very same registration cubicle purporting to be my mother – a 68-year-old woman – with no identification. Thank GOD things had worked out the way they had, although admittedly more by accident than design.

Armed with another seventeen bags – promoting everything from Club La Santa to the latest branded coconut water, not to mention my very own shiny, red VLM duffel bag – we turned another corner.

'Jesus! Look at this place!' I said out loud, the words falling helplessly out of my mouth as we were funnelled straight into runners' shopping utopia. I stood staring at an entire wall covered in handwritten good luck messages scrawled across a cleverly marketed Adidas slogan. I felt like I belonged.

'Take a photo of me writing on this wall, would you, Chris?' I asked, already keen to start adding to my bank of marathon memories. I found an empty half-inch of wall, and in tiny letters, I wrote: *'This one's for you, Tills. Mummy xxx'*

I was suddenly Charlie Bucket in the chocolate factory again as I looked around at rail upon rail of fancy, branded VLM gear. I could feel Chris beginning to sweat at the prospect of an unplanned, costly half-hour. I decided on a zip-up VLM training top. They only had one left – in a size too big – but I wanted it anyway. 'And I'll take a marathon teddy back for Tills,' I said, when we finally reached the counter at the end of the mile-long queue.

Following the Expo's assault on my senses, I became very aware that Chris, quite understandably felt like he wasn't quite a part of this whole marathon merry-go-round, and so we headed off to locate some desperately needed fresh air.

'That was mental, wasn't it! Shall we head back to the hotel?' I asked, trying to keep myself from marathon burnout before I'd even reached the start line.

Only one more sleep to go ...

RACE DAY

17 April 2011

I've just woken up and it's finally here! It's race day! Even yesterday it still didn't seem real, until the Expo jolted me into a whole new marathon-running world, that is.

I got all my kit ready last night. I have:

- Pinned my number onto my vest (CHANGED VESTS & RE-PINNED SEVEN TIMES)
- Loaded my ammunition belt with too many disgusting energy gels (REARRANGED TEN TIMES)
- Charged my watch and iPod (CHECKED ON BOTH AT LEAST FIVE TIMES)
- Packed my bag for the luggage bus (RE-PACKED AND RE-CHECKED MAYBE A HUNDRED TIMES)
- Laid out my socks and even some specially selected hair bobbles ready for this morning's marathon pigtails (CHANGED SOCKS TWICE AND CONTEMPLATED MOST SUITABLE HAIRSTYLE FOR CIRCA AN HOUR)

Nothing has been left to chance. It has all been thoroughly checked and re-checked at least a dozen times over. I've studied the route map, including the different coloured starting zones. There is a red, blue, and a green starting area — most probably due to the fact they have over 40,000 runners to funnel across the official start line. Depending on your number, you're allocated one of the zones. I'm in blue. I've also familiarised myself with the Circle and District Tube lines. Perhaps it's just because it's all completely unknown to me, but this feels like planning a military operation. I can't slip up and leave anything to chance.

It's ridiculously early now, but I already feel insanely awake. I just want to get this marathon underway. We've got to go down and get breakfast soon, but I don't have much of an appetite. Chris will be aghast that I won't be eating my own bodyweight in Danish pastries, but I know what my body needs: a strong coffee and a slice of toast with jam will be more than enough at this ungodly hour. I'll take a banana for the hour-or-so wait beforehand...

Right. He's finally up and ready, so we're off. When I return, it'll all be over, and we will know how this particular journey ends.

I'm about to venture forth into battle with every limiting belief I ever had about myself.

Here goes...

Breakfast was painful. The room was full of apprehensive marathon runners, and their bleary-eyed support crew. The contrast between those of us fuelling up in preparation for running 26.2 miles, and those who were devouring their early-morning cinnamon swirls just to try and wake up was stark. Nowhere more so than on our table.

I sat in quiet apprehension, barely able to chew on my few dry mouthfuls of brown toast with jam. The 'real' coffee was deliberately stronger than I'd normally have it, and it tasted like rocket fuel.

'Is that all you're having?' Chris enquired, as he delicately sliced his plump croissant and lathered each half thickly in cold packet butter.

'Yeah. I'm fine with just toast and a coffee. I'll have quite a long wait before the start, so I may fancy a banana or something in a bit. I can't face it just now,' I said, whilst my stomach did somersaults. I was so tired of having to explain.

Is he deliberately being as slooowwww as possible? I wondered. *Does he not realise I've got a marathon to run? I've no idea how long it'll take to get to the start, and my nerves are already shot. I just want to get there.*

We finally headed out of the hotel lobby and immediately picked up a throng of marathoners all swarming towards the Tube station. *Phew! This may be easier than I thought!* I soon realised that it would be far harder to *avoid* the start of the marathon than it would be to find my way there, and so we joined the endless throng of red-bagged runners.

The London Marathon is possibly the best place in the world to dabble in a spot of people-watching. I looked around as the Tube was already beginning to fill up, and I wondered about the other runners. *Why are these people here? Where have they come from?* An American couple seated in front of me were chatting quietly to their young son. He looked like a well-travelled, mature eight- or nine-year-old. I intuited that Sensible Son would wait with his Supportive Dad whilst Sporty Mum ran the marathon – she gave off a confident vibe that she'd done this plenty of times before: this looked like their 'normal'. I couldn't help but wonder what that felt like.

As I stood, clinging with one hand gripped onto the overhead rail as the Tube rattled and swayed, an elderly woman turned to me. Her beige jacket seemed a little out of place amongst the bright, multi-coloured T-shirts and shiny red luggage bags. I smiled. She looked back at me kindly, and then reached out her hand. 'Here, love. Put this towards whichever charity you're raising money for,' she spoke quietly as she carefully placed a ten-pound note into my hand.

'Good grief! Really? Are you sure?' I said, momentarily stunned by her generosity, and unable to believe that she'd just handed over a tenner to me – a random stranger – based purely on instinct and trust. I didn't want to offend her by explaining that I wasn't a charity runner, and so I thanked her and donated the ten pounds to the Help for Heroes charity.

Everywhere around us the marathon was exerting its magnetic pull, drawing people together, making connections. 'It could be a warm one, today!' an old-timer offered to the younger runner sitting next to him, who was hugging his luggage bag nervously.

As we stepped off the Tube, we swam with the tide once more: it was impossible to do anything else with the sea of people in front of us. We blended perfectly into the magical, meandering vision of colour and movement. I thought back to the many years I'd spent watching the BBC's live Sunday-morning marathon coverage on TV, with the overhead cameras swinging round to capture thousands of everyday heroes collectively on the move. I remembered sitting and gazing into the TV, whilst tucking into my oversized portion of Sara Lee double-chocolate gateau. All those years I'd spent by myself at home, inhaling empty, lonely calories watching the aerial shots on TV. They didn't do it justice.

For once, I wasn't watching from the sidelines: *I'm here! I'm actually here!* My heart sang as I swam amongst the waves of positivity, movement and colour.

Chatter was everywhere, and the hum of excitement, apprehension and hope filled all open space. The greens of the trees somehow looked greener; the blue of the sky looked strangely bluer. It appeared as though everything were illuminated in technicolour. Wherever I looked, the colours seemed brighter, crisper, sharper and clearer. I felt myself being drawn further into the scene that I was now a part of. I knew I wasn't being particularly good company. The sooner I headed off to my start – the blue start – the better.

'Right. This is me!' I said to Chris, stating the bleeding obvious. 'Wish me luck, and all that. Oh, and could you just take one last picture of me with my race number on, before I head off?'

With that, and to my great relief, I was on my own. I looked around me at the vibrant scene. *Hot air balloons! Wow! Look at them all!* I'd never seen so many. Flames fired up from one basket into a giant-sized Virgin Active red balloon, which bobbed around next to an equally vast inflatable Lucozade

Sport bottle. It seemed more like a carnival – a festival of all things good, bright and possible. Like a celebration of being alive. It was certainly unlike any race – or any place – I'd ever been to before.

What do I do now, other than wait? People-watch, and wait. I would wait for the gun to go off, and then I'd be running my very first marathon. I thought of Tilly back home with her grandma and grandad. *Would they be watching on TV?* She's a baby. Years away from knowing what any of this is, or what any of it means, but one day she'd know.

I paced up and down. I queued for the loos. It seemed like nobody else knew what to do either, so they did exactly the same as me. I couldn't keep track of the thousands of charity vests. A guy walked past me in a plain bright-green T-shirt. On the back, it was simply printed '4 U DAD'. *What happened to his poor dad?* I wondered.

It was getting hotter. Perhaps we'd all been distracted by the crowds, the colours, the balloons, the people-watching, and the waiting. Perhaps the older guy on the Tube was right: maybe this *is* going to be a hot one. *Ah well, no time to worry about that just now. Best get into the starting pens before there really is no more time left.*

I climbed over a barrier which was more like an industrial-sized cattle pen. We were the cattle – penned in, anticipating our fate over the coming 26.2 miles ahead of us. And now it was clear that we had the heat to contend with along with the distance itself. I could feel the body heat radiating from the other runners around me. The air felt still and stifling. Wafts of deep heat, cheap deodorant and nervous farts all intermingled, whilst still retaining some of their own identity.

'Is it your first time?' one shy-looking woman said to me, as we jostled restlessly next to each other.

'Yeah. Yeah it is. It's a bit overwhelming, isn't it?' I offered back, trying to bond over our mutual apprehension.

'You can say that again! It's my first time, too …' She seemed to be put at ease by the break in silence. 'Are you going for a time?'

Eh? What does she mean? I'm keen to finish it in one piece, but going for a time? Surely that's a bit ambitious for now. I don't even know if I can complete the bloody thing yet! My imagination wouldn't let me dream that far.

'Oh no, not really. I'll be more than happy to get round!' I replied … And I meant it.

Before we knew it, the claxon sounded, and we were off. Adrenalin coursed through my veins as I geared myself up for the miles and the hours ahead. *Hang on a minute. No one's bloody running! It's half a mile to the official start line – the place where our timing chips are activated and we begin to count down the 26.2 miles – and people are barely even shuffling!* It felt like the slowest mass trudge to the start – and a bit of an anti-climax. I overheard some general grumblings around me, as people just wanted to start running and begin to chip away at the 26.2 miles strewn out across the city of London.

We finally reached the start line, but there were too many pairs of trainers for the congested route to manage. Heels were clipped and curbs were hopped on and off, as faster runners quick-stepped around those who would otherwise be trampled.

The first mile was a jolty hopscotch to find space. I stumbled on a discarded water bottle, and clumsily fell into a man next to me. He grabbed on to my arms tightly as I steadied myself and avoided being face-planted on the pavement. 'SORRY! Sorry. I'm really sorry.' I smiled at him, half expecting an irritated grunt in return, but was pleasantly surprised by a beam instead.

Right. We're REALLY off now. Around five or six miles in and the sea of runners had dispersed, allowing me to find a flow of movement and some rhythm. Those first few miles had flown by without my even realising. *So far, so good!* I reassured myself, as I settled into my steady pace.

Wires hung down irritatingly from my earphones, through my vest and into my heavy iPod, which was clumsily stuck onto my left arm in what looked like a huge luminous pink bandage. I tried to ignore the physical irritations, and instead

focus on gaining motivation from Queen's 'Don't Stop Me Now' on repeat play. For a few miles, it worked … and then it became seriously annoying.

Bloody hell! Is that Iwan Thomas? It is! It's him! I fumbled about with my belt, trying to dig out my phone for a ridiculous attempt at a moving selfie. Although my pace dropped to virtually a walk and I found myself zigzagging all over the road, *CLICK!* I just about managed it. *I've just overtaken Iwan Thomas! He's a flippin' athlete!* I spurred myself on with my spurious aspirations of running grandeur.

Around mile fifteen, and it started to hit me. *Shit, this feels hard.* I'd been distracted by the crowds and the celebs, the sunshine and the carnival atmosphere. All of that was now paling into insignificance as my body began to grumble, telling me it wasn't particularly happy. *Remember all those training runs, Rach. You've done far harder than this. Remember that God-awful twenty-miler when you thought it would never end? It did, and you managed it. You kept going. Remember the guy Jim who came to run alongside you at your lowest point at the Spen 20 race? What would he say now? He'd just keep going. So, that's exactly what you'll do: just keep going.*

A man swerved and swayed right across the road in front of me. *Blimey! What's wrong with him?* He looked drunk.

The distance and the heat were affecting people badly. I looked again and he'd collapsed by the barrier on the other side of the road. 'Get him some water!' one woman shouted, who was momentarily propping him up. 'It's all right, Mark. You're OK.

I'm getting you some water. You're going to be fine.' She knew his name from his vest. I ran on.

I'd just passed the nineteen-mile marker when all sorts of thoughts began rifling through my mind. A cocktail of mind games was now in full throttle. *There are still another seven miles to run, Rach. Another seven bastard miles! How can I break up another seven miles? … But it's only seven miles. Surely I can make another seven miles. Will my legs keep going? What if I can't keep going?* I obsessed over the number seven, trying to chop it up into virtual, manageable chunks. *Two lots of three miles plus one; three lots of two miles plus one.* But any which way I chopped it up, there were still seven miles to go.

Just around the next corner, the crowd was going wild. Shouts of 'GO ON, WILL!' and then, less subtly, 'LOOK! IT'S WILL YOUNG!' passed through the spectators lining the route. I ran alongside a guy who was dressed in black shorts and a black vest (think understated pop-star chic) wearing the biggest headphones in the world, and equally large 'I'm not a pop-star – honest!' oversized sunglasses. Looking like a celebrity who was pretending to try hard *not* to look like a celebrity. It worked. He was running steadily. *Shit! I've just overtaken Will Young!* I'm not sure why this felt like such an accomplishment. I'd no grounds for assuming that poor Will Young could run for a bus, let alone a marathon.

I messed about with my ridiculously non-marathon-friendly gadgets, and my pace dropped to a shuffle as I once again zigzagged all over the road whilst trying to capture my celebrity spots in unnecessary gormless selfies. My iPod wires had become so fully entangled, they kept being yanked sharply out of my ears with every arm-swing. I pulled over to sort my technical equipment out. *Oh, bollocks to it. It's not worth the hassle.* That was it for my music, and any further rousing anthems by Queen, as I stuffed my headphones into my belt.

The scary fainting/drunken sailor episodes were continuing all around me. I couldn't believe I was still standing, still compos mentis, and still running! I stopped just beyond the twenty-mile marker and took a large swig of my homemade flat cola. It was simply water with a couple of cola-flavoured electrolyte tablets mixed in that would replace lost salts throughout the race. I'd been given some free samples at a previous event, and so I was drinking these entirely by accident rather than design: I had no idea that they may well have saved me from dehydration, heat exhaustion, and would potentially save my marathon.

I'd also stopped for a small swig of water at every water station, and when the heat seriously kicked in, I began to douse myself in it at any given opportunity. Still the heat was relentless.

We were into the last six miles. Every single mile marker felt to be getting further and further away. I willed for the next one to come, and to be able to tick off the remaining,

painful miles. *How hard can it be to count to six? How long could it possibly take? How painful might it be?* I was about to find out.

In my training, I'd done a couple of twenty-mile races, but nothing longer. Experienced runners say that the first half of any marathon is up to the twenty-mile point: the second half is the last sickening six. I was just about to commence the 'real' second half of my first marathon, and my wheels were beginning to fall off. I'd never been to this place before; I'd never run this far before, in this kind of sweltering heat before. I'd never asked – or demanded this of my body before. Everything was painful. Remember my hip flexors? They were about to pack up and go home. My legs burned with searing, aching pains. My feet felt to be running on hot coals whilst wearing ill-fitting sandals. I could feel the blisters on my toes swell further with every strike on the road. I knew that my big toenail was hanging on for dear life, and that it wouldn't make it far beyond the finishing line.

I pulled over at mile twenty-two. *Jesus Christ. What can I tell myself to make this be OK? How can I make myself do this?* The crowd stepped in. 'Hey! Don't stop now, lassie!

You're almost there!' one guy patted me on the shoulder. 'Come on, lady!' a woman yelled. She was talking to me. 'Number 9389: DO NOT STOP! KEEP ON RUNNING!' an enthusiastic teenager hollered at me. *That's my number!* I had to run again. If I stopped for any longer, I may not be able to restart. My legs grumbled to the point of belligerence, as affronted as they were at the prospect of having to move again. *Come on, guys. Work with me here. I know you're tired, but we have to see this one through.* I creaked and heaved them into action once more.

Mile twenty-five came into view. *OH. MY. GOD. I'M NEARLY THERE!* I had to pull over again for a short reprieve. *One more mile. Just one more mile. That's all you have to do, Rach. One final effort. JUST ONE MORE MILE …*

I looked up at the sea of people. None had faces – it was a blurry wall of colour and noise. The tree-lined route had all the London iconic landmarks, but I couldn't see anything. I heard the noise – the noise that would not allow me to stop. *When will it end?* My legs were increasing their protest with every second.

I can't see the finish. Where is the finish? I'd temporarily forgotten what a mile looks or feels like. A guy came staggering past me, as if he was using his very last human effort to will his body into the finish. I couldn't stay with him, as my legs had all but abandoned me. A sign read '800m to go …' *Right. OK. I can do this. Come on, legs! Only 800 metres. We can DO this!* We turned a corner. Another bloody corner! *Fuck me! How far can 800 metres even be?*

And there it was: the finish line came into sight. 400 metres … then 200 metres … more noise; screams of goodwill; hollers of encouragement. The Union Jacks swinging proudly; the big red banner stretching across the entire width of the Mall; the timing clocks ticking as I willed myself across the finish.

FINISH

I heaved myself over the striped red timing mats, and wept as my legs virtually gave way beneath me, and I could *FINALLY* press STOP on my watch.

After seven months, four hours and twenty-five minutes – I could stop running.

EPILOGUE

Running and me: it certainly wasn't a love-at-first-sight relationship. The first dates weren't very pretty at all. In fact, we didn't even *like* each other in the early days. Having experienced nothing but humiliation in trainers throughout my teenage years, I could never have predicted that one day, I would run a marathon. And I'd do it again … and again. I couldn't possibly have foreseen that eventually I would fall in love with running until I needed it like I need the air to breathe.

In the early days, as much as I often hated the thought of my daily torturous obligation, there were tiny glimpses of light breaking through. We're not talking thunderbolts here, just little peppery flashes when The Suffering abated sufficiently for me to breathe in the beauty of my surroundings, or absorb the warmth of the sunshine on my skin. Even unlikely moments began to clock up in the Good Memory Bank: when I'd begrudgingly brave the elements to run directly into horizontal, sleeting rain, only to come back home feeling refreshed and alive; times when I'd step back in through my front door after shoehorning myself out, feeling as proud that I'd made the effort as I was relieved it was over – in equal measure. Feeling calmer and somehow happier, yet not knowing or understanding why. Maybe it was just the Prozac kicking in, but maybe there was more to it than that.

My post-pregnancy London Marathon goal defined running, and what it meant to me. What had previously been (at best) mild fondness developed into a far deeper connection – an understanding and appreciation of what running had given me over the years, and could give me over many more. A respect and gratitude grew for what had evolved into becoming my joy and my sanity. It did, unfortunately, cement the demise of mine and Chris's relationship, but it also opened up the door for us to explore our own paths for future happiness. I would go on to meet Gav, my running soul mate, and we would (literally) run off into the sunset together. Sometimes, those nauseatingly cheesy happy endings do happen. We run together, we race together. We hobble down the stairs in sympathy with each other. We drag each other out of bed on cold, wet mornings when it would be *so* much easier not to. We celebrate with each other and we commiserate when things don't quite go to plan. We tag-team training sessions around looking after our girls, and even when we're running separately, we're always together. That's just how it is.

And then we arrive at my most recent chapter. Freedom. Simply that: absolute freedom. Once I allowed myself to be truly free and created a life for myself that I really, genuinely wanted, I began to soar. It was incredible. I felt like I'd just been unshackled and brought back to life: a Duracell Bunny on a high, having ditched the batteries and gone for the direct plug-in option. My own personal freedom came from creating a life that was on *my* terms, nobody else's. One where my running adventures, achievements, PBs, medals, times, races and prizes would be celebrated.

Let's be clear though. This is a story about far more than just running. It's about struggle, and about discovering joy in the midst of struggle. Simple, soul-satisfying joy and contentment, which is greater than any of the short-term fixes I was missold. I was told that happiness came from owning a bigger house, another spare bedroom to store more 'stuff': a flashier car, designer handbags, *those* shoes. I did all of those things, and yet I still felt empty. The happiness was disappointingly fleeting. What I was missing was the deep satisfaction that comes from discovering what I love, what I am capable of, and who I could be – if only I allowed myself to believe it were possible.

I also realised that such discovery is not meant to be easy. Perhaps the reason my running has and continues to give me such a deep sense of joy is exactly this. It symbolises standing up to the bullies – those being FEAR and SELF-DOUBT. I've had a few recent years filled with successes, but far more so filled with failures. Either way, I needed to be brave enough to face the tormentors – those cruel, Bastard Inner Chimps who made me believe that my achievements were not possible for me; that my goals were beyond me.

They never were.

The deep satisfaction I have found is in proving to myself that regardless of the outcome, I can – and will – turn up to the start line, when it would be far easier not to. Time and again, proving to myself that the bullies will never win. They had me brainwashed for a long while.

All the times when things didn't go right – when nothing flowed, when my body has screamed at me for daring to push beyond its comfort zone, when I've got so close to my goal but not quite there, when I was overtaken near the finishing line, when I had to cling on as everything hurt and burned and ached, or when I didn't even make it past the line at all – these are exactly what make the successes so sweet.

I have discovered that inherent in running is the necessity of yin and yang, as in life: triumph/adversity; success/failure; joy/pain. It has been a huge part of my learning to realise that both are required to feel fully alive.

I've had over two decades of inner wrangling and gladiatorial battles with self-doubt. The subsequent reward is simply due recognition for being brave enough to try. For working a way through my anxiety and not letting it win; for conquering my fears – fears of failure, of looking foolish, of the pain – and ultimately for being stronger than the voice inside which says, 'You can't do this.'

Well actually, I can ...

In 2011 I completed the London Marathon in a time of 4:25. I was ecstatic at having completed my own, very personal goal. However, I wanted to do better: I knew I could do better.

I returned in 2012 – having managed to bag myself another ballot place – and I crossed the finish line in 3 hours and 50 minutes, and a few seconds (*the few seconds are important. You'll see why*).

Back then, the London Marathon Good for Age (GFA) qualifying time for my age category was 3:50. I had no idea it existed. I'd never even *heard* of it, let alone allowed myself the self-indulgent fantasy of believing that I was capable of achieving it. I looked again at my time. *Bloody hell! I'm only a few seconds off!* Just as before, I wanted to do better. I *knew*

I could do better. With more training, more discipline and more hard work, I believed I could achieve that standard.

So, I wrote to the race director, Mr Brasher. I explained to him that I fully believed I could smash the 3:50 GFA qualifying time, if he would only give me the chance and shoehorn me in.

One of his staff wrote back to me. Unfortunately, those '*and a few seconds*' were a few seconds too many. She explained to me that if they were to nudge the cut-off qualifying time for me, it would open the floodgates to an endless number of other '*just a few second-ers*' and erode their management of the GFA application process. Disappointed, I understood and accepted their position, and I respected the floodgates argument. I would simply have to try harder, and do better.

In 2013, I didn't secure a place in the London Marathon: the Ballot Gods weren't shining down on me, and so I entered the Edinburgh Marathon instead. I was *still* determined to prove to Mr Brasher that I was true to my word, and that I *could* do better. That year, I'd battled with glandular fever and dramatic (unhealthy) weight loss, and it was touch and go as to whether I'd be fit enough to run the marathon at all, let alone go for a GFA qualifying time. I struggled most of the way around the Edinburgh course, and crawled over the finishing line in 3 hours and 45 minutes, and a few seconds (*these few seconds are once again critical. You'll see why*).

Dear Mr Brasher,

I'm writing to let you know that I have just completed the Edinburgh Marathon in a time of 3:45 and a few seconds. You may recall that I wrote to you last year after completing the Virgin London Marathon in a time of 3:50 and a few seconds.

When I passed the finishing line in Edinburgh and I looked at the clock, I couldn't believe I'd qualified for a VLM Good for Age place for 2014. And then I looked at the VLM website, and noticed that the goal posts had been changed whilst I wasn't looking.

I understand that the qualifying time has been altered for my age category from 3:50 to 3:45, and I am devastated, because I'm sure that had I known this was the case, I could have dug deeper and shaved off those crucial few seconds.

As it stands, I'm writing to you again to ask you for a chance to prove that I can meet this standard.

With kind regards,

Rachel Cullen

So, *TWICE* I was the 'almost' girl. *TWICE* I was seconds away from the cut-off Good for Age qualifying time. *TWICE* I wrote to the VLM race director, asking him to allow me to squeeze through the tiniest of turnstiles and give me a chance.

He wrote back to me. Personally, this time.

Dear Miss Cullen

Thank you for your letter. I am pleased to be able to offer you a place in the 2014 Virgin London Marathon. My assistant will be in touch with you regarding this.

Good luck

Hugh

And that was it: I was in.

I came back in 2014, and I ran hard. I was hoping for somewhere around 3 hours and 30 minutes, and set off at that pace. But I *knew* I could do better. I dug deep, and unbelievably, I crossed the finish line in 3:22. I smashed through all of my self-imposed barriers that had kept me hovering around the GFA qualifying time for the previous two years, requiring me to write incessant begging letters to Mr Brasher.

I didn't need to write to him again, but I did anyway. Just to say thank you for giving me the chance to prove that I could earn myself a Virgin London Marathon Good for Age place in my own right.

I returned in 2015 and completed the course in 3 hours and 17 minutes. As at the time of writing, that remains my London Marathon personal best time. Who knows – dare I dream that one day I may dip under the 3-hour mark?

Either way, I've had a Good for Age place ever since.

AGED 38

May 2017

I am overjoyed to declare my love for and my commitment to running. I fully acknowledge that as hard as our relationship can be at times, I need it. As much as we may fall out, I love it. Whenever times are tough, I go back to it. When times are good, I celebrate with it.

So, at the risk of this sounding like a soppy wedding speech, or a tearful scene on *This is Your Life*, I love running for:

The places I've been
The things I've seen
The people I've met
The times I've cried
When everything flowed
When nothing flowed
The comedy moments
The weekends away
The heat (not so much the cold)
The photos and selfies
The friends I've made
The pride I've felt
The wind in my face
The peace I have known
The lessons I've learnt
The medals
The trophies (yes, there are quite a few)
The newspaper articles
The 'random' connections
Proving I could
Becoming visible
Learning to accept my body
Learning to go the extra mile
Feeling my heart thump out of my chest

The relief when it's over

Turning all the 'whys' into 'why nots'

The support I've had

The love I've felt

My little girl cheering, 'Go, Mummy, go!'

Finding my soul mate

Feeling brave

Feeling alive

My joy

My freedom

My sense of achievement

Belief in what is possible

Belief in myself

My story.

ACKNOWLEDGEMENTS

My deepest thanks go to the following people for their amazing support, encouragement and contribution throughout this whole journey.

To my mum for wrestling with, and finally slaying, the mental health demons that held her prisoner for so long. You finally beat them, and found your joy. Thank you for your endless encouragement in allowing me to find mine, and for believing that I could.

To my dad – for being a stalwart of goodness, decency and protection (despite having no idea of the 'why's').

To all of the friends who have played their part in my story over the years, with particular thanks to Maureen and Paul for their permissions in allowing me to make reference to their beautiful Ness. I know we all miss her still.

To our lovely friends, Helen and Adrian, who have run alongside me (literally) at the highest and lowest points, and Tom and Cheryl, who remind me everyday what a hero looks like. The strength you have shown through your grief has inspired me more than you know.

A huge thanks to all those who have encouraged me in my running, particularly to Pat who showed me that it was possible to smile through the miles! To friends and comrades in the running community who have cheered and hollered at me along the way. Particularly those within the Stainland Lions and Halifax Harriers. You know who you are. And to

Auntie Wendy and Uncle Bill for cheering me on in London. FYI – I'm not *quite* as fast as Paula!

To the guys (and gals) at the charity Threeways, who remind me what it is to turn up and contribute on a daily basis. You guys are amazing, and special thanks to Dave, Callum, Kristan and Bill for the endless laughs amidst the madness. And talking of madness, thank you to my lovely yoga guru, Lianne, who has kept me sane (usually in swan pose) during the injuries and the frustrations. Thank you for sharing your gift.

Enormous thanks to the most amazing editor Beth Eynon, who has relentlessly championed my story since it landed in her inbox on that miraculously fateful day. Thank you, Beth, for your endless commitment, energy and passion to see this project through to fruition. I cannot imagine being on this journey without having you to drive me through the million re-writes, reviews and revisions. Thank you for the pep talks, the virtual hugs and the absolute belief you have shown in my writing, and in me. Also to the wider Blink Publishing team for giving me the opportunity to tell my story, and for every ounce of effort that each one of you has put in to make it possible.

Thanks to my brilliant literary agent Jo Bell for plucking me from the slush pile, and offering me a place to dry out. Thank you for making me and my Yorkshire raincoat laugh out loud. I may be hanging around for a while.

Thanks to Angela, Gary, Tim and Rach for embracing me and Tilly into their family, treating us like their own and cheering all of us on from the sidelines.

And all my love and heartfelt thanks to my husband and soul mate, Gav, for showing me the confidence I never knew I had, the strength I didn't know I could find, and a love I never imagined was possible. Thank you for making me laugh out loud every single day, and for believing in me with such love and conviction. Most of all, thank you for allowing me to be me, and for loving me because of it.

Lastly, thank you to my beautiful girl Tilly for being my reason 'why'. You are the reason why I ran that very first marathon, and the reason why I wrote this book. You are my reason to try harder every single day, and I love you to the moon and back.

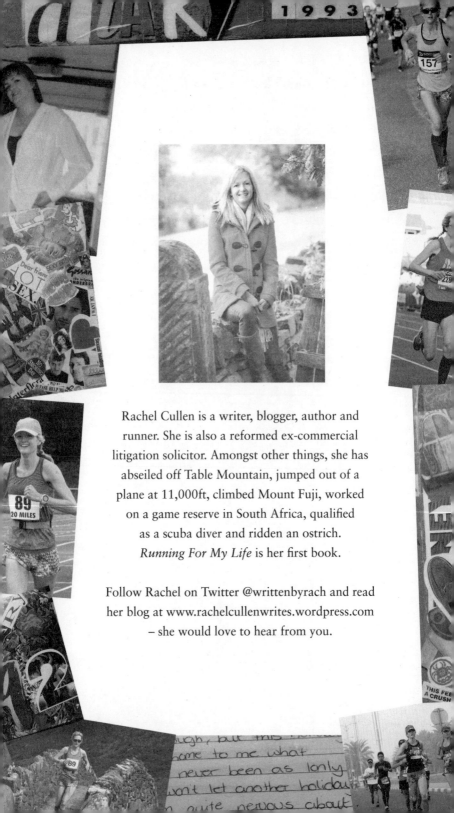

Rachel Cullen is a writer, blogger, author and runner. She is also a reformed ex-commercial litigation solicitor. Amongst other things, she has abseiled off Table Mountain, jumped out of a plane at 11,000ft, climbed Mount Fuji, worked on a game reserve in South Africa, qualified as a scuba diver and ridden an ostrich. *Running For My Life* is her first book.

Follow Rachel on Twitter @writtenbyrach and read her blog at www.rachelcullenwrites.wordpress.com – she would love to hear from you.